Ariadne's Thread

Ariadne's Thread

Story Lines

J. Hillis Miller

Yale University Press

New Haven and London

Designed by Sonia L. Scanlon and set in Sabon type by DEKR Corporation, Woburn, Massachusetts.

Printed in the United States of America by Thomson-Shore, Dexter, Michigan.

Library of Congress Cataloging-in-Publication Data

Miller, J. Hillis (Joseph Hillis), 1928–

    Ariadne's thread : story lines / J. Hillis Miller.

        p.   cm.

    Includes bibliographical references and index.

    ISBN 0-300-05216-2 (alk. paper)

    1.   Fiction—Technique. 2.   Narration (Rhetoric) I. Title.

PN3355.M48   1992

808.3—dc20   91-32842

                    CIP

The paper in this book meets the guidelines for permanence and durability of the Committee on Production Guidelines for Book Longevity of the Council on Library Resources.

10 9 8 7 6 5 4 3 2 1

For Dorothy

Contents

Preface: Interruption ix

Acknowledgments xvii

1 Line 1

2 Character 28

3 Anastomosis 144

4 Figure 223

Notes 259

Index 275

Preface
Interruption

L a fin de l'écriture linéaire est bien la fin du livre.
—Jacques Derrida, *De la grammatologie*

On January 4, 1976, after several months of thinking and making notes, I sat down early one morning in Bethany, Connecticut, to write a brief essay. I planned a twenty-page introduction to a book I was then completing, *Fiction and Repetition*. I thought of calling the introduction "Ariadne's Thread." My idea was to relate the image of the line to the concept of repetition in a quick review of narrative theory. I would then exemplify all that in a brief comparison of Elizabeth Gaskell's *Cranford* with Walter Pater's "Apollo in Picardy." When I reached a hundred pages of manuscript I realized something had gone wrong. I was writing not an introduction but a separate book on narrative theory. The project seemed to have taken on a life of its own and was making demands on me I had not foreseen.

Yielding shamelessly to the fallacy of imitative form, I then planned a book with a separate chapter on each of the seven forms of narrative theory I had initially identified. A final chapter would tie it all together with the comparison of Gaskell and Pater. Each chapter, I thought, would be shorter than the one before, as though the line being traced out were circling closer and closer to the center of a labyrinth. The penultimate chapter, on the straight-line labyrinth in Borges's "La muerte y la brújula," would, I imagined, be only a few lines long, terse, economical, elegant. But each chapter, as I tried to write it, got longer and longer, until the project began to appear virtually interminable, though all I was writing seemed implicit in the initial project. My plan for a shapely labyrinth of a book became as unfulfillable as the original idea of a twenty-page introduction. I had experienced in my own way something like that interruption of logical and ordered thought endured by the Prior Saint-Jean in Pater's "Apollo in Picardy." This is described in one of the epigraphs to the first chapter here.

Now, over fifteen years later, *Fiction and Repetition* has long since been published with a different introduction. Those original twenty pages have grown and subdivided to become the manuscripts of no fewer than four books, of which this is the first. The interwoven simultaneous reading of *Cranford* and "Apollo in Picardy" has been drafted, along with all but one of the chapters as originally planned. The reading of Gaskell and Pater will form the final chapter of the fourth book to grow from this project, on the relations of novels to what is presumed to be outside them—landscape, history, the real world. Although I have written and published other books in the meantime, I have continued to work on the "Ariadne's Thread" project. It has been one of my main preoccupations in teaching and writing. Parts of the project have been published along the way, detached segments of that apparently interminable line. During all this time, Ellen Graham and the Yale University Press have waited more or less patiently for me to fulfill my contractual obligation to submit a manuscript for their consideration.

What happened to make my original plan so unworkable and to swell my modest project to such monstrous dimensions? I would not tell this little story if I did not think it is to some degree paradigmatic or exemplary. No doubt the doubling and redoubling of my project has been, as they say, overdetermined. In part, my delay has been sheer laziness, the inability to bring myself to do the hard work of preparing a typed manuscript from the hand-written drafts, completing the notes, and revising the whole. The project, moreover, has had deep personal connections of which I am only partially aware. It has been mostly written in pen and ink in various notebooks, in the early morning, before anyone else in my family was up. Different parts of it are intimately associated with the places where it was written, the dining rooms in our houses in Bethany and in Deer Isle, Maine, for "Line" and "Character"; a house in Laguna Beach, California, for a chapter on "Topography" for the book on the external relations of narratives; the Bodmer House at the University of Zurich, which Goethe visited, for the chapter here ("Anastomosis") on Goethe's *Die Wahlverwandtschaften;* various houses and hotels in Australia, where the concluding chapter here on Borges's "La muerte y la brújula" was written ("Figure"). Those intimate associations have somehow made me reluctant to part with the material or to make it fully public, just as one would hesitate to publish a private diary.

My real difficulties, however, I have only recently realized, arise from irreconcilable contradictions in the original project. One contradiction arises from the collision between the desire, on the one hand, to write an orderly, logical, rational, logocentric book, a book with a beginning, middle, end, and firm underlying *logos* or ground. This desire was instilled by all my education and culture. On the other hand, the original insights generating this work were not amenable to such ordering. These insights were alogical, though not exactly irrational. I take Pater's hapless Prior Saint-Jean as an allegory of this predicament, though initially I saw him only as a figure for the predicament of the novelists I was studying. The Prior's twelve-volume treatise was to be a monumental and "well-ordered" account of the quadrivium, that is, arithmetic, geometry, astronomy, and music. The quadrivium, in medieval pedagogy, was the application to space, time, and number of the trivium. The latter comprised the purely linguistic sciences of grammar, logic, and rhetoric with which a liberal education began. The Prior's treatise presupposed that it would be possible to "draw tight together the threads of a long and intricate argument" using the trivium to develop the quadrivium, ending with a satisfactory conclusion. This presupposition was invaded by "an argument of an entirely new and disparate species." This new argument was based on insights that "divided hopelessly against itself the well-ordered kingdom of his thought." Though Pater offers several figures for this interruption or self-division, I should define it, as it applies by allegorical displacement to my own difficulties with "Ariadne's Thread," as the invasion of logical thought by rhetorical insight. Rhetoric, in the sense of insight into the role of figurative language in all discourse, for example, narrative, is the odd man out in the trivium. It suspends the forward march of rational thought in grammar or logic. It forbids the straightforward extension to the outer world, in the quadrivium, of linguistic laws acquired in the trivium. This present book could be defined as the partial investigation, through examples, of ways figurative language interrupts and complicates storytelling. No story can be wholly logical or logocentric. My initial mistake was not to recognize that this would necessarily also apply to the story I was trying to tell. It would mean that my book or books would have to take a different form from the ones I had previously written. They would necessarily testify to the impossibility of fulfilling the project they set for themselves rather than end in some triumphant Q.E.D.

I have said that Pater offers several figures for what broke off the Prior Saint-Jean's thinking and made it impossible for him to finish his treatise. All apply obliquely to my own experience in trying to write "Ariadne's Thread." The Prior is invaded by Apollonian illumination that works against the invisible *Logos* of the Gospel of St. John. The Prior's mind then becomes dialogical, subject to a double logos. He is invaded by "a blaze of new light," light directly seen as against the mediated vision of logical thought. This new light is "an interpolated page of life" producing a manuscript "pieced together of quite irregularly formed pages." The Prior's lamentable twelfth volume is, literally, as a material object, a "solecism," that is, "a nonstandard usage or grammatical impropriety," by extension an "impropriety, mistake, or incongruity." "It could never be bound," any more than my scribbled notebooks of different sizes could be bound or published. Pater's Prior Saint-Jean had experienced proleptically or anachronistically the end of the linear book Derrida was to announce in *De la grammatologie,* just as I had participated in my own way in the same ending.

The "end of the book" has recently been defined in another way. Many students of culture see computer technology as signaling the disappearance of the "linear codex book" and its replacement by the "electronic book." The latter will disobey all the traditional presuppositions about authorship, unity, and shapely finitude we have thought of as necessary to a book.[1] One way to define my difficulties with the Ariadne project would be to say that I was trying to write with pen and ink, as a linear sequence, a book that demanded the nonlinear ordering soon to be possible with the electronic book. The computer will assemble a large amount of material in a big database with commentary. Any part of this database will be available at the touch of a button from more or less anywhere. Movement from one place to another will be made according to methods of association, "paths," or Boolean search techniques difficult to reproduce on the printed page. "Electronic space," as against the temporal sequence of word following word, is only by metaphor called a space, for it is by no means a Euclidean spatial array, though it is not linear either. It is a new electronic region, a region of interrelated signs. In this electronic space everything is everywhere. Computer people have given one form of this digital space the somewhat terrifying name "random access memory."[2] It may (or may not) have some vague similarity to the way memory is organized in the human brain.

The original insights sketched in the first chapter here could perhaps best be embodied in the format of that electronic book soon probably to replace the printed book. Traces of this exigency are present not only in the way my original project has subdivided into four different books but also in the way this present book is organized not as a completely logical argument but as a series that might be otherwise. Individual chapters, especially "Character," form a series that is not wholly developmental. Each chapter's sequence could better be thought of as a set of examples that might be ordered in any sequence, as would be the case if it were an electronic book. And in some cases, for example, the discussion of *The Egoist* in "Character," a given example is interrupted in the middle by a new example, in this case by a return to Nietzsche necessitated by what I was trying to say. My attempts to give the whole book a logical order and make it a developing argument (these have been considerable) are interfered with by a desire for assemblage that goes against the grain of sequential logic or storytelling.

The final figure Pater uses for the perturbation of the Prior Saint-Jean's well-ordered thought is also applicable as a figure to my difficulties with the Ariadne project. Until the twelfth volume of his treatise, illustrations were rare, the "simplest indispensable diagrams." In the twelfth volume there was a shift to abundant illustrations breaking up the sequence of letters in "mazy borders, long spaces of hieroglyph" that turn even letters back into pictures. The rearranged letters make on the page "veritable pictures of the theoretic elements of his subject": "Soft wintry auroras seemed to play behind whole pages of crabbed textual writing, line and figure bending, breathing, flaming into lovely 'arrangements' that were like music made visible." The preliminary version of the first chapter here, published as an essay entitled "Ariadne's Thread: Repetition and the Narrative Line," was only the second essay accompanied by illustrations I had written, the first being an essay on the Cruikshank illustrations for *Oliver Twist*. Illustration was now again necessary to what I wanted to say, or show. Moreover, the question of the role of illustrations in novels was one of the seven topics in narrative theory "Ariadne's Thread" identified. I have discussed this topic in a separate book, *Illustration*, another outgrowth of this project. My chief interest there is in the way pictorial illustrations complicate the story's forward march in a novel. Pictures are the product of a separate logos. They make an illustrated novel dialogical, divided against itself, like the Prior Saint-Jean. My sharing in the renewed interest in illustrations for novels, I have come to realize, was a concomitant of radical changes that have recently shifted us from dependence on the printed book to a multimedia culture of cinema, television, and video in which adeptness in "reading" pictures is as much needed as an ability to read the printed word.

But the figure of illustration as interruption applies in another way to my project, that is, to the use of "examples" as illustration of a given theoretical point. Another contradiction in my original project arose from a collision between the desire to give examples while subordinating examples to concepts, whereas the concepts in question included the idea, proved on my pulses through the attempt to write this book, that each example is unique. Theoretical concept and specific example are incommensurate. Each reading act is particular and unique. It does not so much validate a concept as modify or even disqualify it. The reading of an example suspends the straightforward advance of theoretical formulation much as the Prior Saint-Jean's reasonable argument was disturbed by illustrations that even used the letters on the page as the medium of auroral pictures that were like music made visible. My own examples in this book, particularly the ones treated at length—*The*

Egoist, Die Wahlverwandtschaften, and "La muerte y la brújula"—
go beyond the theoretical points they are meant to illustrate. Each
takes on a separate illustrative life of its own, leading me to places
I did not foresee or plan to visit when I began the reading.

What was it, exactly, that invaded my thinking concerning literature about 1975 and made the completion of this project so
difficult? I have said that what happened to me was overdetermined. No doubt it had something to do with the second French
invasion of America, the post-structuralist or deconstructive one
that followed the earlier phenomenological one that brought "criticism of consciousness." Criticism of consciousness was for me,
however, only a momentarily successful strategy for containing
rhetorical disruptions of narrative logic through a dialectic method
in criticism. Such criticism exerted that control by a constant reference back to the continuities of authorial consciousness as origin,
end, and underlying logos of literature. My turn to the rhetoric of
literature in *Fiction and Repetition* and in the Ariadne project was
not only the displacement of one form of Continental thought by
another. It was also the return to an indigenous, abiding fascination
with local linguistic anomalies in literature. This was my original
motivation for the study of literature long before I had heard of
Jacques Derrida, or of Kenneth Burke either, for that matter. This
fascination has remained the chief constant throughout all my
work.

The writing of this book and of the other three to come from
my anxious early morning meditations in 1975–76 has coincided
with major changes in humanistic study that had begun then and
have accelerated since. Perhaps the parts of this project already
printed in earlier forms have even in a small way helped bring
about these changes, as opposed to simply reflecting them. These
changes are familiar to almost everyone now. They include not
only the effect on humanistic study of the computer revolution,
mentioned already, but also the putting in question of traditional
canons; the breakdown of the distinction between literature and
other forms of writing; the rapid redeployment of disciplinary
divisions and borders; the development of women's studies, mi-
nority studies, film studies, the study of postcolonialism; the
triumph of theory; the shift to multilingual study from the separate
study of monolingual national literatures; the return to history and

to the study of popular culture, mass media, "cultural studies" generally. This preface has been an attempt to put this book into the context of these changes. Recent transformations in the procedures and strategies of literary study are one part of these changes.

Acknowledgments

ork on this book has been greatly aided by a Senior Faculty Fellowship from Yale University, a sabbatical research leave from the University of California at Irvine, and two fellowships from the National Endowment for the Humanities, as well as by the generous support of my research by both Yale University and the University of California at Irvine. I am also grateful to students at Yale, Irvine, and other universities, as well as to lecture audiences, all of whom listened patiently and made constructive suggestions. Parts of this book published in preliminary form as articles are the following: "Ariadne's Thread: Repetition and the Narrative Line," *Critical Inquiry* 3 (Autumn 1976): 57–77; "A 'Buchstäbliches' Reading of *The Elective Affinities,*" *Glyph* 6 (1979): 1–23; "The Disarticulation of the Self in Nietzsche," *The Monist* 64 (April 1981): 247–61; "Character in the Novel: A Real Illusion," in *From Smollett to James: Studies in the Novel and*

Other Essays Presented to Edgar Johnson, ed. Samuel I. Mintz, Alice Chandler, and Christopher Mulvey (Charlottesville: University Press of Virginia, 1981), pp. 277–85; "'Herself against Herself': The Clarification of Clara Middleton," in *The Representation of Women in Fiction,* ed. Carolyn G. Heilbrun and Margaret R. Higonnet (Baltimore: Johns Hopkins University Press, 1983), pp. 98–123; "La Figura en 'La muerte y la brújula' de Borges: Red Scharlach como Hermeneuta," trans. María Inés Segundo, in *La Deconstruccion,* a special issue of *Diseminario* coordinated by Lisa Block de Behar (Montevideo: Uruguay: XYZ Editores, 1987), 163–73; "Figure in Borges's 'Death and the Compass': Red Scharlach as Hermeneut," *Dieciocho* 10 (Spring 1987): 53–61; "Translating the Untranslatable," *Goethe Yearbook,* vol. 5, ed. Thomas Saine (Columbia, S.C.: Camden House, 1990), pp. 269–78. All of these have been thoroughly recast, augmented, and revised to reflect my present understanding and to be incorporated into the larger argument of this book. I am grateful for the reuse of this material.

I also thank Ellen Graham, humanities editor of the Yale University Press, for many courtesies and for her patient encouragement of this project.

Ariadne's Thread

1 Line

ine is the thread of Ariadne, which leads us through the labyrinth of millions of natural objects. Without line we should be lost.
—George Grosz

Ich bin dein Labyrinth.—Friedrich Nietzsche, "Klage der Ariadne," *Dionysos-Dithyramben*

Now, in the pictures of this imaginary maze, you are to note that both the Cretan and Lucchese designs agree in being composed of a single path or track, coiled, and recoiled, on itself. Take a piece of flexible chain and lay it down, considering the chain itself as the path: and, without an interruption, it will trace any of the three figures. (The two Cretan ones are indeed the same in design, except in being, one square, and the other round.) And recollect, upon this, that the word "Labyrinth" properly means "rope-walk," or "coil-of-rope-walk," its first syllable being probably also the same as our English name "Laura," "the path," and its method perfectly given by Chaucer in the single line—"And, for the house

1

is crenkled to and fro." And on this note, farther, first, that *had* the walls been real, instead of ghostly, there would have been no difficulty whatever in getting either out or in, for you could go no other way. But if the walls were spectral, and yet the transgression of them made your final entrance or return impossible, Ariadne's clue was needful indeed.

Note, secondly, that the question seems not at all to have been about getting in; but getting *out* again. The clue, at all events, could be helpful only after you had carried it in; and if the spider, or other monster in midweb, ate you, the help in your clue, for return, would be insignificant. So that this thread of Ariadne's implied that even victory over the monster would be vain, unless you could disentangle yourself from his web also.

—John Ruskin, *Fors Clavigera*

String is my foible. My pockets get full of little hanks of it, picked up and twisted together, ready for uses that never come. I am seriously annoyed if anyone cuts the string of a parcel instead of patiently and faithfully undoing it fold by fold. How people can bring themselves to use india-rubber rings, which are a sort of deification of string, as lightly as they do, I cannot imagine. To me an india-rubber ring is a precious treasure. I have one which is not new—one that I picked up off the floor, nearly six years ago. I have really tried to use it, but my heart failed me, and I could not commit the extravagance.

—Elizabeth Gaskell, *Cranford*

Devilry, devil's work:—traces of such you might fancy to be found in a certain manuscript volume taken from an old monastic library in France at the Revolution. It presented a strange example of a cold and very reasonable spirit disturbed suddenly, thrown off its balance, as by a violent beam, a blaze, of new light, revealing, as it glanced here and there, a hundred truths unguessed at before, yet a curse, as it turned out, to its receiver, in dividing hopelessly against itself the well-ordered kingdom of his thought. Twelfth volume of a dry enough treatise on mathematics, applied, still with no relaxation of strict method, to astronomy and music, it should have concluded that work, and therewith the second period of the life of its author, by drawing tight together the threads of a long and intricate argument. In effect however, it began, or, in perturbed manner, and as with throes of childbirth, seemed the preparation for, an argument of an entirely new and disparate species, such as would demand a new period of life also, if it might be, for its due expansion.

Figure 1. Cretan coins referred to by Ruskin. Illustration from John Ruskin, *Fors Clavigera,* 23 (1872). In *Works of John Ruskin,* ed. E. T. Cook and Alexander Wedderburn, vol. 27 (London: George Allen, 1907).

Figure 2. Labyrinth on the southern wall of the porch of the Cathedral of Lucca. Illustration from John Ruskin, *Fors Clavigera,* 23 (1872).

But with what confusion, what baffling inequalities! How afflicting to the mind's eye! It was a veritable "solar storm"—this illumination, which had burst at the last moment upon the strenuous, self-possessed, much-honoured monastic student, as he sat down peacefully to write the last formal chapters of his work ere he betook himself to its well-earned practical reward as superior, with lordship and mitre and ring, of the abbey whose music and calendar his mathematical knowledge

had qualified him to reform. The very shape of Volume Twelve, pieced together of quite irregularly formed pages, was a solecism. It could never be bound. In truth, the man himself, and what passed with him in one particular space of time, had invaded a matter, which is nothing if not entirely abstract and impersonal. Indirectly the volume was the record of an episode, an interlude, an interpolated page of life. And whereas in the earlier volumes you found by way of illustration no more than the simplest indispensable diagrams, the scribe's hand had strayed here into mazy borders, long spaces of hieroglyph, and as it were veritable pictures of the theoretic elements of his subject. Soft wintry auroras seemed to play behind whole pages of crabbed textual writing, line and figure bending, breathing, flaming, into lovely "arrangements" that were like music made visible; till writing and writer changed suddenly, "to one thing constant never," after the known manner of madmen in such work. Finally, the whole matter broke off with an unfinished word, as a later hand testified, adding the date of the author's death, "*deliquio animi.*"
—Walter Pater, "Apollo in Picardy"

What line should the critic follow in explicating, unfolding, or unknotting these passages?[1] How should the critic thread her or his way into the labyrinthine problems of narrative form, and in particular into the problem of repetition in fiction? The line of the line itself? The motif, image, concept, or formal model of the line, however, far from being a "clue" to the labyrinth, turns out, as the passage from Ruskin suggests, to be itself the labyrinth. To follow the motif of the line will not be to simplify the knotted problems of narrative form but to retrace the whole tangle from the starting place of a certain point of entry.

This overlapping of the part, even a "marginal" part, with the whole is characteristic of all such theoretical investigations. The same thing would happen, in a different way, if the problems of narrative form were entered by way of character in the novel, or of interpersonal relations, or of the narrator, or of temporal structure, or of figurative language and mythological references, or of irony as the basic trope of fiction, or of realism, or of multiple plots, and so on. The motif of the line may have the advantage of being a less used point of entry and of being at once a local motif, microscopic, and an overall formal model, macroscopic. The image of the line, it might be noted, has, by an unavoidable recrossing, already contaminated this topological placing of the image of the line. Since this line is more figure than concept (but is there any concept without figure?), the line can lead easily to all the other conceptual problems I have mentioned: character, intersubjectivity, narrator, time, mimesis, and so on. Perhaps it begs the questions less from the start, or begs the questions in a different way.

To begin at the beginning with the physical aspects of the book, the novel as book, its conditions of production and use. The linearity of the written or printed book is a puissant support of logocentrism. The writer, Walter Pater or Elizabeth Gaskell, George Eliot or Charles Dickens, sits at a desk and spins out on the page a long thread or filament of ink. Word follows word from the beginning to the end. The manuscript is set for printing in the same way, whether letter by letter, by linotype, or from tape by computer. The reader follows, or is supposed to follow, the text in the same way, reading word by word and line by line from the beginning to the end. This linearity is broken, in the Victorian novel for example, only by the engravings that juxtapose "illustrations" in another medium to the continuous flow of printed words, or by anything in the words on the page which in one way or another says, see page so and so. An example of this is the repetition from one place to another of the same word, phrase, or image. The physical, social, and economic conditions of the printing and distribution of Victorian books, that is, the breaking of the text into numbered or titled parts, books, or chapters, and publication in parts either separately or with other material in a periodical, interrupts this linearity but does not transform it into something else. The text of a Victorian novel, to remain with that as prime example for the moment, with its divisions into chapters and parts, is like bits of string laid end to end in series. Its publication in parts over a period of time that, in the case of Dickens's big novels, was almost two years in length, only emphasizes this linearity. Publication in parts gives that linearity an explicitly temporal dimension, a dimension already present in the time it takes to follow a novel word by word, line by line, page by page. Victorian readers had to read one part of *Bleak House* and then, after an interval, the next part, and so on. The spurious instantaneous unity or simultaneity of the single volume held in one's hand was further broken by the fact that Victorian novels, even when their scattered parts were gathered in volume form, were often printed in two, three, or even four volumes. The linearity of a novel is always temporal. It is an image of time as a line. Martin Heidegger, in *Sein und Zeit* and elsewhere, has shown how all the language of temporality is contaminated by spatial terms. From Aristotle on, according to Heidegger, this spatializing of time has reinforced the systematic assumptions of logocentric metaphysics. More recently, Paul Ricoeur, in *Temps et récit,* has explored the relation between notions of time in Aristotle and St. Augustine and forms of narrative coherence in our tradition.[2] One must distinguish sharply, however, between effects of discontinuity, spaces or hiatuses between segments of a narrative line, and true disturbances of the line that make it curve back on itself, recross itself, tie itself in knots. Those spaces may have a powerful effect, in one way or another, on the meaning, but they are not in themselves forms of repetition breaking linearity.

The image of the line and the contrary possibility for the line to return on itself have entered deeply into the terminology used to describe written or printed documents. The root of the word *script* itself, as in manuscript, superscript, and so on, is *skeri,* to cut, separate, sift. The Latin *scribere* meant scratch, incise, write. The words *scrabble, crisis, critic,* and *criminal* have the same root. Writing is the scratching of a line, as when one says "drop me a line." In the eighteenth and early nineteenth centuries, when paper was precious, letters were "crossed," that is, written both ways on the paper, one script superimposed at right angles to the other. A text cited by critic or scholar is a "passage," a narrow defile or *detroit,* a way to get from one place to another in the argument. If writing is a form of dividing, sieving, sifting, or discrimination, a book is made of "gatherings" or "folds" bringing the divided back together. The pages are in order, with a margin framing the lines in a white border, "justified," as we say, suggesting some vague ethical or judicial responsibility to keep neat and straight the frontiers between meaningful sign and unmeaning blank. A justified margin is well policed. It does not straggle. A whole book is a collection of gatherings "bound," given a distinct edge or boundary line. In Pater's "Apollo in Picardy" the physical manifestation that the Prior Saint-Jean's lamentable twelfth volume is a "solecism," evidence that the line of logic is irremediably broken, deviated, or distorted, is the irregularity of its pages: "It could never be bound."

If writing is initially a form of scratching or engraving, the cutting of a line, penetration of some hard substance with a marking tool, it may also, after the invention of pencils and pens, be thought of as the pouring out on a flat surface of a long line or filament, lead or ink making a cursive line of characters stamping, cutting, contaminating, or deflowering the virgin paper, according to a not very "submerged" sexual metaphor. What is a metaphorical transfer in this case? Which is the metaphor of which? Is the pleasure of scribbling the "sublimated" or "displaced" pleasure of sex or is the pleasure of sex the pleasure of writing, the pleasure (male?) of penetrating, furrowing, or marking a blank page, the pleasure of extending the genetic line and of making a copy of oneself, saving the seed from fruitless scattering. On the other hand, is the pleasure or function of sex the pleasure of writing in the sense (female?) of texturing or weaving a text, making a pattern? Is the womb a typewriter or is it a sewing machine? Feminist critics have in recent years taken up these traditional "phallogocentric" figures and challenged them.[3] They have had great currency and power. Gerard Manley Hopkins, for example, describes the "mind . . . mother of immortal song" as a gestating weaver: "Nine months she then, nay years, nine years she long / Within her wears, bears, cares and combs the same."[4] The other sexual figure for writing is brought to the surface, for example, not only in a crucial passage in Hardy's *Tess of the d'Urbervilles* but also in a well-known text in Freud's *Problem of Anxiety*:

> Why it was that upon this beautiful feminine tissue, sensitive as gossamer, and practically blank as snow as yet, there should have been traced such a coarse pattern as it was doomed to receive.[5]

> If writing—which consists in allowing a fluid to flow out from a tube upon a piece of white paper—has acquired the symbolic meaning of coitus, or if walking has become a symbolic substitute for stamping upon the body of Mother Earth, then both writing and walking will be abstained from because it is as though forbidden sexual behavior were thereby being indulged in. The ego renounces these functions proper to it in order not to have to undertake a fresh effort of repression, *in order to avoid a conflict with the id*.[6]

The paradox here is that the paper is already thought of as a tissue, a woven surface of crisscross lines or filaments. The word *line* comes from a root *lino* meaning linen, flax. The text is scratched, cut, stamped, poured out, imprinted, or embroidered on a blank integument that is itself already a woven fabric. *Text* comes from *texere,* to weave. Writing lays fabric on fabric in a hymeneal stitching, joining, or breaking, transgressing a line or frontier, tracing on the woven pattern another pattern, coarse or fine.

If letters in the epistolary sense are "lines," written documents that may be copied or cited, in whole or in part, strung together with more or less commentary, frame, or interpolation to make that strange kind of text, the novel in letters, the basis of a written or printed narrative is letters in another sense. Letters in the alphabetic sense are made of lines carved, stamped, or inscribed which turn back on themselves in one way or another to make a knot, a glyph, a character or sign. The intelligibility of writing depends on this twisting and breaking of the line that interrupts or confounds its linearity and opens up the possibility of repeating that segment, while at the same time preventing any closure of its meaning.

A straight line conveys no information beyond the fact that the line is there, like a continuous dial tone on the telephone, a single monotonous tone on the radio, or the straight line on an oscilloscope when it is not monitoring any changes. The latter is frightening when a cardiac monitor becomes disconnected or when the patient dies and the hills and valleys of "blips" become an unbroken straight line. Such a straight line may both be cited exactly and may not be cited. It may be cited because every straight line is like every other straight line in its featureless perfection. It may not be cited because for that very reason it is impossible to tell which line is being cited. The model remains unidentifiable, and so the perfectly straight line conveys no information beyond itself.

Only the curved, crossed, or knotted line can be a sign making the line simultaneously something intelligible, conveying meaning, standing for something else, and at the same time repeatable, already a repetition, so imposing on the sign the aporias of repetition, the blind alleys in thought to which repetition leads. No repetition is exact, but the meaning of a sign depends on taking it as the exact repetition of some other sign. Nonetheless, the meaning of a sign, as linguists have told us, lies not in its exact contours but in the possibility of differentiating it from other signs, adjacent or nearby, in the possibility of recognizing that an "a," however made, is an "a" and not a "b" or a "z." In any sign something is always left over that is not sublimated in its meaning but remains stubbornly heterogeneous, unique, material. This remainder, which links a text to its means of production, repetition, and consumption, its physical base, makes it possible for there to be texts, something other than the nonexistent phantasm of pure spiritualized, immaterial meaning. There is no meaning without some textual base, even if it is only modulated air. At the same time this exigency makes all texts undecidable in meaning. They are undecidable because the role of that physical substratum either as determining meaning or as being safely excludable from the determination of meaning, as trivial or accidental, can never finally be decided for sure. Does it matter, for example, that blue, black, or red ink is used to inscribe a given written document? It might or it might not. No convention or code can ever fully circumscribe these alternatives. Each letter, mark, or sign, as Jacques Derrida has more than once said, must have an ideal iterability in order to be identifiable and have meaning. At the same time each mark is divisible, marked by the possibility of being used, in whole or in part, in different contexts and therefore with different meanings. Derrida names this propensity to wander away from itself, intrinsic to any sign, "destinerrance." The meaning of any sign, as I shall argue in my discussion of Clara Middleton in Meredith's *Egoist,* is always, each time it is used, posited performatively. This positing is an act for which the one who acts must take responsibility. The meaning is not fixed a priori in the sign itself.[7]

The terms for letters or written signs "characteristically" go back to some physical act, some gesture of marking, incising, or stamping, with some suggestion of the possibility of repetition. The word *write* itself comes from Old English *writan,* from Germanic *writan* (unattested), meaning to tear, scratch. All the *graph* words—graph itself, paragraph, paraph, epigraph, graffito, and graft, in both the botanical and economic senses—go back to words meaning pencil, to inscribe, or the inscription itself: Latin *graphium,* pencil, from Greek *graphion,* pencil, stylus, from *graphein,* to write, derived from the root *gerebh-,* scratch. Grammar, diagram, epigram, and so forth belong to the same family. "Sign" is from Latin *signum,* distinctive mark or feature, seal. "Glyph" is from Greek *gluphein,* to carve, from the root *gleubh-,* to cut, cleave. "Mark" comes from Old English *mearc,* boundary, hence landmark, sign, trace. The root is *merg-,* meaning boundary or border, that is, a line traced around the edges of a region. "Character," as in my word "characteristically" above, is from Latin *character,* character, mark, instrument for branding, from Greek *kharakter,* engraved mark, brand, from *kharassein,* to brand, sharpen, by synecdoche or metonymy, or by exchange of result for cause, from *kharax,* pointed stake, from the root *gher-,* to scrape, scratch. I shall discuss "character" in detail in chapter 2. "Letter" comes from Latin *littera,* letter, possibly borrowed from Greek *diphthera,* tablet, leather used to write on, by synecdoche or metonymy again, a transfer from the act to what is acted upon, though with a different structure, from the root *deph-,* to stamp.

From the pointed stake to the incised brand, from the act of stamping to the material on which the writing is stamped to the stamped figure, from act to material cause to effect—what sort of transfers are these? Metonymy of accidental contiguity or the more intrinsic participation of synecdoche? Active or passive, something done or something suffered, a performative act producing something new or a supposition copying something already there? In any case, in any writing somewhere there is an act of violence, a blow, a cut, cleaving, or stamping, perhaps even a division between the cause and its effect. In writing the effect is not commensurate with its cause. The way writing is a troubling or twisting of the logocentric line is inscribed in the terminology which must be used to write or speak of the act or the paraphernalia of writing. *Signum, gleubh-, gher-, gerebh-, gno-*(the root of "narration")—is it only an accident that these words or roots not only "originally" mean the act of cutting, scratching, or pointing but express that act with a strangulated "guh," the throat's closure, plus some consonant? Writing is named by the involuntary sound in the throat caused by the bodily effort required to do it. This sound is primitive or inarticulate speech. Derrida, in *Glas,* has glossed at length this guh—gn, gl, gh, gr.

Ariadne's thread is a line that traces out the corridors of a labyrinth that is already a kind of writing, as Ruskin, in the passage cited above, suggests. Dionysus's "I am your labyrinth," said to Ariadne, marks the moment of the happy ending of her story, the moment of Dionysus and Ariadne's marriage and apotheosis. This moment has entered almost as deeply as the other two crucial moments of Ariadne's life into the classical, Renaissance, and post-Renaissance imaginations, all the way down to Richard Strauss's *Ariadne auf Naxos.* The latter is the latest in a long genealogical line in opera going back through Jiří Benda in the eighteenth century to Claudio Monteverdi in the seventeenth.[8] The other two moments of the story are the one in which the enamored girl offers Theseus the thread with which to save himself, offering in the thread herself, and the one which shows Ariadne betrayed, watching from the shore at Naxos the perjured sails diminishing toward the horizon:

And to the stronde barefot faste she wente,
And cryed, "Theseus! myn herte swete!
Where be ye, that I may nat with yow mete,
And myghte thus with bestes ben yslayn?"
The holwe rokkes answerede hire agayn.
No man she saw, and yit shyned the mone,
And hye upon a rokke she wente sone,
And saw his barge salynge in the se.[9]

Though in one version Ariadne in her forlorn despair hangs herself with her thread, the story is most often given a happy ending. Dionysus rescues Ariadne and marries her. Walter Pater stresses the importance of this episode for art:

Of the whole story of Dionysus, it was the episode of his marriage with Ariadne about which ancient art concerned itself oftenest, and with most effect. . . . And as a story of romantic love, fullest perhaps of all the motives of classic legend of the pride of life, it survived with undiminished interest to a later world, two of the greatest masters of Italian painting having poured their whole power into it; Titian with greater space of ingathered shore and mountain, and solemn foliage, and fiery animal life; Tintoret with profounder luxury of delight in the nearness to each other, and imminent embrace, of glorious bodily presences; and both alike with consummate beauty of physical form.[10]

The story of Ariadne has, as is the way with myths, its slightly asymmetrical echoes along both the narrative lines which converge in her marriage to Dionysus. Daedalus it is who tells Ariadne how to save Theseus with the thread. Imprisoned by Minos in his own labyrinth, he escapes by flight, survives the fall of Icarus, and reaches Sicily safely. Daedalus is then discovered by Minos when he solves the puzzle posed publicly by Minos, with the offer of a reward to the solver: How to run a thread through all the chambers and intricate windings of a complex seashell? Daedalus pierces the center of the shell, ties a thread to an ant, puts the ant in the

Figure 3. Titian, *Bacchus and Ariadne* (1518). National Gallery, London. Photo courtesy National Gallery.

pierced hole, and wins the prize when the ant emerges at the mouth of the shell. Thread and labyrinth, thread intricately crinkled to and fro as the retracing of the labyrinth that defeats the labyrinth but makes another intricate web at the same time—pattern is here superimposed on pattern, like the two homologous stories themselves.

This notion of a compulsion to repeat intrinsic in the pattern of the story is present in the legend of the "dance of Theseus." Theseus, the anti-Dionysus of the myth, man of reason and Apollonian clarity, nevertheless cannot free himself from his bondage to the Dionysian irrationality of the maze or from the unreason of Ariadne herself, however much he tries to forget her. When Theseus has escaped from the Daedalian labyrinth and, later on, has abandoned Ariadne, he goes to the island of Delos, makes sacrifice to Apollo and to Aphrodite, and institutes in their honor a dance, performed by his consort of youths and maidens saved from the Minotaur. The dance in its intricate turnings is a ritual copy of the

Figure 4. Tintoretto, *Bacchus and Ariadne* (1578). Venice, Palazzo Ducale. Photo Alinari.

labyrinth. It becomes a religious institution at Delos and is performed periodically henceforth in honor of Aphrodite. The Delians call it "Geranos," the crane dance, by analogy, apparently, to the movements of that bird.[11]

Along the other line, the line of Dionysus, in one direction there is the story of Erigone, in the other that of Pentheus and the Baccantes, subject of the extraordinary late play by Euripides, still controversial in purport. The story of Pentheus, doubter of Dionysus, murdered by his Bacchus-maddened mother, is well known, that of Erigone more obscure. Daughter of Icarius, one of the two Erigones, she is seduced by Dionysus who repays her father with wine. Icarius's people murder him when they believe they have been poisoned by the wine. Led to her father's unburied corpse by the barking dog Marra, Erigone hangs herself on a nearby tree. Dionysus, in revenge, drives all the daughters of Athens mad so that they hang themselves. Erigone is made into the constellation of the Virgin.

Again the slightly askew matching of the three stories is striking.

Dionysus is in each case the ambiguous seducer-rescuer in a family story involving defeat or death for the father figures and a complex role for the female figures as murderous mothers, self-slaying victims, and transfigured mates for the god. Dionysus liberates the latter from their repression by fathers or by self-righteous perjuring lovers. The relation among the various stories cannot be wholly rationalized. The need for a permutation of the somewhat mysterious elements of the story is intrinsic to the story itself. It is as if no telling of it could express clearly its meaning. It has to be traced and retraced, thread beside thread in the labyrinth, without ever becoming wholly perspicuous. Each telling both displays the labyrinthine pattern of relations again and at the same time leaves its "true" meaning veiled. Generations of scholars have quarreled over the meaning of Euripides' *Bacchae*. Even Daedalus, fabulous artificer, could not with all his cunning escape from the labyrinth he had made to hide Pasiphaë's monster son, product of her unnatural lust. Daedalus escaped his labyrinth only by flying out of it, by cutting the Gordian knot, so to speak, rather than by untying it, though at the cost of his too bold son, the rash youth Icarus, defier of the sun. All these stories turn on enigmatic oppositions: making, solving; hiding, revealing; female, male, united in ambiguous or androgynous figures, like Dionysus himself, or like Ariadne, who is perhaps too aggressive to be purely "feminine," in the male chauvinist sense of the word, or like Arachne, devouring phallic mother, weaver of a web, "erion" in Greek. *Erion* also, as Jacques Derrida observes in *Glas*, means wool, fleece, the ring of pubic hair.

The conflation of Arachne and Ariadne is implicit in Ruskin's image of the labyrinth's victim eaten by the "monster in midweb." The superimposition of the myths of Ariadne and Arachne, two similar but not wholly congruent stories, both involving images of thread or of weaving, is already present in Shakespeare's splendid portmanteau word "Ariachne's" in Act 5 of *Troilus and Cressida*.[12] As "This is, and is not, Cressid," so Ariachne is and is not Ariadne and at the same time is and is not Arachne. She is both and neither at once. To the similarity and dissimilarity of stories in the same mythical or narrative line must be added the lateral repetition with a difference of distinct myths, here called attention to by the accidental similarity of the names. This clashing partial homonymy perfectly mimes the relation between the two stories.

The convergence of two narrative lines in the marriage of Dio-

nysus and Ariadne, that of Dionysus, that of Ariadne, is traditionally symbolized by the starry crown Dionysus gives her. This crown
is immortalized after her death as the corona in the region of the
constellation Taurus. It is also symbolized by the ring Dionysus
slips on Ariadne's finger. Ring of the marriage tie, knotting the
two stories, rings of stars, each ring deifying the fragmented and
linear sequence of episodes in a round or recurrence, the round of
eternal return: "o wie sollte ich nicht nach der Ewigkeit brünstig
sein und nach dem hochzeitlichen Ring der Ringe—dem Ring der
Wiederkunft?" ("Oh, how should I not lust after eternity and after
the nuptial ring of rings, the ring of recurrence?").[13] This double
ring, marriage ring and crown of stars, is rather a spiral, coil-
shaped, labyrinth-shaped, or ear-shaped. Even an exact repetition
is never the same, if only because it is the second and not the first.
The second constitutes the first, after the fact, as an origin, as
model or archetype. The second, the repetition, is the origin of the
originality of the first. Ariadne, originally herself goddess of love,
is doubled, in Tintoretto's magnificent painting, by Venus. Venus
gives Ariadne the crown, and, in another doubling, the marriage
ring of Ariadne and Dionysus matches the small labyrinth-shaped
ears of the lovers. These ears appear in Nietzsche's revision, for
the version in the *Dionysos-Dithyramben,* of Dionysus's response
to the lament of Ariadne, sung grotesquely by the magician-shaman
in *Zarathustra,* 4.5:

Sei klug Ariadne! . . .
Du hast kleine Ohren, du hast meine Ohren:
steck ein kluges Wort hinein!—
Muß man sich nicht erst hassen, wenn man sich lieben soll? . . .
Ich bin dein Labyrinth.

Be clever, Ariadne! . . .
You have small ears, you have my ears:
Put a clever word unto them!
Must people not first hate themselves if they are to love them-
    selves? . . .
[Or: Must one not first hate himself if he is to love himself?
The phrase in German has two possible readings.]
I am your labyrinth.[14]

I am your labyrinth! Ariadne's lament is pervaded by the imagery of Dionysus's penetration of her inmost being: *"willst* du *hinein,* / ins herz, einsteigen, / in meine heimlichsten / Gedanken einsteigen?" (*"Wouldst* thou *deeply,* / into the heart, climb in, / into my most secret / thoughts climb in").[15] When Dionysus speaks, he offers himself in turn as a maze for her to penetrate and retrace with her thread. This reciprocity, in which each is the container or labyrinth for the other, is echoed by the matching of their small spiral-shaped ears, as in Tintoretto's painting. It is echoed also in the mirroring oscillations of meaning in the enigmatic wisdom Dionysus puts in Ariadne's ear. This is the wisdom of a doubling interpersonal relation between the sexes. It is a relation of simultaneous love and hate that is at the same time the narcissistic mirroring of an androgynous self by itself, in self-hate and self-love: "Muß man sich nicht erst hassen, wenn mann sich lieben soll." The line of Ariadne's thread is at once the means of retracing a labyrinth that is already there and is itself the labyrinth, a "rope-walk," according to Ruskin's false etymology, spun from the belly of a spider in mid-web, Ariadne anamorphosed into Arachne. The line, Ariadne's thread, is both the labyrinth and a means of safely retracing the labyrinth. The thread and the maze are each the origin of which the other is a copy, or each is a copy that makes the other, already there, an origin: Ich bin dein Labyrinth.

The tangles of love and hate and the question of who penetrates whom, in a love that, in its intensity of self-abnegation, is a fatal labyrinthine betrayal, is expressed at a crucial moment of *The Golden Bowl* in a reference to Ariadne's thread. It will be remembered that the biblical source of James's title contains the image of a broken or untied line: "Also when they shall be afraid of that which is high, and fear shall be in the way, and the almond tree shall flourish, and the grasshopper shall be a burden, and desire shall fail: because man goeth to his long home, and the mourners go about the streets: Or ever the silver cord be loosed, or the golden bowl be broken, or the pitcher be broken at the fountain, or the wheel broken at the cistern" (*Ecclesiastes* 12:5–6). Desire and the failing of desire in death, broken containers of the bounty of life, interrupted lines for holding or drawing those vessels—the biblical passage "contains" already elements of the Ariadne story. James's reference to Ariadne comes just after Mrs. Assingham, one of James's most brilliant "ficelles," or auxiliary characters, has smashed the bowl and has left Maggie to confront her adulterous

husband and to offer him the "help" of a delay. She sets the
outrageous price he must pay for her complicity in her own betrayal. He must allow her penetration into the winding corridors
of his inmost self. He must be her labyrinth: "It had operated
within her now to the last intensity, her glimpse of the precious
truth that by her helping him, helping him to help himself, as it
were, she should help him to help *her*. Hadn't she fairly got into
his labyrinth with him?—wasn't she indeed in the very act of
placing herself there for him at its centre and core, whence, on that
definite orientation and by an instinct all her own, she might
securely guide him out of it?"[16] Maggie, like Ariadne/Arachne, is
both the source of the thread that will make it possible for her
husband to escape his labyrinth and at the same time a central
energy spinning a web to entangle him. His labyrinth is both his
own and the one she has made inescapable for him by penetrating
it and retracing it.

The image of the line, it is easy to see, cannot be detached from
the problem of repetition. Repetition might be defined as anything
that happens to the line to trouble its straightforward linearity:
returnings, knottings, recrossings, crinklings to and fro, suspen-
sions, interruptions. As Ruskin says in *Fors Clavigera,* the Daedalian labyrinth, made from a single thread or path curved and
recurved, may serve as a model for everything "linear and complex" since. The phrase is an oxymoron. It names a line that is not
simply linear, not a straightforward movement from beginning to
middle to end. In what follows, I shall explore the way linear
terminology and linear form used to discuss realistic fiction subverts itself by becoming "complex"—knotted, repetitive, doubled,
broken, phantasmal.

To put down first, pell-mell, like the twisted bits of string in the
pockets of the narrator of *Cranford,* some line images as they are
associated with narrative form or with the everyday terminology
of storytelling: narrative line, life line, by-line, main line, drop me
a line, "break up their lines to weep," linotype, what's my line?,
genealogical line, genetic strain, affiliation, defile, thread of the
story, ficelle, lineaments, crossroads, impasse, dénouement, cor-
nered, loose thread, marginal, trope, chiasmus, hyperbole, crisis,
double bind, tie that binds, circulation, recoup, engraving, beyond
the pale, trespass, crossing the bar, missing link, marriage tie,

couple, coupling, copulation, plot, double plot, subplot, spin a yarn, get an angle on, the end of the line.

It may be possible gradually to untwist these hanks, to lay them end to end in a neat series, to make an orderly chain of them, knot added to knot in macramé, or to crochet them into a fabric making a visible figure, a figure in the carpet. Initially to be emphasized is how rich and complex is the family of terms involving the line image—figures of speech, idioms, slang, conceptual words, or narrative motifs like Hercules at the crossroads. Dozens of examples spring to mind in proliferating abundance, like a tangled skein of yarn bits. This is especially the case if the line is extended slightly to include the adjacent figures of cutting, weaving, and setting limits, drawing boundary lines. How can one find the law of this tangled multitude or set limits to it? The notions of legislation (imposed from without or found within) and of boundary are themselves already images of the line. (*Lex* is from the root *lege,* to collect. It is the same root as that for *logic* and *coil.*) The thing to be defined enters into and contaminates the definer, according to a recurrent aporia.

One can see that the line image, in whatever region of narrative terms it is used, tends to be logocentric, monological. The model of the line is a powerful part of the traditional metaphysical terminology. It cannot easily be detached from these implications or from the functions it has within that system. Narrative event follows narrative event in a purely metonymic line, but the series tends to organize itself or to be organized into a causal chain. The chase has a beast in view. The end of the story is the retrospective revelation of the law of the whole. That law is an underlying "truth" that ties all together in an inevitable sequence revealing a hitherto hidden figure in the carpet. The image of the line tends always to imply the norm of a single continuous unified structure determined by one external organizing principle. This principle holds the whole line together, gives it its law, controls its progressive extension, curving or straight, with some *arché, telos,* or ground. Origin, goal, or base: all three come together in the gathering movement of the logos. *Logos* in Greek meant transcendent word, speech, reason, proportion, substance, or ground. The word comes from *legein,* to gather, as in English collect, legislate, legend, or coil.

What is the status of these etymologies? Identification of the true meaning of the word? Some original presence rooted in the ground of immediate experience, physical or metaphysical? By no means. They serve rather to indicate the lack of enclosure of a given word. Each word inheres in a labyrinth of branching interverbal relationships going back not to a referential source but to something already, at the beginning, a figurative transfer, according to the Rousseauistic or Condillacian law that all words were originally metaphors. The searcher through the labyrinth of words, moreover, often encounters for a given word not a single root, but rather forks in the etymological line leading to bifurcated or trifurcated roots or to that philologist's confession of archeological ignorance: "Origin unknown." No reason (that I can see) prevents there being bends or absolute breaks in the etymological line. The realm of words is a free country. Or is it? No reason (that I can see) forbids deploying a given sound or sign to uses entirely without affiliation to its figurative roots. Or is this impossible? What coercion does the word itself, as a material base, exert over the range of meanings one can give it? Can one bend, but not break, the etymological line? In any case, the effect of etymological retracing is not to ground the word solidly but to render it unstable, equivocal, wavering, groundless. All etymology is false etymology, in the sense that some bend or discontinuity always breaks up the etymological line. If the line suggests always the gatherings of the word, at the same time, in all the places of its use, the line contains the possibility of turning back on itself. In this turning it subverts its own linearity and becomes repetition. Without the line there is no repetition, but repetition is what disturbs, suspends, or destroys the line's linearity, like a soft wintry aurora playing behind its straightforward logic.

Linear terminology describing narrative tends to organize itself into links, chains, strands, figures, configurations, each covering one of the topographical regions I have identified as basic to the problematic of realist fiction: time, character, the narrator, and so on. To identify line terminology used for stories, bit of string by bit of string, will be to cover the whole ground, according to the paradox of Ariadne's thread. That thread maps the whole labyrinth, rather than providing a single track to its center and back out. The thread is the labyrinth, and at the same time it is a repetition of the labyrinth.

The bits of string I have gathered may be organized in nine areas of linear terminology.

First come the physical aspects of writing or of printed books: letters, signs, hieroglyphs, folds, bindings, and margins, as well as letters in the sense indicated in the phrase "drop me a line."

A second region of linear terminology involves all the words for narrative line or diegesis: dénouement, curve of the action, turn of events, broken or dropped thread, line of argument, story line, figure in the carpet—all the terms, in short, assuming that narration is the retracing of a story that has already happened. Note that these lines are all figurative. They do not describe the actual physical linearity of lines of type or of writing. Nor do most of them even describe the sequence of chapters or episodes in a novel. Most name rather the imagined sequence of the events narrated.

A third topic is the use of linear terms to describe character, as in the phrases "life line," or "what's my line?" Physiognomy is the reading of character from facial lineaments. The word *character* itself is a figure meaning the outward signs in the lines on a person's face of his inward nature. A character is a sign, as in the phrase "Chinese written character."

A fourth place is all the terminology of interpersonal relations: filiation, affiliation, marriage tie, liaison, genetic or ancestral line, and so on. One cannot talk about relations among persons without using the line images.

Another region is that of economic terminology. The language of interpersonal relations borrows heavily from economic words, as in "expense of spirit in a waste of shame," or when one says "pay him back" or "repay him with interest" or speaks of someone as "out of circulation." Many, if not all, economic terms involve linear imagery: circulation, binding promise or contract, recoup, coupon, margin, cutback, line your pockets, on the line (which means ready for immediate expenditure), currency, current, and pass current.

Another area of narrative terminology involves topography: roads, crossroads, paths, frontiers, gates, windows, doors, turnings, journeys, narrative motifs like Oedipus murdering Laius at the place where three roads cross or Hercules at the crossroads.

Another topic for investigation is illustrations for novels. Most nineteenth-century novels were of course illustrated by etchings or engravings, that is, by pictures printed from plates incised with lines. Ruskin in *Ariadne Florentina* (1873–75) has investigated this use of the line to make a repeatable design.[17]

Another region for investigation is figurative language in the text

of a novel. The terminology for figures of speech is strongly linear,
as when one speaks of tropes, of topoi, of chiasmus, of ellipsis, of
hyperbole, and so on.

A final topos in the criticism of fiction is the question of realistic
representation. Mimesis in a "realistic" novel is a detour from the
real world that mirrors that world and in one way or another, in
the cultural or psychic economy of production and consumption,
leads the reader back to it.

Each of these topological areas invites separate discussion. The
image, figure, or concept of the line threads its way through all the
traditional terms for storywriting or storytelling. Line images make
the dominant figure in this particular carpet. The peculiarity of all
these regions of criticism is that there are no terms but figurative
ones to speak of any of them. The term *narrative line,* for example,
is a catachresis. It is the violent, forced, or abusive importation of
a term from another realm to name something which has no proper
name. The relationship of meaning among all these areas of terminology is not from sign to thing but a displacement from one
sign to another sign that in its turn draws its meaning from another
figurative sign, in a constant displacement. The name for this displacement is allegory. Storytelling, usually thought of as the putting
into language of someone's experience of life, is in its writing or
reading a hiatus in that experience. Narrative is the allegorizing
along a temporal line of this perpetual displacement from imme-
diacy. Allegory in this sense, however, expresses the impossibility
of expressing unequivocally, and so dominating, what is meant by
experience or by writing. My exploration of the labyrinth of narrative terms is in its turn to be defined as a perhaps impossible
search for the center of the maze, the Minotaur or spider that has
created and so commands it all.

The reasons for this impossibility may be variously formulated.
Perhaps it might be better to say, since what is in question here is
the failure of reason, that the inability of the mind to reach the
center of narrative's maze and so dominate it may be encountered
from various directions. One way is in the blind alley reached when
any term or family of terms is followed as far as it will go as a
means of talking about objective aspects of specific novels. No one
thread (character, realism, interpersonal relation, or whatever) can
be followed to a central point where it provides a means of over-
seeing, controlling, and understanding the whole. Instead it
reaches, sooner or later, a crossroad, a blunt fork, where either

path leads manifestly to a blank wall. This double blind is at once the failure to reach the center of the labyrinth and at the same time the reaching of a false center, everywhere and nowhere, attainable by any thread or path. These empty corridors are vacant of any presiding Minotaur. The Minotaur, as Ruskin saw, is a spider, Arachne-arachnid who devours her mate, weaver of a web that is herself. This ubiquitous figure both hides and reveals an absence, an abyss.

The impasse in the exploration of a given novel or of a given term in narrative criticism occurs differently in each case, yet in each case it is experienced as something irrational, alogical. The critic suffers a breakdown of distinctions—for example, that between figurative and literal language, or between the text and that extratextual reality the text mirrors, or between the notion that the novel copies something and the notion that it makes something happen. The critic may be unable to decide, of two repeating elements, which is the original of which, which the "illustration" of the other, or whether in fact they repeat or are rather heterogeneous, inassimilable to a single pattern, whether they are centered, double-centered, or acentric. The critic may be unable to tell whether a given textual knot is "purely verbal" or has to do with "life." The reader may experience the impossibility of deciding, in a given passage, who is speaking, the author, the narrator, or the character, where or when, and to whom. Such a passage in its undecidability bears the indelible traces of being a written document, not something that could ever be spoken by a single voice and so returned to a single *logos*. Always, in such passages, something is left over or missing, something is too much or too little. This forbids imputing the language back to a single mind, imagined or real. In one way or another the monological becomes dialogical, the unitary thread of language something like a Möbius strip, with two sides and yet only one side. An alternative metaphor would be that of a complex knot of many crossings. Such a knot may be in one region untied, made unperplexed, but only at the expense of making a tangle of knotted crossings at some other point on the loop. The number of crossings remains stubbornly the same.

The critic, in a further frustration, may experience the impossibility of detaching a part of narrative form from the whole knot of problems and so understanding that. He cannot separate one piece and explore it in isolation. The part/whole, inside/outside division breaks down. The part turns out to be indistinguishable from the whole. The outside is already inside. Character in the

novel, for example, may not be defined without talking about
interpersonal relations, about time, about figures of speech, about
mimesis, and so on.

The critic may also experience the impossibility of getting outside
the maze and seeing it from without, giving it its law or finding its
law, as opposed to trying to reach a commanding center by exploration from within. Any terminology of explication is already
folded into the text the critic is attempting to see from without.
This is related to the impossibility of distinguishing analytical terminology, the terms the critic needs to interpret novels, from terminology used inside the novels themselves. Any novel already
interprets itself. It uses within itself the same kind of language,
encounters the same impasses, as are used and encountered by the
critic. The critic may fancy himself safely and rationally outside
the contradictory language of the text, but he is already entangled
in its web. Similar blind forks or double binds are encountered in
the attempt to develop a general "theoretical" terminology for
reading prose fiction and, on the other hand, in the attempt to
eschew theory, to go to the text itself and, without theoretical
presuppositions, to explicate its meaning.

Criticism of a given novel or body of novels should therefore be
the following of one or another track until it reaches, in the text,
one or another of these double blinds, rather than the attempt to
find a presupposed unity. Such a unity always turns out to be
spurious, imposed rather than intrinsic. This can be experienced,
however, only through the patient work of following some thread
as far, deep into the labyrinth of the text, as it will go. Such an
effort to read is not the "deconstruction" of a given novel. It is
rather a discovery of the way the novel deconstructs itself in the
process of constructing its web of storytelling. These blind alleys
in the analysis of narrative may not by any means be avoided.
They may only be veiled by some credulity making a standing place
where there is an abyss—for example, in taking consciousness as
a solid ground. The thinly veiled chasm may be avoided only by
stopping short, by taking something for granted in the terminology
one is using rather than interrogating it, or by not pushing the
analysis of the text in question far enough so that the impossibility
of a single definitive reading emerges.

The impasse of narrative analysis is a genuine double blind alley.
It results first from the fact that there is in no region of narrative

or of its analysis a literal ground—in history, consciousness, society, the physical world, or whatever—for which the other regions are figures. The terminology of narrative is therefore universally catachresis. Each is a trope breaking down the reassuring distinction between figure and ground, base of so much theoretical seeing.

The other fork of this double blind is the fact that the terminology of narrative may by no effort be compartmentalized, divided into hanks of different colored thread. The same terms must be used in all regions. All the topoi overlap. Neither the critic nor the novelist can, for example, talk about sexual relations without at the same time using economic terminology (getting, spending, and so on), or without talking about mimetic representation (reproduction), or about topography (crossings), and in fact about all the other topics of narrative. The language of narrative is always displaced, borrowed. Therefore any single thread leads everywhere, like a labyrinth made of a single line or corridor crinkled to and fro.

Take, as an example of this, the letter X. It is a letter, a sign, but a sign for signs generally and for a multitude of relations involving ultimately interchanges among all nine of my places. X is a crossroads, the figure of speech called chiasmus, a kiss, a fish, Christ, the cross of the crucifixion, an unknown in mathematics, the proofreader's sign for a broken letter, a place marked on a map (X marks the spot), an illustration (as when we say, "See figure X"), the signature of an illiterate person, the sign of an error or erasure ("crossed out"), the indication of degrees of fineness (as in the X's on a sack of flour or sugar), the place of encounters, reversals, and exchanges, the region of both/and or either/or ("She is my ex-wife"), the place of a gap, gape, or yawning chasm, the undecidable, the foyer of genealogical crossings, the sign of crossing oneself, of the X chromosome, of crisis, of the double cross, of star-crossed lovers, of cross-examination, of cross-stitching, of cross-purposes, of the witch's cross, of the criss-cross (originally Christ-cross), and of the cross child. X is, finally, the sign of death, as in the skull and crossbones, or the crossed-out eyes of the cartoon figure who is baffled, unconscious, or dead: X X. In all these uses, the "ex" means out of, beside itself, displaced. The real and visible rises, exhales, from the unreal, or does the unreal always appear as the intervening veil or substitute for the absent real, as, in stanza 18 of Wallace Stevens's "Man with the Blue Guitar," daylight comes "Like light in a mirroring of cliffs, / Rising upward from a sea of ex."[18]

Daylight, the visible and nameable, is always doubly derived, secondary. It rises from the sea and then is further displaced by its mirroring from the cliffs in a wandering like that of all those terms I have been examining. This movement makes the source itself unreal, a sea of ex. Stevens speaks, in section 13 of "An Ordinary Evening in New Haven," of the approach of night, from which the light comes and to which it returns, as "the big X of the returning primitive."[19] The real and the unreal, the metaphorical and the literal, the figure and the ground, constantly change places, in oscillating chiasmus, for "ex"ample in Stevens's contradictory explanation of "sea of ex" in his letters. To Renato Poggioli he wrote: "A sea of ex means a purely negative sea. The realm of has-been without interest or provocativeness." To Hy Simons: "Sea of Ex. The imagination takes us out of (Ex) reality into a pure irreality. One has this sense of irreality often in the presence of morning light on cliffs which then rise from a sea that has ceased to be real and is therefore a sea of Ex."[20] Which is unreal, which real, the sea or the light? It cannot be decided. Whatever one sees is unreal and creates as its ground a phantasmal real, which becomes unreal in its turn when one turns to it.

I shall come full circle, to conclude this chapter, to one of the texts with which I began, *Cranford*. *Cranford* is about a village in danger of becoming entirely populated by old maids and fastidious bachelors. The village is in danger of dying out through a failure of family lines to continue. This will happen through a failure of sexual doubling or genealogical crossing. The masculine power of capitalization seems to have been lost in an effeminate or effeminizing doubling, as in Freud's recognition that the multiplying of the images of the phallus means its loss: "As Miss Pole observed, 'As most of the ladies of good family in Cranford were elderly spinsters, or widows without children, if we did not relax a little, and become less exclusive, by-and-by we should have no society at all.'"[21] The passage in question in *Cranford* has to do with generation and with the passing on of names from generation to generation in family crossings. It has to do with the letter f, in fact with a double f. F is genealogically derived from G, gamma in Greek, which is another kind of crossing, the fork in the road, a truncated X, like Y. The f is a doubling of that turn, a *digamma* or "double gamma," as it was called in Greek. The cursive or minuscule gamma is y-shaped: γ, while the capital gamma is like a right-angled turn: Γ. In the passage in *Cranford* the f or double g is further doubled in an effete purity of family names and family bloodlines that almost, but not quite, makes further genealogical crossings impossible. It is as though the double f or quadruple g were the true double blind or end of the line, as it ends my line of argument in this chapter.

The passage, in its admirably quiet but devastating irony, speaks for itself, though it should be noted that it is doubled, dialogical. It is alogical, not only in its irony, but in its use of that Möbius strip form of language called indirect discourse. The passage has quotation marks around it. It is presented as spoken by Mrs. Forrester at the convocation of Cranford ladies brought together to decide whether to call upon the parvenue Mrs. Fitz-Adam, née Mary Hoggins, a farmer's daughter. Mrs. Forrester's words are not presented directly, however. They are expressed in the third person past tense of indirect discourse as if what she says were, absurdly, printed in a newspaper as reported from a parliamentary debate. The words on the page, the tenses and the pronouns, are neither the narrator's nor Mrs. Forrester's. The language belongs properly to no one. It is a double diegesis, that kind of narration Plato so deplored in *The Republic*. In fact the passage is a double double diegesis, if the reader thinks, as she should, of the narrator of *Cranford* as an invented character not identical to Elizabeth Gaskell. The words on the page could be spoken, in the real world of person to person dialogue, by no man or woman. They are a pure invention of writing, like the double f in the names ffaringdon or ffoulkes. The passage is not so much dialogical, with two originating voices, like an ellipse with two focii, as alogical, parabolical, hyperbolical,[22] thrown permanently off-base. It has no conceivable ground in any logos, not even in a double one:

"She had always understood that Fitz meant something aristocratic; there was Fitz-Roy—she thought that some of the King's children had been called Fitz-Roy; and there was Fitz-Clarence now—they were the children of dear good King William the Fourth. Fitz-Adam!—it was a pretty name; and she thought it very probably meant 'Child of Adam.' No one, who had not some good blood in their veins, would dare to be called Fitz; there was a deal in a name—she had had a cousin who spelt his name with two little ffs—ffoulkes—and he always looked down

upon capital letters, and said they belonged to lately-invented
families. She had been afraid he would die a bachelor, he was
so very choice. When he met with a Mrs. ffaringdon, at a water-
ing-place, he took to her immediately and a very pretty genteel
woman she was—a widow, with a very good fortune; and 'my
cousin,' Mr. ffoulkes, married her; and it was all owing to her
two little ffs."[23]

The chapters that follow explore the three corridors of narrative
theory's labyrinth most in question in Ariadne's story as Nietzsche
tells it: the question of self ("Character"), the question of interpersonal relations ("Anastomosis"), and the role of figurative language in the spinning of any narrative line ("Figure"). The other
topics will be mapped in other places.

2 Character

hat a Character Is

If I must speak the schoolmaster's language, I will confess that character comes from this infinite mood, that signifieth to engrave, or make a deep impression. And for that cause, a letter (as A. B.) is called a character.

Those elements which we learn first, leaving a strong seal in our memories.

Character is also taken from an Egyptian hieroglyphic, for an impress, or short emblem; in little comprehending much.

To square out a character by our English level, it is a picture (real or personal) quaintly drawn, in various colors, all of them heightened by one shadowing.

It is a quick and soft touch of many strings, all shutting up in one musical close; it is wit's descant on any plain song.

—*Sir Thomas Overbury His Wife*

It is in modern philosophy, in the fully realized metaphysics of the Subject, that ideology finds its real guarantee: that is to say, in the thought of being (and/or of becoming, of history) defined as a subjectivity present to itself, as the support, the source, and the finality of representation, certitude, and will. . . . The *ideology of the subject* . . . is fascism, the definition holding, of course, for today.

—Philippe Lacoue-Labarthe and Jean-Luc Nancy, "The Nazi Myth"

In following in another place the corridor marked "diegesis,"[1] I have already encountered the problem of character. The exploration of any key term in the criticism of fiction necessarily crisscrosses with the others. The question of character occupies so large a region in the maze of narrative terminology that it calls for separate exploration. The assumption that the primary function of novels is to present characters is a red thread running through reigning assumptions about what is important in realistic fiction and about what procedures should be used in interpreting it. Examples from English and American criticism include the work of F. R. Leavis and W. J. Harvey, or the influential studies of the novel by Barbara Hardy, or the discussions of the topic by Martin Price.[2] The list could be extended indefinitely. It would include even essays by those who have doubts about traditional notions of character and traditional ways of representing it in fiction. A salient example is Virginia Woolf's attack on Edwardian realism, "Mr Bennett and Mrs Brown."[3]

The assumption that one should talk about the characters when discussing novels is deeply ingrained in English and American culture. To analyze the character of the characters seems so natural—so much part of nature, not cultural at all—that it is difficult to get students in courses in fiction to talk or write about anything else. The reasons for this are both cultural and literary. They derive from the "real" expectations of people in their living together in society at a certain historical moment, the time of the novel, which coincides with the time of the rise of capitalism. At the same time they derive from readers' expectations about this particular form of literature, itself embedded in modern history. Most English and American readers of novels, even those trained experts who are for one reason or another writing essays on a given novel, pass through the language of a novel as if it were transparent glass. They begin talking about the characters in the story as if they were real people, seen perhaps through that glass and perhaps distorted by it, but not created by language. This is as true of most "post-structuralist" readings—Lacanian, new historicist, or recent Marxist readings, for example—as it is for old-fashioned humanist discussions, such as those by Leavisites, New Critics, or Boothians.

Such discourse talks about the characters in the novel in the same way as the narrator of that novel normally talks about them. Usually there is a change from the past to the present tense in the critic's language. The critic writes, for example: "Dorothea Brooke convinces herself that marrying Casaubon would be like marrying Milton . . . ,'" and so on. The language of the critic extends and continues the language of the narrator. That shift to the present tense, however, grants each moment of the characters' lives an odd species of eternal presence. Dorothea, in the critic's language, goes on indefinitely intending to marry Casaubon. All the other moments of her life also go on eternally happening over and over, within the pages of the book. This use of the present tense implicitly recognizes that Dorothea comes to exist through an act of reading that may be repeated innumerable times. Once this process of transfer and assimilation is performed, the critic is free to yield to the illusion generated by the story, filling in gaps in the narrator's analysis, extrapolating from it, paraphrasing it. This is the "How many children had Lady Macbeth?" fallacy made the basis of a strongly institutionalized form of criticism.

Such criticism is an odd form of mystification. The critic has caught a trick of language from the text, as one catches a disease. The reader has been contaminated by the narrator's language and speaks unwittingly as though he or she were one of the invented characters in the novel, the narrator, even though the critic knows perfectly well that Dorothea Brooke can be encountered only in the pages of *Middlemarch*. Far from being more a means of engagement in the "real world" than discussion of the rhetorical strategy of the novel, such criticism is often a spontaneous evasion into unverifiable fictionalities that makes of the critic himself or herself implicitly a fiction. If I speak or write of fictional characters as if they were real people, have I not myself passed through the mirror into the wonderland of fiction?

To change the metaphor of the transparent glass: it is as difficult to pay attention to the language of a work of fiction as to study the threads of a tapestry rather than look at the blazoned picture it represents. To be sure, many critics of various sorts these days are paying that attention. The figure of the threads of the tapestry, however, like all such visual figures for the way novels work, is misleading. A novel is a curious kind of tapestry in which the fact that its picture is made of thread is likely to be woven into the picture in multiple ways. The picture is "of" its own medium. A work of fiction often allegorizes problems of language in terms of the characters and their interaction. This allegorizing is likely to be explicitly signaled in many details of the work. An example is Meredith's *Egoist,* to be discussed in detail later in this chapter. In such novels, in a different way in each case, the picture in the tapestry calls attention to its own threads and to their modes of weaving.

Nevertheless, for readers who belong still to the tradition for which realistic fiction was written, such fiction has as perhaps its most salient characteristic the ability to create powerful phantasms of personalities. We feel we know Elizabeth Bennet, Dorothea Brooke, Plantagenet Palliser, Michael Henchard, or Joe Christmas in the same way we know our friends or members of our own families. We may feel we know the fictional characters even better. One of the powerful attractions of reading novels is the way the reading of a novel produces the powerful illusion of an even more intimate access to the mind and heart of another person than the reader can ever have in real life.

Nevertheless, the effect of encountering and knowing a character or person or another self in a novel is an illusion, as, in a different way, it is in real life. Belief in unitary selfhood is as much an ideological construct as the other basic concepts of Western "logocentrism" with which it is inextricably connected—cause, ground, the subject-object dichotomy, and so on. But if realistic novels have been a puissant reinforcement in the West for the last four hundred years of the illusion of selfhood, they have at the same time constantly and explicitly deconstructed that illusion. Novels show belief in unitary selfhood to be an effect of the misreading of signs. In this chapter I shall explore this self-dismantling as it is expressed in one region of the imagery of the line in narrative terminology—lengths of yarn tied in one hank, corridors in one part of the labyrinth retraced by Ariadne's thread.

Life line, what's my line? lineaments, character—these terms discussed in the first chapter are cited here as examples of the way the terminology defining selfhood is tied to the network of linear terms for narrative. The word *character* is itself a linear figure, as whoever wrote "What a Character Is" in *Sir Thomas Overbury His Wife* knew. (It may have been Donne, Dekker, or Webster, or perhaps Overbury himself.) A character is a carved design or sign.

The word is a noun made from the Greek verb *kharassein,* to brand, cut, or scratch, as with a pointed stick (*kharax*). What is involved in borrowing a word for a "character" in the sense of a letter or incised sign to name "character" in the sense of personality or selfhood?

It might be claimed that the figurative etymology of this or of any other conceptual word does not say anything one way or the other about the extralinguistic existence of the entity. This is true, but etymology does say something about the procedure involved in naming that presumed entity. Identification of the root metaphor identifies the figurative transfer that was necessary to develop the conceptual term for the entity in question. The word *character,* like the word *lineaments* and the word *person* (from the Latin word for mask), involves the presumption that external signs correspond to and reveal an otherwise hidden inner nature. The visible design made by the features of a face—nose, mouth, eyes, lines of fore- head, cheek, or chin—are taken as a hieroglyphic sign telling ac- curately what that person is like inwardly. What was originally a synecdoche, part for whole, or a metonymy, contingent visible element as sign for a secret adjacent element, in a complex which must be assumed to be homogeneous for the figure to work, grad- ually comes to be the "literal" name for what it used only to figure. What is problematic about the figure is obvious. Does a man's face really correspond to his inner nature? Does he really "have" an inner nature, separate from the signs that point to it? This problem is likely to be forgotten when the figure is literalized.

A further question involved in any such figure is also likely to be forgotten. The figure is a catachresis. It does not substitute for any existing literal term. What kind of existence does something have which can in no way be named except figuratively? The figure is hypostatized as the name of an entity supposed actually to exist— the unified self. The terminology for the soul and for the faculties of the soul is an important example of this figure. It is particularly important for the interpretation of novels. There is no way to talk about psychological entities except in figure, no literal language for the self, as the example of *The Egoist* will show. This is so because the features of the self can never be encountered directly, as objects of sense experience. These features can only be inferred, indirectly, from signs. Many novelists in the realistic tradition have in one way or another dramatized this disquieting fact.

Does this mean that the "self" is a fiction? Does the self not exist as an independent, substantial, extralinguistic entity, either in

real life or in fiction? It depends on what one means by "exist," though there is no doubt some dubiety about the existence of an entity that cannot be straightforwardly sensed and named, as a table or a leaf apparently can. Whatever can only be named in figure may be only a figure, a phantasmal effect of the displacements and exchanges of language. On the other hand, such a thing may exist, but in a realm inaccessible to direct seeing and naming. Or, it may be, the self exists as the product of a promissory performative contract, just as a new state does after a declaration of independence. The self must then take responsibility for the self it has made. It must keep or break the promise and take the consequences for what it does. The "self" is one of the most important and problematic of such strange entities generated by speech acts.

It might be argued that these uncertainties do not matter. The assumption of character in the sense of selfhood is a noble error that is essential to the holding together of society, as well as essential to any coherent storytelling. One definition of madness, however, is the taking literally of a figure of speech and then living in terms of that figure. The madman misinterprets himself and other people according to false literalizations. Anyone who says that the study of rhetoric (in the sense of training in the deciphering of beguiling illusions generated by various figures of speech) has nothing to do with life has no understanding of life. Catastrophic difficulties are likely to follow from taking figures of speech literally, as thousands of pages of psychiatric literature abundantly illustrate.

Perhaps, it might nevertheless be answered, the concept of selfhood is a benign error if it is a collective one, if it is shared by a whole society. Selfhood is an indispensable illusion, it might be argued, if it functions as the supreme fiction holding together the members of a given society, just as belief in totemism holds together a given preliterate tribe. I answer that collective madness, based on the literal living out of a figure of speech, is the most dangerous insanity of all, as a moment's reflection will show. It is dangerous both to the members of the group and to those outside it. Collective madness can lead to the solemn "justified" slaughter of tens of thousands of "others." This becomes ultimately, by a regular law, the self-slaughter of the group. William Golding's *Lord of the Flies* is a parable of this self-destructive fatality of misread signs. Freud's late paper "Constructions in Analysis" ends by identifying the illusions and hallucinations of the hysteric with the collective delusions of mankind: "If we consider mankind as a whole and substitute it for the single human individual, we discover that it too has developed delusions [Wahnbildungen] which are inaccessible to logical criticism and which contradict reality."[4] Lacoue-Labarthe and Nancy name such delusions "myths"—for example, the myth of the Aryan Subject in National Socialism.[5] Belief in the myth of the subject is by no means a benign or politically innocent error.

On the other hand, to live without the illusion of selfhood, to feel one's selfhood doubled, tripled, dissolved, as though by demonic possession, as Kierkegaard described it,[6] to live in the nakedness of truth, were such a thing possible, would be another kind of madness. To be human is to live precariously balanced between madness and madness, between extremes both extremely dangerous. The function of the novel in the economy of modern bourgeois society, I suggest, has been the paradoxical one of reinforcing, to some degree even creating, the linguistic error of a belief in unitary selfhood, while at the same time putting that belief in question, demystifying in one way or another the error. Novels hold their readers in the *malconfort* of that balance. The psychic or social function of this simultaneous affirmation and putting in question remains to be interrogated.

Challenge to belief in fixed substantial selfhood has been a persistent topic of post-Renaissance thought. This is so in spite of the theological, legal, contractual, and ethical stakes involved. How can I be judged by an angry or merciful God, or be haled before the law, or be held to a contractual commitment, or be obligated to keep a promise, if I do not remain the same person from hour to hour and day to day, long enough at least to be held responsible for what I do? Such modern philosophical movements as phenomenology and existentialism are grounded on one or another concept of the ego, "transcendental" or otherwise.

After Nietzsche and Freud, however, it would seem difficult to take the existence of the unitary self as an a priori firmly established. Even earlier, Cervantes, Sterne, and Diderot, for example, among many other novelists, had already in one way or another put the unified self in question. A long tradition in British empirical philosophy, extending from Locke through Hume into the nineteenth century, challenged or redefined the notion of fixed selfhood.

In a notorious passage in the chapter on "Personal Identity" in *A*

Treatise on Human Nature Hume puts the emphasis on the insensible temporal changes whereby a self ceases to be itself. Since we
have no valid standing place outside these changes from which we
can measure them, discussions of personal identity cannot be part
of philosophy. They are disputes about language: "all the nice and
subtle questions concerning personal identity can never possibly be
decided, and are to be regarded rather as grammatical than as
philosophical difficulties. Identity depends on the relations of ideas;
and these relations produce identity, by means of that easy transition they occasion. But as the relations, and the easiness of the
transition may diminish by insensible degrees, we have no just
standard, by which we can decide any dispute concerning the time,
when they acquire or lose a title to the name of identity."[7]

To move to more recent philosophy: neither Husserl nor Heidegger nor Sartre, in the twentieth-century phenomenological tradition, hold to an idea of the self in the sense of an original and
originating ego that remains the same through time. Husserlian
intentionality is by no means the same as intention in the sense of
"I intend to do so and so." Heideggerian *Dasein* is explicitly
opposed to the Cartesian self-conscious "I." For Sartre the "I"
reinvents and reaffirms itself from moment to moment in order to
persist in ethical or political commitment. Nor can one accept the
now outmoded interpretation of "modernism" that sees a self
assumed to be solidly there in earlier epochs endangered or "alien-
ated" by recent social or historical forces. A suspicion that the self
may be no more than a social, legal, or linguistic fiction, however
necessary a fiction, has been present in one way or another at all
times in our history. Dubiety about the existence of the unitary self
is an intrinsic part of the Western tradition, along with a complex
interlocking set of different ways to define it and affirm it. This
copresence of affirmation and denial has, however, taken special
forms in the nineteenth and twentieth centuries in the West. These
will be my primary, but not exclusive, focus here.

What I have said so far in this chapter is preliminary, hypothet-
ical, proleptic. "Character" is made up of the reading of a series
of examples in which the word or the concept of character, and
adjacent words or concepts (subject, self, the ego, and the like),
are not so much defined as used. My effort is an example of what
Jacques Derrida calls "palaeonomy": "I use the word 'palaeonomy'
to explain the way we should use an old word; not simply to give

up the word, but to analyze what in the old word has been buried or hidden or forgotten. And what has been hidden or forgotten may be totally heterogeneous to what has been kept."[8] Only a series of careful readings, as opposed to the stark propositions of theory, will, I hold, enter within the problematic of character, as a word, concept, or thing, all three of these and not quite any one of them. So much is at stake here that the interpreter must move slowly, interrogating exemplary passages in detail. Though much has been written about the self in recent years, resistances of one sort or another make it still difficult to achieve full clarity about it. My examples are not dialectically, chronologically, or cumulatively arranged. Nor would it be quite right to define them as perspectives on a central topic, character, concentrically or eccentrically arranged around some mysterious center, the "truth about the self." Each example, rather, might be better thought of as one path through a complex forest of possible ways to think, speak, or write about "character." Or, each might be thought of as a unique crystallization of possibilities inherent in the word or concept *character* and its near neighbors, *self, ego, I*. Nietzsche, *The Oxford English Dictionary*, Benjamin, Baudelaire, Derrida, Trollope, George Eliot, Poe, Rabelais, Wittgenstein—the passages by these authors read here form a repertoire, by no means exhaustive, of possible ways of thinking about character. More elaborated readings of Nietzsche and Wittgenstein bracket briefer discussions of the others. The cumulative effect of reading the examples one by one is not so much a gradually attained mastery of the topic as a gradually attained sense of what the terrain is like. The examples are bound together more by what Wittgenstein calls "family resemblance" than by a conspicuous repetition from one to another of the same patterns of thought or language. The culmination of the chapter is a fuller reading of the presentation of Clara Middleton's character in George Meredith's *Egoist*.

Nietzsche

Of all modern writers, Friedrich Nietzsche, in Book 3 of *The Will to Power*, presents perhaps the most systematic dismantling of selfhood in its relation to the other metaphysical concepts entwined with it.[9] He inherits, recapitulates, and extends the long Western tradition of dubiety about the substantiality of the self. Decomposition of the idea of selfhood is of course one of Nietzsche's main themes throughout his work, beginning with *The Birth of Tragedy* (1872) and the incomplete *Philosophenbuch* (1873). The topic threads its way through all he wrote. But Book 3 of *The Will to Power* contains, among other things, a concentrated effort of demystification directed against the concept of the self. The topic recurs throughout Book 3 as a patient and constantly renewed process of disarticulation, for which there is no "central" expression. Section 477 nevertheless contains most of the elements involved. This section also brings out the way the image of the line is essential both to the fiction of the self and to its undoing. Nietzsche's thought here, in its connection with other sections of Book 3, has considerable complexity. It is not all that easy to rethink it, or to hold all its features clearly in one's mind, partly for reasons that I shall specify at the end of this section:

> I maintain (Ich halte) the phenomenality of the *inner* world, too: everything of which we *become conscious* is arranged, simplified (vereinfacht), schematized, interpreted through and through—the *actual* process of inner "perception," the *causal connection* (*die Kausalvereinigung*) between thoughts, feelings, desires, between subject and object, are absolutely hidden from us—and are perhaps purely imaginary. The "apparent *inner* world" is governed by just the same forms and procedures as the "outer" world. We never encounter "facts": pleasure and displeasure (Lust und Unlust) are subsequent and derivative intellectual phenomena—
>
> "Causality" (Die "Ursächlichkeit") eludes us; to suppose a direct causal link (ein unmittelbares ursächliches Band), as logic does—that is the consequence of the crudest and clumsiest observation. *Between* two thoughts *all kinds of affects* play their game (*Zwischen* zwei Gedanken spielen *noch alle möglichen Affekte* ihr Spiel): but their motions are too fast, therefore we *fail* to *recognize* them, we *deny* them (deshalb *verkennen* wir sie, *leugnen* wir sie)—
>
> "Thinking," as epistemologists conceive it, simply does not occur: it is a quite arbitrary fiction (eine ganz willkürliche Fiktion), arrived at by selecting *one* element from the process and eliminating all the rest, an artificial arrangement (eine künstliche Zurechtmachung) for the purpose of intelligibility—
>
> The "spirit," something that thinks: where possible even "absolute, pure spirit"—this conception is a second derivative of

that false introspection which believes in "thinking": first an act is imagined which simply does not occur, "thinking," and secondly a subject-substratum in which every act of thinking, and nothing other than thinking, has its origin (seinen Ursprung): that is to say, *both the deed and the doer are fictions* (sowohl *das Tun, als der Täter sind fingiert*).[10]

The parts of the concept of the self Nietzsche wants to put in question are bound into one around the central "substratum" of the subject. Nietzsche unties these bonds, "analyzes" the knotted elements. In so doing he demolishes that central substratum too. When the links chaining the parts together vanish, the phantom of their origin in a single substantial thing called the subject also vanishes, like a ghost at daybreak. This disarticulation is also performed by reversing the apparent order of origination and derivation. The usual sequence—putting subject first, and its thoughts second as derived from the thinker; putting the thoughts themselves in sequence, each causing the next, in logical order; asserting a causal connection between the outer world and inner sensations or thoughts caused by the outer world—all three are condemned as metalepses, substitutions of before for after. They are reversals of the actual order of temporal priority. To say sensations cause thoughts puts the earlier later and the later earlier, so creating the false appearance of a necessary sequence.

Essential to Nietzsche's procedure is the presupposition that the mind's fundamental activity is interpretation. All interpretation, for Nietzsche, is false interpretation. It is an aberrant reading dependent on simplifying, schematizing, omitting, transferring, substituting, exchanging, a making equal of things that are not equal. To put this another way, all interpretation is the fabrication of figures of speech and then commission of the aboriginal human error of taking these figurative equivalences as literally true of extralinguistic reality.

Nietzsche's disentangling of the various knots involved in the idea of selfhood follows no preestablished order of priority. Order and priority are among the things being undone. Rather, each particular effort of untying, in the different sections of Book 3, assumes that some other one has already been accomplished and can be used as the basis for the present effort. The result is a constant process of undoing without any fixed starting place. The knot of presuppositions being untied was constructed by the same circular process of a round robin positing. The notion of self depends on theological assumptions, but those theological assumptions depend on the notion of self, and both depend on the idea of causality, the idea of substance, and the idea of ground. Those ideas in turn make no sense without the theological assumptions—and so on, in a perpetual round. It is appropriate therefore that the untying should reverse this procedure, untying it by performing its magic performatives backward.

The purpose of the false construction of the self, for Nietzsche, is to make continued human life possible. It also yields the pleasure of an exercise of the artistic will to power over things. This gives us the illusion of knowing things, whereas in fact, as Vico long ago said, we can know only what we have made. "The sense for the real," says Nietzsche in section 495, "is the means of acquiring the power to shape things according to our wish. The joy in shaping and reshaping—a primeval joy! We can comprehend only a world that we ourselves have made. (Die Lust am Gestalten und Umgestalten—eine Urlust! Wir können nur eine Welt *begreifen,* die wir selber *gemacht* haben)" (E, 272; G, 424).

The assumption that the external world is a construction is taken for granted in section 477. It is posited as the solid base on which a secondary positing may be deposited: "I maintain the phenomenality of the *inner* world, too." As Nietzsche says in section 482: "We set up a word at the point at which our ignorance begins, at which we can see no further, e.g., the word 'I,' the word 'do,' the word 'suffer':—these are perhaps the horizon of our knowledge, but not 'truths'" (E, 267; G, 863). The inner world, the world of the "I," is like the external world man has constructed for himself in the primeval joy of his artistic shaping. The inner world too, the world of "thoughts, feelings, desires (Gedanken, Gefühlen, Begehrungen)," is phenomenal. It is an appearance, a fiction, a work of art: "The 'apparent *inner* world' is governed by just the same forms and procedures as the 'outer' world." It too is the result of schematizing, omitting, simplifying, a figurative making equal of the unequal. In short, it is the result of an act of interpretation. It is a misreading.

Nietzsche's procedure of deconstruction for the inner world of subjectivity is the same as that for the apparent outer world of things. Four different procedures of dismantling are simultaneously employed in section 477 and in other related passages.

First: the individual entities of which the soul is supposed to be constituted—thoughts, feelings, faculties, and so on—are held by Nietzsche not to exist as such. They are the fictitious products of acts of simplifying construction: "We never encounter 'facts': pleasure and displeasure are subsequent and derivative intellectual phenomena." The same thing may be said for all the other "facts" of the inner world.

Second: according to Nietzsche no two feelings or thoughts are the same, or continue, or ever recur. They are made to appear to do so by a making simple, regular, and manageable like that which motivates our creation of a fictitious outer world: "In order for a particular species to maintain itself and increase its power, its conception of reality must comprehend enough of the calculable and constant (Gleichbleibendes) for it to base a scheme of behavior on it" (E, 266; G, 751); "In *our* thought, the essential feature is fitting new material into old schemas (= Procrustes' bed), *making* equal what is new (das Gleich-*machen* des Neuen)" (E, 273; G, 462). This "making equal" of what is unequal is registered in the primordial act of naming. Man makes up the name "leaf" for what does not exist, since no two leaves are the same, nor does any one remain the same from moment to moment. At the same time this making equal is the primordial act of fabricating figures of speech. Making equal what is unequal is the basis of figuration. Naming and figuration are the "same." This means the beginning is catachresis, since the initial names are figures brought in from some other semantic region to cover an ignorance, but they do not substitute for any literal words. The second act of deconstruction Nietzsche performs on the self, then, is to undo this construction of regularity by denying that any two phenomena of the inner world are ever the same. No feeling or thought may continue or ever recur, holds Nietzsche.

A third disarticulation is to undo the supposed causal links that appear to bind together in tight chains these fictitious entities as they follow one another in the mind. Much of Nietzsche's attention in section 477 and the other "similar" sections is focused on the undoing of the concept of causality. Here the image of tying and untying is fundamental. The apparently firm causal links between one thought or feeling and the next are said to be hidden or perhaps nonexistent: "to suppose a direct causal link between thoughts, as logic does—that is the consequence of the crudest and clumsiest observation." Events in the inner world of consciousness follow one another without any connection, causal or otherwise, between them. Each is self-enclosed. It is separated by a gap from all other thoughts and feelings. It is only made into any sort of pattern with those others by an arbitrary act of artistic construction: "Everything of which we become conscious," says Nietzsche in section 478, "is a terminal phenomenon (Enderscheinung), an end—and causes (verursacht) nothing; every successive phenomenon in consciousness is completely atomistic" (E, 265; G, 729).

A fourth process of decomposition is related to the third. It is not so much an untying as a reversal. This reversal is one of the most powerful arguments Nietzsche makes against the coherence of the inner world and against the possibility of unifying it around the idea of the self. If the apparent entities of the inner world do not exist as such, if nothing in the inner world continues or recurs or is the same as any other, and if the apparent causal lines between these fictitious entities are themselves fictitious, these apparent lines themselves are more than merely fictitious. They are also drawn backward. The apparent causal links of the inner world are the result of that preposterous figure of speech that puts the early late and the late early: metalepsis. There are two forms of this in the inner world. One is the mistaken ascription to events in the "outer" world of causal power over the events in the "inner" world. This apparent sequence from outer to inner, from object to subject, is a reversal of the true order. Inner precedes outer and projects that outer as the illusory cause of its states. This means that the distinction between inner and outer, on which the whole set of assumptions depends, breaks down. It too is an illusion, a fiction, a work of art. There is no solid "object" to cause "subject." There is only one single "phenomenal" realm within which all these fictitious entities and the lines between them are constructed.

Nietzsche's procedure of deconstruction here is to reverse what has been reversed. He performs a metalepsis of the metalepsis, a chiasmus of the chiasmus. He reveals thereby the fictitious, projective nature of the supposed "cause" in the "outer" world. This is implicit in section 477, but it is most explicitly performed in another well-known section, 479:

> *The phenomenalism of the "inner world."* Chronological inversion (Umdrehung), so that the cause (die Ursache) enters consciousness later than the effect.— We have learned that pain is projected to a part of the body without being situated there— we have learned that sense impressions naively supposed to be

conditioned by the outer world are, on the contrary, conditioned by the inner world; that we are always unconscious of the real activity of the outer world— The fragment of outer world of which we are conscious is born after (nachgeboren) an effect from outside has impressed itself upon us, and is subsequently (nachträglich) projected as its "cause." (E, 265; G, 804)

If the outer world is no prior cause, but is rather a later projected illusion cast back as the supposed source of some "inner" event, feeling, or thought, the same inversion is spontaneously practiced by consciousness to make sense of the temporal order of the inner world taken in itself. "We believe that thoughts as they succeed one another in our minds stand in some kind of causal relation (kausalen Verkettung)" (E, 264; G, 728), but in fact "the sequence of thoughts and feelings is only their becoming visible in consciousness. That this sequence has anything to do with a causal chain (einer Kausal-Verkettung) is completely unbelievable: consciousness has never furnished us with an example of cause and effect" (E, 284; G, 732).

Nietzsche unties the links of cause and effect in the inner world, in this fourth process of decomposition, by seeing them as a gross oversimplification of an enormously complex set of rapid occurrences. As he says in section 477: "Between two thoughts all kinds of affects play their game: but their motions are too fast, therefore we fail to recognize them, we deny them." Moreover, Nietzsche argues that these oversimplified links go in the wrong direction. He reverses the metalepses once more and defines the inner causes too as fictitious entities projected backward after the effects to account for them. Projection is a switch of prior and posterior in which the effect is made the cause of its cause, the cause the effect of its effect:

> In the phenomenalism of the "inner world" we invert the chronological order of cause and effect. The fundamental fact of "inner experience" is that the cause is imagined after the effect has taken place— The same applies to the succession of thoughts:— we seek the reason (Grund) for a thought before we are conscious of it; and the reason enters consciousness first, and then its consequence— Our entire dream life is the interpretation (die Auslegung) of complex feelings with a view to possible causes— and in such a way that we are conscious of a condition only

when the supposed causal chain (Kausalitäts-Kette) associated

with it has entered consciousness. (E, 265; G, 804)

Nietzsche's thought here is not easy to grasp. The paradox is that we are not, and cannot be, conscious of the "facts" of the inner world as such, nor even of effects, such as pain, or a thought, that seem to exist only as facts of consciousness. We cannot be conscious of our consciousness as such. The reason is that consciousness only works in terms of comprehensible imaginary causal chains. We project backward a fictitious cause and only then can the thought or the feeling enter consciousness. It enters consciousness in the thoroughly aberrant form of a fictitious effect of a fictitious cause: "The effect always 'unconscious': the inferred and imagined cause (Ursache) is projected (projiziert), *follows* in time" (E, 271; G, 473). An effect of which we are not yet conscious becomes the cause of an imaginary cause, and that imaginary cause then generates belatedly the consciousness of an effect that fits that imaginary cause. It does this in the sense of being purely imaginary, "phenomenal," too. If dreams are inventions of phantasmal causes for conditions that we can only become aware of in the dream, in the form of equally phantasmal effects, as when a book falling to floor is read by the dream as a shot fired by a burglar breaking in to the house, or vice versa, our entire "waking" life is also no more than a sequence of regularized and recurrent dreams. The human condition is to be, in the striking phrase from the early essay "On Truth and Lies in a Nonmoral Sense," "as if (gleichsam) hanging in dreams on the back of a tiger."[11]

The function of language in the human economy is to make the regularizing and equalizing of our collective dreamlife possible. The names that are already there for anyone born into the human dream are the tools with which the metalepses that make waking dreams are constructed. As Nietzsche argues in "On Truth and Lies in a Nonmoral Sense," the "origin" of language was the performative violence of catachresis, naming in figure what cannot be named literally. This act of naming is "performative" because it works. It is a speech act that has effects for the individual, for society, and for history. The users of a given language then construct by elaborate transfers of metaphor and metonymy a whole beehive or columbarium of concepts and classifications. This process is the indispensable means of making the mad waking dream that seems to the one living within it his or her familiar, sane, conscious life:

> The whole of "inner experience" rests upon the fact that a cause of an excitement of the nerve centers is sought and imagined—and that only a cause thus discovered enters consciousness: this cause in no way corresponds to (ist schlecterdings nicht adäquat) the real cause—it is a groping (ein Tasten) on the basis of previous "inner experiences," i.e., of memories (Gedächtnisses). But memory also maintains the habit of all interpretations, i.e., of erroneous causality (irrtümlichen Ursächlichkeit)—so that the "inner experience" has to contain within it the consequences of all previous false causal fictions. . . .
>
> "Inner experience" enters our consciousness only after it has found a language (eine Sprache) the individual understands—i.e., a translation (Übersetzung) of a condition into conditions familiar to him—; "to understand" means merely: to be able to express something new in the language of something old and familiar. (E, 265–66; G, 804–05)

Finally, only after this elaborate act of untying, moving backward to undo knot after knot that has woven the web of the inner world, does Nietzsche come at last, at the end of section 477, to the ur-fiction on the ground of which the whole airy structure has been built: the notion of the unity, substantiality, and perdurability of the self. Having patiently dismantled, one by one, the entities of the inner world—feelings and thoughts—and loosing the apparently determining causal lines between those entities, Nietzsche turns finally to the supposed subject, the "Ich" or "I" that apparently does the thinking and feeling. It is easy to see that the concept of the self does not have a leg to stand on. It vanishes like all the other imaginary entities and imaginary lines between entities of the inner world.

Nietzsche's thinking here is again complex. It involves several elements simultaneously. A number of texts must be cited to demonstrate the entire network of connections involved in the rejection of the self. Each such section repeats the denial but follows a slightly different track out from this point, tracing a different consequence of positing the self or denying it. Section 477 ends by fictionalizing the subject. A cascade of other passages repeats this gesture in different ways:

—This conception is a second derivative of that false interpretation which believes in "thinking": first an act is imagined which simply does not occur, "thinking," and secondly a subject-substratum in which every act of thinking, and nothing other than thinking, has its origin: that is to say, both the deed and the doer are fictions. (E, 264; G, 674)

There exists neither "spirit," nor reason, nor thinking, nor consciousness, nor soul, nor will, nor truth: all are fictions (Fiktionen) that are of no use. (E, 266; G, 751)

"The subject": interpreted from within ourselves, so that the ego (das Ich) counts as a substance, as the cause of all deeds, as a doer (Täter).
   The logical-metaphysical postulates, the belief in substance, accident, attribute, etc., derive their convincing force from our habit of regarding all our deeds (Tun) as consequences of our will—so that the ego, as substance, does not vanish in the multiplicity of change.—*But there is no such thing as will.* (*Aber es gibt keinen Willen.*) (E, 269–70; G, 536–37)

No such thing as the will! How can the philosopher of will, par excellence, in a book now called *The Will to Power,* deny the existence of the will? Will there is, for Nietzsche, but not in the sense of an intention directed by a conscious, unified, substantial self. Will is rather, for him, a name for the forces, inner and outer (but the distinction no longer holds), that make things happen as they happen. Will as force (the will to power) is the product of difference, of the differentiation of energies, as an electric current flows only if there is a difference of potential between two poles. The "poles," however, exist not as things in themselves but as their difference from one another, just as a phoneme, in structural linguistics, is its differences from other phonemes. Will in the ordinary sense of volition, as when we say, "I will to do this," is one element in the complex tangle of elements that are untied and disintegrated by Nietzsche when the self is annihilated.
   In the series of passages in which this occurs, there is not a chiasmus or the righting reversal of an aberrant metalepsis, but rather a constant reversal of cause and effect, origin and result. The elements in question constantly reverse themselves, like Yeats's Hermetic egg that continually turns inside out without breaking its shell, or like a Gestaltist diagram in which figure and ground

constantly change places before the beholder's eyes. Whichever element one looks at is the figure grounded on the other as preexisting foil, but the next instant foil becomes figure.

In this case, the notion of the self is a final result of multiple fabrications leading to the fiction of thinking and then to that of a thinker. First we imagine an act which does not exist, thinking, and then we posit a fictitious entity, the self, to do the thinking. To deconstruct the notion of the "I" that thinks Nietzsche must patiently untie all the liaisons constituting the act of thinking and then, finally, the doer will dissolve in the dissolution of his deed. On the other hand, in other sections on the self, the self is seen as the originating fictitious postulate on the basis of which causality, will, substance, and so on are projected. Origin and end constantly change places in Nietzsche's presentations. Whatever one looks at appears secondary in relation to some prior act of positing that must be assumed already to have taken place. The act of origination is never present as such. It has always already taken place, over there, earlier. The whole structure of elements sustains itself in a constantly moving airy confabulation of self-generating and self-sustaining fictions, like a man lifting himself by his own bootstraps. The deconstruction of any one element disperses the whole fabrication, like an architectural edifice of clouds, leaving not a wrack behind. The interdependence of all and the lack of a single originating hypothesis on which the rest depend explain also the contradictions in Nietzsche's formulations, the way what is cause in one fragment becomes effect in another, and vice versa.

The figure of interpretation (Auslegung) is essential to Nietzsche's procedure. "Experience" is defined as a text that has been interpreted, or as an act of interpretation: "Against positivism, which halts at phenomena—'There are only *facts (Tatsachen)*'—I would say: No, facts is precisely what there is not, only interpretations" (E, 267; G, 903). The figure of text and its interpretation is, however, a figure. It is a displacement, a distortion, in short, itself an interpretation. The text in question here, that is, the various entities of the inner world making up a given person's "character"—feelings, thoughts, volitions, the "self"—is not a document waiting to be read. It is created by the act of interpretation that reads it. Interpretation posits the signs and reads them, in a single act. This is an act of autogeneration, autosuspension, and, ultimately, of autodestruction, since, for Nietzsche, any act of interpretation always contains the seeds of its own undoing. The phenomena of the inner world of character are not facts to be named. They are themselves entities that only exist as hypotheses, that is, as suppositions, signs, interpretative fictions open to further reading. This reading takes place spontaneously, not as the result of the volition of some thinking "I." Intrinsic to all this projection is the positing of an interpreter behind the interpretation, namely the self: "'Everything is subjective,' you say; but even this is interpretation (Auslegung). The 'subject' is not something given, it is something added and invented and projected behind (Dahinter-Gestecktes) what there is.—Finally, is it necessary to posit an interpreter behind the interpretation? Even this is invention (Dichtung), hypothesis" (E, 267; G, 903).

This positing of an arch-interpreter, the self, in turn, in a circularity or circulation that is essential here, becomes the basis of the language system within which our thinking remains imprisoned. This imprisonment is for man's own good, since the original motivating force behind the whole construction was the simplifying, making calculable and regular, necessary to life: "However habitual and indispensable this fiction (that the ego 'causes' thoughts) may have become by now—that in itself proves nothing against its imaginary origin (Erdichtetheit): a belief can be a condition of life and *nonetheless* be *false*" (E, 268; G, 915); "*Truth is the kind of error* without which a certain species of life could not live. (*Wahrheit ist die Art von Irrtum,* ohne welche eine bestimmte Art von lebendigen Wesen nicht leben könnte.) The value for *life* is ultimately decisive" (E, 272; G, 844).

Essential to language is the rigorous chain of grammatical constructions. Grammar imposes upon us belief in the entities our way of making sentences implies, so "that when there is thought there has to be something 'that thinks' is simply a formulation of our grammatical custom that adds a doer to every deed" (E, 268; G, 577). That doer, in turn, is the result of another aspect of language, namely, its turning or troping, making equal or similar what are unequal or dissimilar. By this the same name is given to two entities which are in fact not the same. This is the primordial act of interpretation. It creates language, the self, and all the entities based on the model of the self, in one fell swoop of metaphorizing: "The 'subject' is the fiction that many *similar* (*gleiche*) states in us are the effect of one substratum: but it is *we* who first *created* (*geschaffen*) the 'similarity' ('Gleichheit') of these states; our *adjusting* them (Zurecht-*machen*) and *making* them similar (Gleich-*setzen*)

is the *fact, not* their similarity (—which ought rather to be *denied*)"
(E, 269; G, 627). The making similar that is hypostatized in the
fiction of a substantial, enduring self becomes, "in turn" once more,
the model for a "similar" projecting and hypostatizing, by analogy,
of all the features of the inner and outer worlds that are presupposed in the initial positing of the self: substance, the "reality" of
the external world, causality, will, the reality, unity, and persistence
of such feelings as "being in love," and so on:

> Through thought the ego is posited; but hitherto one believed
> as ordinary people do, that in "I think" there was something of
> immediate certainty (Unmittelbar-Gewissen), and that this "I"
> was the given *cause* of thought, from which by analogy we
> understood all other causal relationships. (E, 267–68; G, 915)

> The concept of *substance* is a consequence of the concept of the
> *subject: not* the reverse! If we relinquish the soul, "the subject,"
> the precondition (Voraussetzung) for "substance" in general,
> disappears. (E, 268; G, 627)

> Must all philosophy not ultimately bring to light preconditions
> (Voraussetzungen) upon which the process of *reason* (*Vernunft*)
> depends?—our *belief in the "ego"* (*das "Ich"*) as a substance, as
> the sole reality from which we ascribe (zusprechen) reality to
> things in general? The oldest "realism" at last comes to light: at
> the same time that the entire religious history of mankind is
> recognized as the history of the soul superstition. (E, 269; G,
> 898–99)

This inextricable tangle of hypostatized presuppositions, and
presuppositions of presuppositions, each element presupposing all
the others and being presupposed by them in turn, in a perpetual
turning or displacement, is the prison house of language. It draws
a line in the sense of a limit, a frontier. This border our thinking
cannot by any means cross. We can hardly even see it as a frontier,
since as soon as we think, we are already inside the line, by no
means at its edge. We remain enclosed within it. We are hardly
able, even by a tremendous effort of thinking against thinking, to
see or think the line as a limiting edge to our thought.

> Here [with our belief in the ego as substance] *we come to a limit*
> (*eine Schranke*): our thinking itself involves this belief (with its
> distinctions of substance, accident; deed, doer, etc.); to let it go

means: being no longer able to think (nicht-mehr-denken-dür-fen). (E, 269; G, 899)

We cease to think when we refuse to do so under the constraint of language (in dem sprachlichen Zwange); we barely reach the doubt that sees this limitation as a limitation (eine Grenze als Grenze).

Rational thought is interpretation according to a scheme that we cannot throw off (abwerfen). (E, 283; G, 862)

The predicament Nietzsche describes leads to the recurrent comedy, perhaps especially prevalent in our own time, in which a novelist, poet, artist, philosopher, or cultural critic—Joyce, Williams, Picasso, Heidegger, or Foucault—makes a tremendous effort to cross the line, to get "beyond metaphysics," or "beyond man," beyond the traditions of realism in fiction, beyond the conventions of representational mimesis in painting or poetry, beyond assumptions about "character in the novel," but succeeds only in pushing out the limits of the margin a little, like a balloon slightly expanded. The thinker or artist remains still enclosed within the invisible englobing surface. Like the finite but unbounded universe hypothesized by cosmologists, language is a prison, airy and spacious indeed, but still a prison, though it is a prison whose walls we can never encounter, much less demolish.

There is nothing in English literature of the same period quite so like Nietzsche's dissolution of the self as the mournful litany of denials and dissolvings in the conclusion to Walter Pater's *Renaissance*. But there are instructive differences too:

And if we continue to dwell in thought on this world, not of objects in the solidity with which language invests them, but of impressions, unstable, flickering, inconsistent, which burn and are extinguished with our consciousness of them, it contracts still further: the whole scope of observation is dwarfed into the narrow chamber of the individual mind. . . . It is with this movement, with the passage and dissolution of impressions, images, sensations, that analysis leaves off—that continual vanishing away, that strange, perpetual weaving and unweaving of ourselves.[12]

Though Pater may seem to give more substantial reality to impressions, as "facts" of inner experience, than Nietzsche does, he elsewhere recognizes, like Nietzsche, that impressions too are

signs, interpretations, results of complex acts of simplification
rather than aboriginal causes. But Pater remains enclosed within
the subject-object, inner-outer, dichotomy that Nietzsche puts in
question. Nevertheless, Pater in "Apollo in Picardy," like Nietzsche
in passages I shall cite, replaces the hard substantial single self with
the notion of constantly changing multiple selves enclosed in perpetual struggle for power within the receptacle of a consciousness.
The self for both Nietzsche and Pater is the momentary effect of a
combat of forces, forces that function as signs. The ego is a pure
projection, changing from instant to instant as the balance of these
forces shifts, in "continual transitoriness and fleetingness (bestän-
dige Vergänglichkeit und Flüchtigkeit)" (E, 271; G, 474). Since the
"I" is a phantasmal projection, product of an interpretation, it is
not only constantly shifting, never fixed for a moment, expanding,
contracting, changing its center of gravity. It is also capable of
subdividing into two or more centers, each of which appears to be
a self.

Nietzsche's dismantling of the notion of the substantial self culminates in the idea that a single body may be inhabited by multiple
selves. Nietzsche's figure for this "dialogism" (in the sense of submission to more than one logos) is a dynamic, physical one. The
inner world acts like an enclosed collocation of matter and energy.
The system of forces inhabiting a single body may produce in its
interactions the illusion not just of one self, but of many:

> No subject "atoms." The sphere of a subject constantly *growing*
> or *decreasing,* the center of the system constantly *shifting*; in
> cases where it cannot organize the appropriate mass, it breaks
> into two parts. On the other hand, it can transform (umbilden)
> a weaker subject into its functionary without destroying it, and
> to a certain degree form (bilden) a new unity with it. No "sub-
> stance," rather something that in itself strives after greater
> strength, and that wants to "preserve" ("erhalten") itself only
> indirectly (it wants to *surpass* [*überbieten*] itself—). (E, 270; G,
> 537)

> The assumption of *one single subject* is perhaps unnecessary;
> perhaps it is just as permissible to assume a multiplicity of
> subjects, whose interaction and struggle (Zusammenspiel und
> Kampf) is the basis of our thought and our consciousness in
> general? A kind of *aristocracy* of "cells," in which dominion

resides? To be sure, an aristocracy of equals, used to ruling jointly and understanding how to command?

My hypothesis: The subject as multiplicity (Das Subjekt als Vielheit). (E, 270; G, 473)

Nietzsche here doubles the monological self into two or more "logoi." His notion of dialogism is a powerful lever to displace our traditional "logocentrism." Dialogism, two-mindedness, is, as Shakespeare shows in *Troilus and Cressida,* unreason, madness. It is not appropriate to speak of it under the category of logos, in the sense of reason, measure, ratio, mind, ground. Nietzsche does not do so. He substitutes for the family of logocentric terms another set of terms involving will, power, force, and interpretation, the latter in his special sense of a life-enhancing simplification and making calculable. Reason, consciousness, and logic are almost accidental consequences of the work of interpretation. They may become a dangerous constriction when new "illogical" interpretations become necessary for man's self-preservation. In defiance of the presumed univocity of logic, each person's body is the locus of a set of warring interpretations, or at best, according to an alternative Nietzschean metaphor, the body is a complex political entity within which there is perhaps momentarily one "ruler" within the struggle for power. But this ruler is dependent on the ruled and obliquely ruled by them. Such a "state" is a shifting balance of antagonistic forces from which the illusion of single selfhood arises as a figment. This epiphenomenon, moreover, fluctuates constantly, however fixed it appears to falsifying interpretation that wants to say, "I am I, a single self, remaining always the same":

The *body* and physiology the starting point: why?— We gain the correct idea (Vorstellung) of the nature of our subject-unity, namely as regents at the head of a communality (not as "souls" or "life forces"), also of the dependence of these regents upon the ruled and of an order of rank and division of labor as the conditions that make possible the whole and its parts. In the same way, how living unities continually arise and die and how the "subject" is not eternal: in the same way, that the struggle expresses itself in obeying and commanding, and that a fluctuating assessment of the limits of power is part of life (ein fließendes Machtgrenzen-bestimmen zum Leben gehört). (E, 271; G, 475)

Nietzsche's interrogation of the idea of selfhood reaches, by a complex series of dissolutions, a definition of the self as projected, constantly changing virtuality, like the center of gravity of a moving mass. This phantasmal center, moreover, has been doubled, fragmented, multiplied, dispersed into who knows how many separate momentary centers. Each is inhabited by a will to power over the whole, a desire to dominate and be itself the center. Nietzsche's position on the self may be distinguished both from Freud's and from Lacan's. For Freud also the self is a multiplicity, but it is a multiplicity of unequals or incommensurables: the ego, the id, the superego, arranged in layers shading off into the unconscious and the pre-conscious, that is, into areas that are in principle unavailable for face-to-face encounter. Or rather, these various entities are copresent in the strange topography of the self like overlapping populations speaking different languages and carrying on different activities. Freud's topology is quite different from Nietzsche's image of sharply defined multiple centers engaged in a feudal territorial war:

> Let me give you an analogy; analogies, it is true, decide nothing, but they can make one feel more at home. I am imagining a country with a landscape of varying configurations—hill-country, plains, and chains of lakes—, and with a mixed population: it is inhabited by Germans, Magyars and Slovaks, who carry on different activities. Now things might be partitioned in such a way that the Germans, who breed cattle, live in the hill-country, the Magyars, who grow cereals and wine, live in the plains, and the Slovaks, who catch fish and plait reeds, live by the lakes. If the partitioning could be neat and clear-cut like this, a Woodrow Wilson would be delighted by it. It would also be convenient for a lecture in a geography lesson. The probability is, however, that you will find less orderliness and more mixing, if you travel through the region. Germans, Magyars and Slovaks live interspersed all over it; in the hill-country there is agricultural land as well, cattle are bred in the plains too.[13]

For Lacan, on the other hand, the unconscious is more explicitly a matter of language. The multiplicity of the self for Lacan is, even more explicitly than for Freud, constituted by its relation to others and to the Other, for example by the "gaze." Lacan's ultimate model for this was also a topological one, and also one that defied the ordinary power of a Euclidian spatial imagination. This is the image of the Borromean knot, used in some difficult late seminars to map the self in its relation to the other and to the Other.[14]

Nietzsche's model differs from those of both Freud and Lacan. Nietzsche sees a self-enclosed battleground of different powers within the self. These powers are all of the same nature, like citizens in a commonwealth. They are arranged in a fluctuating hierarchy of ruling and obeying that is all out in the open. There is no concept of the unconscious as such in Nietzsche. What takes its place is the notion that the language forms we are born into impose on us systematic errors of interpretation. These make our waking life a perpetual slumber within erroneous dreams, as we sleep on the back of that tiger. Nietzsche's effort, like that of so-called deconstruction, is to wake us up, but the powers of sleep are manifold and almost irresistible. The wake-up call is almost certain to put us back to sleep again.

How this happens in Nietzsche may be seen by asking who is the agent of Nietzsche's procedure of deconstruction? The track I have followed through Book 3 of *The Will to Power* began with section 477. That passage begins with the words "I maintain" (Ich halte). Who is this "Ich" who dismantles any notion of a substantial "Ich"? Who is the ego who says, "The subject as multiplicity is one of my hypotheses, something I posit or hypothesize"? The aporia of Nietzsche's strategy lies in the fact that Nietzsche must use as the indispensable lever of his act of disarticulation a positing of the entity he intends to demolish. He must affirm the thing he means to deconstruct in order to deconstruct it. The deconstruction therefore deconstructs itself. It is built over the abyss of its own impossibility. In order to proceed with the undoing Nietzsche must begin with an act of positing that is the main target of the undoing. The whole series of untyings "I" have traced out, knot by knot, is strung on that initial positing.

If causality, substance, and so on, are posited on the positing of the ego, the denial of those concepts is not a replacement of falsehood by truth, the "facts," things as they are. It is an alternative series of positings based by metaphorical displacements on the initial positing of the deconstructing self: "I hold." In unbinding all those knots Nietzsche does not produce a line straight and true, free of all intrication, open to eyesight and measurement, a ruler by which all crooked thinking can be measured and made straight. He produces only another complicated knot, fold on fold, implicated within itself, a labyrinth of new figures. This reversal, whereby the analysis unties itself, and at the same time creates another labyrinthine fiction whose authority is undermined by its own creation, is characteristic in different ways of all deconstructive discourse, discourse that attempts to put in question and displace such basic presuppositions of our culture as that of the self. The way the fiction of selfhood survives its dismantling, or is even a necessary presupposition of its own dismantling, is a striking example of this remaking of what is unmade. This turning inside out, rather than any intrinsic logical complexity, makes it difficult to hold Nietzsche's argumentation clearly in one's mind, as I began this section by asserting. The particular form of this turning inside out I have followed with Nietzsche, moreover, is essential to the "realistic novel" as a genre, as "I" shall show in the example of *The Egoist*. But first I shall read passages from other authors to get a fuller sense of what is at stake in affirming or questioning selfhood or "character." The series of texts by Nietzsche on inner experience discussed above are on the topic of self-interpretation. They have as their goal an untying of the complex knot by which I interpret myself as a unitary and persisting ego. A novel, after all, presents other characters, that of the narrator, those of the protagonist, for the reader's interpretation. The interpretation of others is not the same thing as self-interpretation. It works by different rules or in any case by a significant extension and displacement of the rules by which I interpret myself.

The word *character,* in its complex structure of meanings, itself contains the possibility of the two interpretations of selfhood I have just identified. To that word I shall now return in order to interrogate further—with the help of the *Oxford English Dictionary,* Benjamin, Baudelaire, Derrida, Trollope, George Eliot, Poe, and Wittgenstein—the contradictory assumptions about character posited by the word itself. Only by following through actual uses of the word *character* can we learn "what a character is." To label each section of this chapter with the proper name of the author of the passage or text discussed is, I am aware, implicitly to accept one version of what the chapter puts in question. At least in recent centuries in the West, but of course also earlier—for example, in classical Greece and Rome or for those who established the canon of the Bible—we have a deep and elaborately institutionalized need to be able to say "So and so wrote this and must take responsibility for it" (for instance, Moses wrote the Pentateuch), even if that means no more than assigning responsibility to some imagined personage for being the conduit through which an inspiration flowed, divine words were dictated.

The Oxford English Dictionary

The entry in the OED for *character* indicates clearly how a complex structure (that does not wholly cohere as a structure) is inscribed within the word and within the history of its usage. The OED divides the nineteen separate meanings of the word into "literal senses" and "figurative senses." A complex web of figurative substitutions connected not as a linear chain but in multiple, mutually sustaining crisscrossings is hidden behind this apparently straightforward bifurcation.

The "original" Greek word *charakter* already has a triple meaning involving a figurative transfer first from the instrument for marking or graving to the engraving itself, the impress, stamp, or distinctive mark, then to what that sign is taken as a sign of, the distinctive nature of the thing branded. Among other meanings, as Marc Shell has noted, *charakter* meant the upper die used by the coinmaker as well as the impressed mark on the coin made by the die.[15] The Greek noun was derived from the verb *charassein*, to make sharp, cut furrows in, engrave. The verbal action seems to have preceded the name of the thing performing the action or the thing resulting from the action. *Charassein* is one of those primordial words naming a basic human act of transforming the physical world, making it humanized, significant, marked by man or woman, in this case marked with the mark which makes it a mark, a sign, a "character." The verb, however, was already double. It named both the act of making the engraving tool sharp and the act of engraving itself.

The range of meanings and examples for the English word *character* in the OED remains within the limits of the Greek word. Nevertheless, to borrow the final musical image from the definition of character in *Sir Thomas Overbury His Wife*, the OED elaborates on those three possibilities in the Greek, like "wit's descant on any plain song." The entry is of great interest, as are the entries for the adjacent words *characteristic, characterize,* and so forth, not least because the reader can see that the problems implicit in the shift from one member of the family of meanings to another are blandly sidestepped by the lexicographical convention of listing the meanings according to certain presupposed categories, literal as against figurative, concrete against abstract, and so on.

The entry for *character* weaves between three or four functions of the word: to name a visible mark already present "naturally" on something as a distinguishing feature; to name a mark put on something by a human being to mark it, as a brand on a cow; to name a system of signs or an element in such a system (in which case the matter receiving the mark is not named by the mark); to name the complex of invisible qualities the mark indicates, usually, though not always, human "character" in the ordinary sense the word is used today, for example in the criticism of fiction, as when we speak of character in the novel or of Dorothea Brooke's character. In any given use of the word there is likely to be a constant somewhat enigmatic play back and forth among these various functions of the word, so that its figurative genealogy is never wholly lost.

There is much figurative play already among what the OED calls the literal senses of the word *character*. The word may mean "a distinctive mark impressed, engraved, or otherwise formed; a brand, stamp," in which case the character is not, in the ordinary sense at least, part of a system of signs (though the question of how signs make or do not make a system is one aspect of the enigma of character). I may brand my sheep with a distinctive squiggle that is part of no alphabet and yet distinguishes my sheep from any other person's. It is not necessarily part of a fully developed code. It is a sign and not a sign.

This meaning is given by the OED a figurative variant, the cases where the word is clearly not literal but contains a "distinct reference to the literal sense." The example given comes from the first part of Marlowe's *Tamburlaine,* 1.2: "Thou . . . by characters graven on thy brows . . . Deserv'st to have the leading of an host." The lines on one's forehead are literal marks. They may only by figure be called a brand or stamp, and yet they have meaning. They signify the "character" of the man or woman who bears them. All the problem of physiognomy, to which I shall return, is present in this citation. The example also manifests an uncomfortable wavering in the apparently clear and unambiguously helpful distinction between figurative and literal. This has allowed the editors of the OED cheerfully to put some meanings of "character" in one bin and some in the other, though their first "literal" meaning has already a figurative variant.

One understands that by "literal" uses of the word *character* the
OED means uses that name the actual mark, stamp, or brand itself.
Yet there is already a play on words here, since the "literal" uses
name that aboriginal figuration whereby a physical mark stands
for something else, "means" it. The mark ceases thereby to be
simply or literally itself, since it has become literally a letter, a
character, a sign, that is, a figure. The literal is already irreducibly
figurative. All the so-called figurative senses distinguished by the
OED are extensions, variations, or reformulations of this initial
figuration. The enigma of character in the sense of a person's
"character" or of a "character" in a novel is present already in the
word itself in the sense of a brand or stamp or furrowed marking,
whether there by nature or deliberately engraved by human effort.

The seven "literal" uses of the word *character* include, beside
(1) "Brand or stamp," already discussed, with its figurative variants, six additional meanings: (2) "A distinctive significant mark
of any kind; a graphic sign or symbol" (the distinction from 1
seems to be that the second kind of mark need not be incised); (3)
"A graphic symbol standing for a sound, syllable, or notion, used
in writing or in printing; one of the simple elements of a written
language; e.g. a letter of the alphabet"; variants, especially in the
plural: "Shorthand. *Obs.*"; (4) "Writing, printing"; (5) "A cab-
balistic or magical sign or emblem; the astrological symbol of a
planet, etc."; (6) "A symbol, emblem, figure; an expression or
direct representation. *Obs.*"; (7) "A cipher for secret correspondence." If a character is a mark or brand, it is also a letter of the
alphabet and the alphabet as a whole, whether the alphabet of a
public or a secret cipher. A character is also an emblem of one sort
or another. The last (obsolete) use of the word overlaps with the
meaning of *hieroglyph* and explains why the definition in *Sir
Thomas Overbury His Wife* says that "character is also taken from
an Egyptian hieroglyphic, for an impress or short emblem; in little
comprehending much." (The word *impress* here anticipates Wittgenstein's use of the word *impression,* discussed below.)

The three submeanings under the fourth literal meaning are of
especial importance for my purposes here. If character may mean
writing or printing generally, it may therefore mean (b) "The series
of alphabetic signs, or elementary symbols, peculiar to any language; a set of letters," for example, "the Chinese written character"; or (c) "The style of writing peculiar to any individual;
handwriting"; or (d) "Kind or style of type or printed letter." A

strange text by Poe, "Autography," to be read below, plays on this region of the meaning of character, but the fundamental paradox is evident from these three submeanings. A character is both peculiar, particular, distinctive, and at the same time it is repeatable, generalizable, able to be used and reused in a variety of circumstances, as the Chinese written character is peculiar to the Chinese and yet may be used to express a limitless variety of meanings, though perhaps not *all* meanings, since some meanings may defy translation into Chinese. An alphabet, like a grammar, is ruthlessly indifferent, mechanical. Each letter has meaning only in its difference from other letters, and those differences impersonally determine all the limitless meanings that may be expressed according to that code. On the other hand, each configuration of signs in the code generates an individual reference that traduces the generality of the alphabetic code. The characters graven on Tamburlaine's brow refer to Tamburlaine in all his uniqueness. Whether or not Tamburlaine preexists the signs that point toward him is just the question all this chapter is meant to raise.[16]

An implied analogy among four operations is at work within the system of meanings of the word *character*. All four involve interpreting something hidden by deciphering manifest signs. All are alike in involving the problem of chirography, signature, or autograph; the problem of physiognomy; the interpretation of human character generally; the problem of reading texts, whether literary or not, whether written in a known or in a secret cipher. Each may by lateral transfer be a sign for the others, a figure for their figuration, in an intimate chain or network of correspondences. To interpret someone's character (handwriting) is to interpret his character (physiognomy) is to interpret his character (personality) is to interpret his character (some characteristic text he has written), in a perpetual round of figure for figure. To read character is to read character is to read character is to read character.

The twelve meanings of *character* explicitly labeled "figurative" by the OED are no more than extensions of these primary figurations. Mostly but not exclusively they have to do with character in the sense of human personality. The first of the figurative senses, sense 8, may seem the same as sense 1. b, but the difference is that the character in question in sense 8, "A distinctive mark, evidence, or token; a feature, trait, characteristic," is rather 1. b inside out, the moral or spiritual character which may or may not be in this case signified by a visible character in the sense of marks "graven on thy brows." Though this use of the word is said to be "archaic in gen. use," the last example is from Stevenson's *Dr. Jekyll and Mr. Hyde* (1886): "Complete moral insensibility and insensate readiness to evil, which were the leading characters of E. H." Sense 8. b, according to a more or less regular law of these figurative senses, applies sense 8 to nonhuman things: "Now *esp.* in *Natural History* one of the distinguishing features of a species or genus," as in one of the examples (1776): "The most striking character is the two upright petals at the top."

Senses 9 through 19 ring the changes on the possibilities of character as personality, individual or general, with figurative transfers back to things human beings have made. If each person is assumed to have a character that can express itself in the characters graven on his or her brow, each person can also imprint a character, a pervasive signature, on handwriting, or on anything he or she has made, a book he or she has written, a house or a piece of furniture, a system of monetary exchange. The originally figurative meaning, in a personality or character, becomes the literal meaning of which other visible, physical meanings are the figures or projected transfers, in a perpetual round in which the *other* meaning is always the literal one and the present one a displaced, that is, nonpresent figure:

9. "The aggregate of the distinctive features of any thing; essential peculiarity; nature, style; sort, kind, description" ("Natural stupidity is by no means the character of Mahomet's book" [Carlyle, 1840]).

10. "The face or features as betokening moral qualities; personal appearance" (here is the physiognomic meaning).

11. "The sum of moral and mental qualities which distinguish an individual or a race, viewed as a homogeneous whole; the individuality impressed by nature and habit on man or nation; mental or moral constitution."

12. "Moral qualities strongly developed or strikingly displayed; distinct or distinguished character; character worth speaking of." Sense 12. b is sense 12 "*transf.*" to a face or a portrait.

13. "The estimate formed of a person's qualities; reputation: when used without qualifying epithet implying 'favorable estimate, good repute.'" Sense 13. b is sense 13 "*transf.* of things," as in *Jevons' Money* (1875): "Such an impression . . . as shall establish its character as current money of certain value," and sense 13. c is an

obsolete idiom: "*By character*: by repute or report. *In* [*great*] *character*; in [good] repute," as in Jane Austen's *Persuasion* (c. 1815): "I had known you by character long before."

14. "A description, delineation, or detailed report of a person's qualities." This is the sense used by the author of *Sir Thomas Overbury His Wife*: "To square out a character by our English level, it is a picture [real or personal] quaintly drawn, in various colors, all of them heightened by one shadowing." Sense 14. b is sense 14 "*transf.* of things. *Obs*," and sense 14. c is "*esp.* A formal testimony given by an employer as to the qualities and habits of one that has been in his employ."

15. "Recognized official rank; status; position assumed or occupied (now influenced by sense 17)."

16. "A person regarded in the abstract as the possessor of specified qualities; a personage, a personality," as in *Tom Jones* (1749): "Eminent characters have . . . played the fool."

17. "A personality invested with distinctive attributes and qualities, by a novelist or dramatist; also, the personality or 'part' assumed by an actor on the stage." Here at last is the sense of a character in a novel. It is one meaning woven into a complicated web of other "literal" and "figurative" senses. Sense 17. b is a variant idiom: "*In* [or *out of*] *character*: In [or at variance with] the part assumed; hence *gen.* in [or out of] harmony, appropriate, fitting."

18. "*Colloq.* An odd, extraordinary, or eccentric person."

19. "*Attrib.* or in *comb.*, as *character-drawing, -monger*, etc., also character-actor."

The OED makes it sound as if any given use of the word *character* could be pigeon-holed neatly in one or another of the multitudinous meanings and submeanings, literal, figurative, and transferred, which it has distinguished. But any given use of the word will involve a complicated interplay among various meanings, literal and figurative, all more or less but not quite determined by the context. The possibilities of meaning in a word always exceed its context and shimmer to some degree with the other possibilities, as the mind follows one strand after another of the spiderweb of interconnected meanings. Among those meanings is "character" as when we speak, for example, of the title character of *Lord Jim*. But the entire complex of meanings inheres as a set of possibilities, in however indirect and even negative a way, in any use of the word apparently limited to sense 17, as my further particular examples will indicate.

In "Schicksal und Charakter (Fate and Character)," Walter Benjamin has put his finger on one latent implication of the uses of the German word *Charakter* to name the marks on a person's face as signs of inner "character." This is the permanent inaccessibility of both character and that "other" or alter ego of character, "fate." Neither can ever be confronted directly, only known through the signs for them. This does not necessarily mean that neither fate nor character exists, but it does mean that if either exists it can never be thought of as an object or thing that can be directly perceived, fall before some witness's eyes in the present. Here is Benjamin's formulation:

> Like character, fate too, can be apprehended only through signs, not in itself (nur in Zeichen, nicht in sich selbst überschaut werden), for—even if this or that character trait, this or that link of fate, is directly in view (unmittelbar vor Augen liegen), it is nevertheless the relationship (der Zusammenhang) that is meant by these concepts, never accessible except through signs (Zeichen) because it is situated above the immediately visible level (weil er über dem unmittelbar Sichtbaren gelegen ist). The system of characterological signs is generally confined to the body, if we disregard the characterological significance of those signs investigated by the horoscope, whereas in the traditional view all the phenomena of external life, in addition to bodily ones, can become signs of fate. However, the connection between the sign and the signified (der Zusammenhang zwischen Zeichen und Bezeichnetem) constitutes in both spheres an equally hermetic (verschlossenes) and difficult problem, though different in other respects, because despite all the superficial observation and false hypostatizing of the signs, they do not in either system signify character or fate on the basis of causal connections (nicht auf Grund kausaler Zusammenhänge). A nexus of meaning (ein Bedeutungszusammenhang) can never be founded causally, even though in the present case the existence of the signs may have been produced causally by fate and character.[17]

Both fate and character, for Benjamin, manifest themselves only indirectly, through signs that, even if they may have been caused by what they signify, do not signify in a causal way. This means that they are not open to empirical verification, as is the case with a material causal concatenation. An example of the latter is the way the symptom of a disease, say a fever, is caused by the disease and may be shown to be so. The whole chain from disease to symptom is open to study and measure. But fate and character reveal themselves through signs that stand for something to which there is no possibility of direct access.

Though character and fate belong to different spheres, or appear to, one internal, the other external, the notion of character cannot be wholly detached from that of fate, though Benjamin attempts to distinguish sharply between them. The confluence of fate and character as vector forces draws out the storyline of a person's life and makes it narratable, something that may be accounted for, recounted, brought out into the open for all to read. Hidden inner character may be the way someone's mysteriously occult outer "fate" inscribes itself most effectively within the world, immanently, by writing itself within and on a person's body, personality, and behavior. This is perhaps what Novalis meant by that aphorism Thomas Hardy cites in *The Mayor of Casterbridge*: "Character is fate."

The key word in Benjamin's analysis is *Zusammenhang,* or in a crucial place, *Bedeutungszusammenhang.* This does not quite mean "nexus of meaning," as the translation has it, but rather the hanging together, the cohering of meaning, their intimate bringing together, not their mere confluence or linking. *Bedeutungszusammenhang* may mean the hanging together of the signs of fate or character to make a readable configuration. Or it may mean the hanging together of the sign with the hidden feature of character or fate for which it "stands," which it replaces or points toward. This happens according to that functioning of signs as pointers that Benjamin's word *Zeichen* brings more to the fore than does the English word *sign*. Probably Benjamin has the second meaning of Bedeutungszusammenhang more in mind, because he has just said that the signs of either fate or character do not signify on the basis of causal connections, "nicht auf Grund kausaler Zusammenhänge bedeuten." Such signs have meaning, but not as a result of causal connections, and so they cannot be read in that way, by comparison of cause and caused. The sign can never be set against a manifest signified.

Benjamin here recognizes that the fundamental problem of the concept of character, like that of fate, is linguistic or semiotic. Both character and fate depend on the peculiar notion of a sign that has

meaning but whose meaning remains forever hidden from direct
encounter. The true nexus here is a non-nexus, the disconnection
of the word or sign, as sign, from its motivation and meaning.

Baudelaire

Another example, from Baudelaire, of the brand of character on a
person's face shows how the apparently firm distinction between
inside character and outside fate, just discussed apropos of the
passage from Benjamin, breaks down in a given case. So does the
apparently necessary distinction between literal and figurative uses
of signs. I give it first in Baudelaire's sinewy and vigorous French:

> Il existe des destinées fatale; il existe dans la littérature de chaque
> pays des hommes qui portent le mot "guignon" écrit en carac-
> tères mystérieux dans les plis sinueux de leurs fronts. Il y a
> quelque temps, on amenait devant les tribunaux un malheureux
> qui avait sur le front un tatouage singulier: "pas de chance." Il
> portait ainsi partout avec lui l'étiquette de sa vie, comme un livre
> son titre, et l'interrogatoire prouva que son existence s'était
> conformée à son écriteau. Dans l'histoire littéraire, il y a des
> fortunes analogues. . . . Y a-t-il donc une Providence diabolique
> qui prépare le malheur dès le berceau? Tel homme, dont le talent
> sombre et désolé nous fait peur, a été jeté avec *préméditation*
> dans un milieu qui lui était hostile.

> There exist fatal destinies; there exist in the literature of each
> country men who carry the word *guignon* [persistent bad luck,
> "jinxed"] written in mysterious characters in the sinuous folds
> of their foreheads. A short while ago, they brought into court
> an unhappy man who had on his forehead a curious tattoo: "pas
> de chance [no luck]." He thus carried everywhere with him the
> regimen of his life, as a book its title, and the interrogation
> proved that his existence was in conformity with that inscription.
> In the history of literature, there are analogous fortunes. . . . Is
> there therefore a diabolical Providence that prepares unhappiness
> from the cradle? Such a man, whose somber and desolate talent
> frightens us, has been thrown with *premeditation* into a milieu
> that was hostile to him.[18]

One can see the intricate contradiction written into that "no
luck," "pas de chance," inscribed on the poor man's forehead. On
the one hand, the mysterious character of the tattoo tells some-

thing, indeed tells the essential thing, about the man's inner character. He is the sort of man who always has bad luck. He is a loser. He has even chosen to have his inner character, or his awareness of his inner character, tattooed on his forehead, as a kind of self-fulfilling prophecy. *Petit Robert* cites in its entry for "guignon" another passage from Baudelaire: "Il n'y a pas de guignon. Si vous avez de guignon, c'est qu'il vous manque quelque chose. (There is no such thing as chronic bad luck. If you are always unlucky, it is because you lack something)." Persistent bad luck is a matter of character all right, though it is not a positive trait but rather something absent from that character, like a missing chromosome, or like dice with a blank in place of the six. On the other hand, the "no luck," it may be, is not something that arises from the man's character at all. It may arise from the lack of conformity between his inner character, with its missing trait, and his outer circumstances.

Like all those evanescent beings in Walter Pater's "imaginary portraits," Denys L'Auxerrois, Sebastian van Storck, or Duke Carl of Rosenmold, victims of an imperfect repetition, Baudelaire's Poe has been thrown by a malign fate into a milieu that does not fit his talents and nature. In other circumstances, in another context, the tattoo might have read: "always lucky." The "no luck" refers not to the man's character but to his fate. Or rather it refers to the malign crossing of the two. There is no absolute distinguishing of character from fate. Characters (in the sense of letters) that seem to refer exclusively to inner nature always necessarily refer also to external circumstances, whether those are accidental mishaps or whether they are deliberately imposed by some benign or malign Providence. (But how could you be sure which it was in a given case?) A throw of the dice makes its own meaning, but it has that meaning only in relation to all the other throws, the players, the rules of the game, and so on.

Derrida

Both Benjamin and Baudelaire, in what they say of the contradictory inherence of fate in character, seem by "fate" not to mean unlucky contingent external circumstances. An example of the latter is George Eliot's assertion that Dorothea's sufferings, in *Middlemarch*, result from the fact that Dorothea is a potential Saint Teresa born into nineteenth-century England, when there are no convents to found. Fate for Benjamin and Baudelaire is rather the mysterious "other" of character. A man's or a woman's fate is an inextricable part of his or her character, its double or ghost, but never confrontable in itself. A person's fate can only be encountered when it is too late, in the ambiguous signs for it. These signs are not even properly to be called signs if we mean by a sign an unambiguous pointer that gives the sign-reader direct access to what is indicated.

In a recent interview, part of an issue of *Topoi* on the topic of the ego that shows the last word has still not been said on the subject of the subject, Jacques Derrida speaks of the encounter within the project of phenomenological description of an "other" of subjectivity. This "other" is an inextricable part of that subjectivity but may by no means be encountered directly. It cannot be sensed, perceived, or experienced as part of the living present. The "other" in question is a part of consciousness that consciousness can by no stratagems become conscious of. It thereby exceeds the phenomenological project, though the attempt to fulfill that project catches a glimpse of it:

> C'est à l'intérieure, si on peut dire (mais justement il y va d'une effraction de l'intérieure) du présent vivant, cette "Urform" de l'expérience transcendantale, que le sujet compose avec du non-sujet ou que l'"ego" se trouve marqué, sans pouvoir en faire l'expérience originaire et présentative, par du non-"ego" et surtout de l'"alter-ego." L'"alter ego" ne peut pas se présenter, devenir une présence originaire pour l'"ego." Il y a seulement une apprésentation analogique de l'"alter ego." Celui-ci ne peut jamais être donné "en personne," il résiste au principe des principes de la phénoménologie, à savoir la donnée intuitive de la présence originaire. Cette dislocation du sujet absolu depuis l'autre et depuis le temps ne se produit pas, ne conduit pas "au-delà" de la phénoménologie, mais, sinon en elle, du moins sur son bord, sur la ligne même de sa possibilité.[19]

It is within, one might say (but it is precisely a question of the effraction of the within) the living present, that "Urform" of the transcendental experience, that the subject conjoins with the non-subject or that the "ego" is marked, without being able to have the originary and presentative experience of it, by the non-"ego" and especially by the "alter ego." The "alter ego" cannot present itself, cannot become an originary presence for the "ego." There is only an analogical a-presentation of the "alter ego." The "alter ego" can never be given "in person," it resists the principal of principles of phenomenology, namely the intuitive given of originary presence. This dislocation of the absolute subject from the other and from time does not come about, nor does it lead, "beyond" phenomenology, but rather, if not in it, then at least on its border, on the very line of its possibility.[20]

We tread on shadowy ground here, since my discussion has been moving toward the claim that characterological signs do not stand for anything beyond themselves. Benjamin's Schicksal, Baudelaire's guignon, and Derrida's alter ego are existences, "somethings," that are outside the circuit of any sign system in which the sign, for example, a person's face, stands for something hidden, but nevertheless namable, his or her "character." But the somethings in question are not compatible with the idea, made explicit by Wittgenstein in passages discussed below, that the marks of a person's character mean themselves, stand for themselves, generate their own meaning. In Benjamin, Baudelaire, and Derrida another, third, possibility, hinted at intermittently already, comes more visibly to the surface. It comes to the surface as something that can never surface as sense data or phenomena. This possibility surfaces (without surfacing) as the notion that the "ego" is "marked" by an other than the ego that is yet inextricably part of the ego, perhaps its most important part. Such a "mark" is another species of that figure, catachresis, one of my guiding threads here. It also exemplifies the "insignificance" and divisibility of the letter or of any other conglomeration of signs, such as those making up someone's "character," paradoxical condition of its iterability and stability of meaning, that is an important theme in Derrida.[21] In my own argument here the insignificance, materiality, divisibility, and consequent proneness to migration or wandering ("destinerrance," in Derrida's coinage) of each "character," in all its senses, including that of alphabetic letter, are the condition of its openness to a new performative positing giving it a new meaning in a new context. My discussion of Clara Middleton in Meredith's *Egoist* will exemplify that.

The obscure idea of an "other" within the self will come up again here in chapter 3, "Anastomosis," and in an essay called "Topography" in a future book. The attempt to express what might be meant by this third possibility is a recurrent part of Derrida's project. This part has received relatively little attention in commentary, perhaps because it is difficult to grasp or perhaps because it does not correspond to presuppositions about what Derrida is presumed to be saying, for example, false notions about what he means by our enclosure within the "free play" of language. The notion that the self is marked by something that exceeds any marks or traces is a fundamental part of Derrida's work—for example, in his essays on Blanchot in *Parages* or in the admirable essay "Fors."[22] Far from intending to "go beyond the subject" or "liquidate the subject," Derrida, as his interview with Nancy makes explicit, has wanted rather to displace the topography of the subject, or to recognize that it has always been displaced, from the magisterial originary centrality it has, for example, in phenomenology. For Derrida subjectivity becomes an effect, a "place," or a function rather than an originary cause, as when he asks, in the interview cited above, whether "the structure of every subject is not constituted in the possibility of this kind of repetition one calls a return, and, more importantly, if this structure is not essentially 'before the law,' the relation to law and the experience of it, if there is such a thing," and then goes on to say of the place of the subject in Althusser's theory of ideology: "This place is that of a subject constituted by interpellation, by its being-interpellated (again being-before-the-law), the subject as a subject subjected to the law, the subject as a subject subjected to the law and held responsible before it" (113). "Law" here is another name for that "alter ego," the unavailable subject within the subject that generates the subject and to which the subject has a categorical obligation.

Trollope

Something like Derrida's idea of an other within the self is also to be found in a writer who seems as different from Derrida as one could get, Anthony Trollope. In *An Autobiography* Trollope speaks of the superior importance, for him, of character over plot in constructing a novel. When he begins a novel, he has no certainty about how the story is going to come out. He has only a strong conception of the characters:

How short is the time devoted to the manipulation of a plot can be known only to those who have written plays and novels;—I may say also, how very little time the brain is able to devote to such wearing work. There are usually some hours of agonising doubt, almost of despair,—so at least it has been with me,—or perhaps some days. And then, with nothing settled in my brain as to the final development of events, with no capability of settling anything, but with a most distinct conception of some character or characters, I have rushed at the work as a rider rushes at a fence which he does not see.[23]

The impetus, verve, or élan for the creation of a novel, for Trollope, does not come from the plot, but from the strong "conception" in the novelist's mind of a character or characters. The sexual metaphor latent in the word *conception* suggests that the novelist is the female matrix receiving the stamp of the pattern of a character. This figure is made explicit in another remarkable passage, about which there would be much to say, but I limit myself to the matter at hand. The passage follows almost immediately after the one just quoted:

At such times [when he has been "at some quiet spot among the mountains" and free to write] I have been able to imbue myself thoroughly with the characters I have had in hand. I have wandered alone among the rocks and woods, crying at their grief, laughing at their absurdities, and thoroughly enjoying their joy. I have been impregnated with my own creations till it has been my only excitement to sit with the pen in my hand and drive my team before me at as quick a pace as I could make them travel. (*Autobiography,* 176)

The imprint of the characters' configuration in whatever novel Trollope has "in hand" is a power of autoaffection. Trollope soaks himself in the emotions that are the spontaneous correlatives of what might be called the hieroglyphs of character. He produces grief out of grief, laughter out of absurdities, joy out of joy, in a closed circuit of intersubjectivity enfolded within a single subjectivity. Writing novels is also an act of self-impregnation. Trollope sits pen in hand (as he has his characters "in hand") and moves forward in a joyful burst of engendering creativity. The progeny of this creative act is the words on the page. These embody in his own character, or handwriting, where they may be read by others, those signets of character that he has conceived in his mind.

What was the source of those configurations in the first place? How did they enter into the circuit of the novelist's self-impregnation? An earlier passage in *An Autobiography* gives the answer. Character is the essence of a good novel, plot a mere carrier of the characters, because the conception of the characters is the basis of the communication between author, text, and readers. The novelist makes his particular configurations of character out of personality "traits" that are already known to his readers. They are known not as the property of this or that real person, but as general components of character that may be possessed by many persons, just as seventeenth-century "characters" were portraits of types— the miser, the glutton, and so on—made up of various elements from a basic alphabet of character. This might be compared to the way a complex Chinese character or Egyptian hieroglyph is made of the juxtaposition or superimposition of several traits that may appear in many other characters, but which make a unique configuration and a unique meaning in this particular assemblage. Another analogy is the way a piece of metal is stamped with a particular combination of the known repertoire of faces, legends, and symbols to produce a coin worth so much in the monetary system of evaluation and exchange to which it belongs. The word *trait* comes from the obsolete French *traict, tret,* for draught, stroke, touch, line, from Latin *tractus,* drawing, draught. The word *trait* of course repeats in miniature the complex web of meanings for "character." *Trait* names one line or element of a character in its various senses, and includes "a stroke made with pen or pencil, a short line, a touch (in a picture), a line, passage, or piece of writing. *Obs.*"; "A line or lineament of the face; the feature"; or "a particular feature of mind or character; a distinguishing quality; a characteristic" (OED). The passage in Trollope plays on these meanings, as on the meanings of *character:*

> A novel should give a picture of common life enlivened by humor
> and sweetened by pathos. To make that picture worthy of atten-
> tion, the canvas should be crowded with real portraits, not of
> individuals known to the world or to the author, but of *created*
> *personages impregnated with traits of character which are*
> *known.* To my thinking, the plot is but the vehicle for all this;
> and when you have the vehicle without the passengers, a story
> of mystery in which the agents never spring to life, you have but
> a wooden show. (*Autobiography,* 126; my italics)

Again (or already, since this passage comes first in *An Auto-biography*), the sexual metaphor appears. The characters in a novel spring to life when each has been imprinted with an assemblage chosen from known traits of character that make up the common genetic code in the community of readers for which the novel is written. These assemblages of known traits are capable of impregnating novelist, novel, and readers with the conceptions of those characters. These are then disseminated again, in a circular generation of character by character, sign by sign. In this circulation the characters in a novel, like the characters of living persons, are only one element in a system of exchanges based on a set of character traits transcending any individual character, fictive or real, just as a money economy is based on an ideal set of monetary measures—the dollar, the pound, the lira, or whatever, and their corresponding divisions. The "known traits of character" are, so to speak, the small change on the basis of which the novelist mints his larger facsimile coins. The common possession of these little coins, their free circulation within society, from readers to novelist to novel and back again to the readers, is the fund or reserve out of which the novel is conceived. This common pool guarantees the novel's function in the psychic economy of the society to which it belongs, just as all speech and all writing are made of a finite lexicon of words, out of which all sentences have to be made.

Behind this freely circulating pool of a strange kind of money there may or may not be a basis in capital to support or ground the circulation of character traits as they are stamped in one combination or another on real or imaginary faces. The confidence that certain characteristic marks are signs of certain inner states (grief, absurdity, joy) exists already as legal tender within the society. The novelist forges his fictitious or counterfeit coins stamped with the proper traits from the world of these known traits. Only if he does this will his characters pass current within society, though known as after a fashion counterfeit. They will do this because the dies with which they are imprinted are modeled accurately on elements from the conceptions of character the novelist's readers already have.

Such novels have as one function to reinforce the credence of their readers that the marks of character stamped on their neighbors' faces are genuine signs of worth, true evidence of inner qualities. Such stamps are coin of the realm and have, so to speak, the Queen's backing. They are as safe as the Bank of England. The character of the counterfeit coin, as always, depends on the character of the "real" coin. The counterfeit makes the real coin seem more real, while at the same time subtly raising questions about the distinction between real and counterfeit. All coin is counterfeit in the sense that it is the stamping of matter with signs of value that matter does not intrinsically have. The value is ascribed to it by the collective faith of the people for whom it is a medium of transfer, figuration, or exchange. If this is true, is not a counterfeit coin "real" too as long as it passes without question from hand to hand, though it does of course inflate the currency?

A moment ago I raised the question of whether this odd kind of money has or has not a basis in a reserve of capital. What I have said thus far makes it sound as if common character traits as they are combined to create this or that fictive character are a superficial and to some degree factitious assemblage. They are supported only by a tacit agreement to accept a combination of such character traits as a valid simulacrum of a possible real person. This would, so it seems, deprive Trollope's characters of the depth and integrity of selfhood necessary for moral choice and responsibility.

All Trollope's novels are concerned with this question. In subtle and varied ways they show valid ethical choice being made on the basis of a hidden self within the self. This means Trollope's good characters *must* choose to act as they do act. Moreover, they are shown as in one way or another knowing this. They not only choose correctly. They choose on the basis of an odd kind of knowledge. Even if they cannot confront directly the unique inner grounds of their choices, they do know they are right. One example is the way Septimus Harding, in one of Trollope's earliest novels, *The Warden*, decides to resign the wardenship. He does this, in defiance of everyone's advice, on the basis of a self within the self he calls his conscience. This forms a kind of groundless ground for ethical decision. "I have little but an ungrounded conviction of my own," says Harding, but later he can assert that he decides on the basis of that self within himself, his "conscience." The working out of this conception of an alter ego or "other" within the self, as it is dramatized from novel to novel by Trollope, is surprisingly complex and various. An example from much later in Trollope's career is the admirable story in *He Knew He Was Right* of a counterproof of what I have been saying. The hero of that novel thinks he has the kind of valid inner conviction that, for example, guides Harding, but he is mistaken. The full demonstration of all this cannot be given here, but enough has been said to indicate that Trollope's conception of character puts together the notion of a combinatory calculus of socially accepted features of character with the notion of an elusive ground for character that does not manifest itself in any known traits of character and is unique for each person. Trollope's use of the term *character* coexists with a conception of human personality that cannot be expressed within the system of the word's possible meanings.

George Eliot

Trollope makes explicit the sexual metaphor latent in taking character as an imprint transferable from one person and text to another. Character traits are like a genetic code keeping a family resemblance alive from generation to generation. Other novelists remain within different regions of the word *character,* sometimes without mentioning the word. The eleventh chapter of George Eliot's *Daniel Deronda,* for example, describes Gwendolen's first encounter with Grandcourt. The chapter's epigraph applies to the confrontation of people or objects George Eliot's theory, so Nietzschean in its configuration, that all epistemology is interpretation of signs. For her too all interpretation of signs is likely to be false interpretation, the projection of presuppositions rather than objective reading. "The beginning of an acquaintance whether with persons or things," says this epigraph, "is to get a definite outline for our ignorance."[24]

The metaphor of reading implicit here becomes explicit toward the end of the chapter's first paragraph. This comes after a description of Grandcourt as Gwendolen sees him "by the light of a prepared contrast." This is the ignorance she inscribes within the outline of Grandcourt's visible features:

> [Grandcourt's] complexion [says the narrator] had a faded fairness resembling that of an actress when bare of the artificial white and red; his long narrow grey eyes expressed nothing but indifference. Attempts at description are stupid: who can all at once describe a human being? even when he is presented to us we only begin that knowledge of his appearance which must be completed by innumerable impressions under differing circumstances. We recognise the alphabet; we are not sure of the language. (DD, 97–98)

Character as alphabet, as facial features, and as moral disposition are here juxtaposed and interwoven. The first is a figure of the second, and the second a figure of the third, in a train of displacements and aberrant readings in which the word *alphabet* corresponds to the word *traits* in the passage from Trollope. Each is the name of the "known" elemental signs of character out of which a given character, that of Grandcourt, for example, is constructed and then, most likely, misread, for how can we ever be "sure of the language"? The story of Gwendolen's disastrous marriage to Grandcourt turns on her inability to read Grandcourt's character from his face until it is too late, though the narrator has had no difficulty in relating the two. The narrator, however, is granted clairvoyant penetration through the signs to the consciousness behind it.

According to a torsion characteristic of Eliot's narrative style the passage affirms its own "realism" at the same time that it undermines that realism. "Grandcourt" is of course whatever phantasm is produced by the our reading of the words on the page. He exists only as the words on the page. By shifting, however, to the problem of "describing" in words a "real" human being empirically encountered, Eliot obliquely argues for the empirical existence of Grandcourt. The reader is likely to be taken in, since the figurative shift is carefully effaced, smoothed over. At the same time, Eliot presents a figure for that figure. A "real" person's facial features, body, and gestures are letters of an alphabet making a difficult text. At two removes, in a figure of a figure, with considerable indirection, the reader is returned to the primary situation he or she is in as reader of those characters on the page. These are his or her only means of access to the characters of Grandcourt or of any other personage of *Daniel Deronda*. The apparent figure names the literal situation. It is the literal situation of reading a figure, in a reversal characteristic of discourse in which the word or concept of character functions.

In these various displacements the situation does not change. The movement is not a shift from fictive to real to a figure for that real. It is a shift from figure to figure to figure, each a different version of the "same" confrontation by some interpreter of signs to decipher. This shift moves from point to point within the system of meanings (all figures for a particular mode of figuration) for the word or concept *character*.

Two more elements may be added to this system of reading character by characters of various sorts: astrology and palmistry. The characters in these pseudo-sciences are inscribed by the invisible lines between the stars or by those mysterious lines (which must mean something!) on the palm of à man's or a woman's hand. The characters read by the palmist are nearby, written on part of the person's body. Astrological signs are hyperbolically distant. These come together in a curious passage in *L'arrêt de mort* (*Death Sentence*) by Maurice Blanchot:

> I had sent a very beautiful cast of J.'s hands to a young man who was a professional palm reader and astrologer (à un garçon qui s'occupait—professionnellement—de chirologie et d'astrologie), and I had asked him to establish the greater coordinates of her fate (les grandes coordonnées de ce destin). J's hands were small and she didn't like them; but their lines seemed to me altogether unusual—cross hatched, entangled, without the slightest apparent unity. I cannot describe them, although at this very moment I have them under my eyes and they are alive (elles vivent). Moreover, these lines grew blurred sometimes, then vanished, except for one deep central furrow (un profond sillon central) that corresponded, I think, to what they call the line of fate (la ligne de chance). That line did not become distinct except at the moment when all the others were eclipsed; then, the palm of her hand was absolutely white and smooth, a real ivory palm, while the rest of the time the hatchings and the wrinkles made it seem almost old; but the deep hatchet-stroke still ran through the midst of the other lines, and if that line is indeed called the line of fate, I must say that its appearance made that fate seem tragic (et si cette ligne s'appelle bien ligne de chance, je dois dire que son aspect rendait cette chance tragique).[25]

The English translation, by using only the word *fate*, obscures the play between *destin* and *chance* in the French. Is J.'s fate a destiny calculated by something or someone, or is it merely "chance," bad luck? Can one distinguish between chance and destiny? Readers of *L'arrêt de mort* will know how important hands and faces, along with life masks and casts of hands, are in both stories in this strange double "récit." Are these hand casts (which "live" on before the narrator's eyes after J.'s death) an emblem of the life pattern of J., the mortally ill heroine of the first story? Or are they an emblem of her life in its relation to others or to some external fate? They could even be, as they are for Geoffrey Hartman, an emblem of Blanchot's narrative itself, with its curious indirections, repetitions, crossings, and recrossings furrowed by the decisive chasm of death.[26] Or the casts could be read as an existential image of human life generally. Life for everyone, not just for J., is not so much bounded by death as cloven by it through and through, even when that cleaving is obscured by the manifold distractions, shapeless wanderings, encounters, and recurrences that make up every individual history. The lines on J.'s palm may mean all of these things.

The character of a person's palm, in any case, joins face, handwriting, and literary style as an index of his or her character and of the person's predestined fate or haphazard chance in whatever context. The distinction between character and fate breaks down in the gradual slippage from patterns of signs, the lines on a person's face or hands, that are close to the person's character (presumably inside the body), to patterns of signs that are further and further away, as far, ultimately, as the stars. In all these cases, however, the signs are exterior to what they signify, and there is never any possibility of direct access to that signification.

Poe

Yet another mode of character reading is displayed, with an explicit reference to hieroglyphs, in an odd essay by Edgar Allan Poe, "Autography." The essay displays clearly the contradiction within the concept of character it is my goal in this chapter to display. This contradiction might be phrased by saying that the manifest signs of character must both presuppose and constitute what they signify. The signs of character are both constative, or referential, and performative, or constitutive. All the examples in this chapter show the impossibility of affirming or practicing one of these penchants without at the same time affirming and practicing the other.

Poe's "Autography" was published in three parts, the first two in the *Southern Literary Messenger* in February and August 1836, the third, entitled "A Chapter on Autography," in two sections in *Graham's Magazine*, November and December 1841. A reading of this essay will lead further toward an understanding of the issues involved in the concept of character in fiction.

The fiction of Poe's essay involves a visit to the editor of the *Messenger* by a certain Joseph Miller, whose name, in the course of the interview, undergoes permutations through the whole alphabet, from Joseph A. Miller to Joseph B. Miller to Joseph C. Miller, all the way to Joseph Z. Miller. This Miller has "a passion for autographs." His enemies claim he has obtained these by inditing "sundry epistles to several and sundry characters of literary notoriety . . . with the sinister design, hope, and intention of thereby eliciting autographed replies—the said epistles presumed to be indited by me, each and individually being neither more no less than one and the same thing, and consisting . . . of certain silly inquiries respecting the character of certain . . . cooks, scullions, chambermaids, and boot-blacks."[27] Whatever he says, it appears rather that Mr. Miller has sent not requests for "characters" of various servants, but examples of his own "character" in the form of literary compositions with notes asking criticisms and other such literary requests. He has thereby enticed the chief American literati into providing signed replies. The replies only (which it is scarcely necessary to say are all fictions) are given. In the first of the three parts of the essay a sample signature is appended. The replies are either burlesques of the supposed writer's usual style, or are rendered otherwise absurd by reference to the nonsensical questions imagined to have been propounded by Mr. Miller. The autographs are twenty-six in all—corresponding to the twenty-six variations in the initial letter of the hoaxer's middle name" (15:176). The second two parts of the essay give further "genuine autograph facsimiles" (what, one might ask, is a genuine facsimile?) for other American literati with lively and often malicious discussion of the authors' "characters" as indicated by their "characters" in the sense of handwriting. Ralph Waldo Emerson, for example, is a "mystic for mysticism's sake." This is indicated in the way "his MS. is bad, sprawling, illegible, and irregular—although sufficiently bold" (15:260).

Poe's "Autography" plays throughout on four different meanings of character: as signature, as style of handwriting, as the characteristics of the content of the writing by a given author, and as the moral features of the person who has signed his name to that writing, who writes a certain hand, and whose compositions have certain qualities. Each of these features is congruent with the others, the displaced image of them. The whole system is governed by the notion that each person has a fixed and inalienable nature that expresses itself chirographically in these various kinds of "character." Of a certain C. M. Sedgewick, for example, Poe says: "The penmanship of Miss Sedgewick is excellent. The characters are well-sized, distinct, elegantly but not ostentatiously formed; and with perfect freedom of manner, are still sufficiently feminine. . . . Strong common sense and a scorn of superfluous ornament, one might suppose, from Miss Sedgewick's hand-writing, to be the characteristics of her literary style" (15:149–50). Of L. H. Sigourney's handwriting Poe says: "The characters are free, well-sized, and handsomely formed, preserving throughout a perfectly uniform and beautiful appearance, although generally unconnected with each other. Were one to form an estimate of the character of Mrs. Sigourney's compositions from the character of her hand-writing, the estimate would not be very far from the truth. Freedom, dignity, precision, and grace of thought, without abrupt or startling transitions, might be attributed to her with propriety" (15:146).

The reader will see the equivocal play with the word or the concept of character here. The "literal" meaning of the sentence refers to the figurative correspondence between Mrs. Sigourney's handwriting and the qualities of her compositions, but the terminology is all moral and psychological. The sentences are a brief portrait or "character" of Mrs. Sigourney. This kind of analysis still flourishes today. It gives the pleasure of superior insight and clairvoyant control. The writer betrays himself or herself inadvertently in handwriting and makes himself or herself the helpless victim of the pitiless knowledge of the expert in autography. The chirographer sees into the style both literary and personal of the author by way of the style of his or her handwriting and surveys it somewhat mischievously from above. A final example is what is said of a certain hapless Timothy Flint: "The writing of this letter has a *fidgetty* appearance, and would seem to indicate a mind without settled aims—restless and full of activity. Few of the characters are written twice in the same manner, and their *direction* varies continually. Sometimes the words lie perpendicularly on the page—then slope to the right—then, with a jerk, fly off in an opposite way" (15:151).

The third section of Poe's essay, "A Chapter on Autography," published five years after the first two, gives, along with the analyses of one hundred more signatures of literati, mostly forgotten minor worthies, the most explicit statement of Poe's theory of handwriting. "A strong analogy," says Poe, "*does* generally and naturally exist between every man's chirography and character. . . . Next to the person of a distinguished man-of-letters, we desire to see his portrait, next to his portrait his autograph. In the latter, especially, there is something which seems to bring him before us in his true idiosyncrasy—in his character of *scribe*" (15:178). Face, body, and gesture; portrait; autograph—all correspond "generally and naturally," but since it is the idiosyncrasy of a writer to write, his handwriting will be a special index to his character.

What Poe calls the "*philosophy* of this subject" (15:178) is expressed most fully apropos of Charles Anthon, professor at Columbia College. Each man or woman, Poe assumes, has an innate or fixed character. This will be expressed readably in the individual's handwriting if his or her experience of life has not conspired to change that writing so that it becomes a mysterious hieroglyph, that is, a sign without identifiable governing signification:

> It is in the chirography of such men as Professor Anthon that we look with certainty for indication of character. The life of a scholar is mostly undisturbed by those adventitious events which distort the natural disposition of the man of the world, preventing his real nature from manifesting itself in his MS. The lawyer who, pressed for time, is often forced to embody a world of heterogeneous memoranda, on scraps of paper, with the stumps of all varieties of pen will soon find the fair characters of his boyhood degenerate into hieroglyphics which would puzzle Doctor Wallis or Champollion; and from chirography so disturbed it is nearly impossible to decide anything. In a similar manner, men who pass through many striking vicissitudes of life acquire in each change of circumstance a temporary inflection of the handwriting; the whole resulting, after many years, in an unformed or variable MS. scarcely to be recognized by themselves from one day to the other. (15:181)

The figure of hieroglyphics here is an odd one. A hieroglyph is a fixed sign or character that cannot be deciphered only because the code has been lost, while the handwriting of the man of the world is a sign without certain reference to the character of its writer. The latter is a sign that is no sign, or at any rate not a sign governed by any ascertainable code. Such a sign has no fixable proper meaning because it has been cut free of the character of the man or woman whose character, signature, or property it properly is. Such a sign is like hieroglyphics before Champollion has come to crack their code, but in this case there is no code.

The figure of the hieroglyph is incongruous. It indicates the presence in Poe's thinking, or at any rate in the text he wrote, of something different from the manifest system of a theory of character governed by the central presence of a fixed personality expressing itself in face, portrait, and chirography. Along with this is the shadow of an assumption that there might be a system of signs governed by no such fixed center. Such signs would be like hieroglyphs with no stone of translation. They would generate their own meaning adventitiously. Such signs would have a meaning in excess of any authorizing consciousness and its patterning matrix of character. Such marks are signs, but about their signification "it is nearly impossible to decide anything." This interfering interplay of two incompatible theories of the sign could be followed, like a track or spoor to be interrogated and deciphered, throughout Poe's work, for example, in the detective stories, in "The Philosophy of Furniture" (14:101–09), or in Poe's various essays on "Secret Writing" (14:114–49). The proprieties and somewhat covert improprieties of Poe's "philosophy of character" are, however, properly primarily in question here. The example of Poe suggests, as do others of my examples, that even a resolute commitment to a single theory of character—for example, the one that posits a preexisting, nonlinguistic self—will not keep out its differential other, the notion that characters (in the sense of signs) generate character (in the sense of selfhood). The one is not the opposite of the other but its inseparable ghostly companion, like a double reflection in a double-paned window at night.

Rabelais

To palmistry and astrology may be added, with the help of a splendidly exuberant passage from Rabelais, physiognomy, phrenology, the reading of tea leaves, augury (the reading of the entrails of sacrificial animals), the study of the auspices (telling the future by the behavior of birds), and a limitless repertoire of other such superstitions. All these are analogous in presupposing an analogy between some manifest hieroglyphic design and some always hidden personal design that it characters forth. These figures of figures, analogies, displacements, function around an always absent center.

I cite the whole passage to conclude my sequence of brief discussions of a series of passages by different authors, before the fuller discussion of Wittgenstein and then Meredith. The hyperbolic multiplication of sciences of character by Rabelais suggests that there would be no end to the various ways human beings have supposed that character and fate can be deciphered from cryptic signs.

The meaning of all hidden character signaled by manifest characters is absence or loss. Rabelais's way of putting this is to suppose that the secret revealed by all divining is cuckoldry, the loss of a loss. This fate is traditionally seen as irresistibly funny. Yet it is worse even than the castration all men, so we are told, fear, since it bereaves a man of what both confirms that fear and assuages it. In chapter 25 of Book 3 of *Gargantua and Pantagruel,* "Panurge consults Herr Trippa." The name is perhaps a play on Agrippa. The chapter is a spectacular list of all the ways of reading character by character, but all these characters mean infallibly the same thing.

"But listen to me," Epistemon went on; "here's something you can do, even before we return to our king, if you'll take my advice. Here, near the isle Bouchart, lives Herr Trippa; and he, as you know, predicts all future events by the arts of astrology, geomancy, chiromancy, metopomancy, and other sciences of that kidney. Let us consult him about your business. . . ."

Immediately on his arrival Herr Trippa looked him in the face and said: "You have the physiognomy and metaposcopy of a cuckold, of a notorious and infamous cuckold, I say." Next, after considering Panurge's right hand all over, he said: "This broken line that I see here just above the *Mons Jovis* was never on anybody's hand that wasn't a cuckold."

Then with a stylus he hastily pricked a certain number of odd points, joined them together by geomancy, and said: "Truth itself is no truer, and certainty couldn't be more certain than that you'll be a cuckold very soon after your marriage." After this he asked Panurge for the horoscope of his nativity; and when Panurge gave it to him, he promptly drew his heavenly house complete. Having considered its position and the aspects in their triplicities, he heaved a great sigh and said: "I had already clearly foretold that you will be a cuckold. You couldn't fail to be one. But here I have abundant confirmation. What is more you'll be beaten by your wife and she'll rob you. For I find the seventh house malignant in all its aspects and exposed to the assaults of all the signs bearing horns, such as Aries, Taurus, Capricorn, and others. In the fourth I find Jupiter in decline, and a tetragonal aspect of Saturn, associated with Mercury. You'll be soundly peppered with the pox into the bargain, my good man. . . ."

Herr Trippa picked up a tamaris branch.

"That's the thing," said Epistemon; "Nicander calls it the divining tree."

"Would you like a fuller knowledge of the truth," asked Herr Trippa, "by pyromancy, by aeromancy—much esteemed by Aristophanes in his *Clouds*—by hydromancy, or by lecanomancy, which was most celebrated of old amongst the Assyrians and attempted by Hermebus Barbarus? In a basin full of water I'll show you your future wife being rogered by two rustics."

"When you poke your nose up my arse," said Panurge, "don't forget to take off your spectacles."

"I can do it by cataptromancy," continued Herr Trippa, "by means of which Didius Julianus, Emperor of Rome, foresaw all that was to come to him. You'll need no spectacles. You'll see her being poked in a mirror, as clearly as if I were to show her to you in the fountain of Minerva's temple, near Patras. Or by coscinomancy, which was once religiously practised among the ceremonies of the Romans. Let's have a sieve and tongs, and you shall see devils. By alphitomancy, described by Theocritus in his *Pharmaceutria,* and by aleuromancy, mixing wheat with flour. By astragalomancy. I have the pictures here ready. By tyromancy. I have a Bréhémont cheese handy. By gyromancy. I'll twist you round and round in circles, and you'll fall to the left every time, I promise you. By sternomancy. And your chest's no beauty, as it is, I swear. By libanomancy. All you need is a little incense. By gastromancy, which was for long employed by the lady Jacoba Rhodogina, the ventriloquist, in Ferrara. By cephalonomancy, which the Germans used to practise, roasting an ass's head on burning coals. By ceromancy, in which by melting wax in water you'll see the figure of your wife and her belly-drummers. By capnomancy. We'll put poppy seeds and sesame on burning coals—a very pleasant method! By axinomancy. All you have to bring me is a hatchet and some jade, which we'll put on the embers. That was a fine use of it that Homer made against Penelope's suitors! By onymancy. Let us have oil and wax. By tephramancy. You'll see ashes exposed to the air, which will show your wife in a fine state. By botanomancy. I have some sage here for the purpose. By sycoinancy. Oh the divine art of using fig leaves! By ichthyomancy, once both praised and frequently practised by Tiresias and Polydamas, and formerly practised with equal success in Diana's pond, in the wood sacred to Apollo, in the land of the Lycians. By choeromancy. Bring us a herd of swine and you shall have the bladder. By cleromancy as sure as they find the bean in the cake on the night before Epiphany. By anthropomancy, which was employed by Heliogabalus, Emperor of Rome. This isn't a pleasant practice, but you'll stand it well enough, since you're fated to be a cuckold. By sibilline stichomancy. By onomatomancy; what's your name?"

"Chewturd," answered Panurge.

"Or perhaps by alectryomancy. I'll draw a pretty circle here, and while you look on and consider I'll divide it into twenty-four equal portions. On each I'll put a letter of the alphabet, and on each letter I'll place a grain of wheat. Then I'll let a fine virgin cock loose among them. You'll see him eat the grains lying on the letters C.O.Q.U.S.E.R.A. [will be a cuckold] I promise you that. It's just as prophetical as it was in the Emperor Valens' time. When he wanted to know the name of his successor, the fatidic and alectryomantic cock ate the grains on letters [the first letters of the name Theodosius]."

"Would you like to know the answer by the arts aruspicine or extispicine? By auguries taken from the flight of birds, from the croaks of birds of omen, or from the dance of the gobbling ducks?"

"By the art of crappisine," replied Panurge.

"Or perhaps by necromancy. I'll quickly have someone raised from the devil for you, someone who died a short time ago, as Apollonius of Tyana did for Achilles, and as the Witch of Endor did in the presence of Saul. He shall tell us the whole business, just as the dead man who was called up by Erictho predicted to Pompey the whole course and issue of the battle of Pharsalia. Or if you are afraid of the dead, as all cuckolds naturally are, I will just employ sciomancy."

"Go to the devil, you raving lunatic," cried Panurge. "Get yourself buggered by an Albanian, and earn yourself one of their pointed hats. Why the devil don't you tell me to hold an emerald or a hyena-stone under my tongue? Or to collect a store of lapwings' tongues or of green frogs' hearts? Or to eat the heart and liver of some dragon, so that I may hear my destiny from the voice of the swan and the song of the birds, as the Arabs did of old in the land of Mesopotamia?"[28]

A man's character is ungraspable, but it is always the secret of an absence, a loss. I must say "man" here, since the example from Rabelais depends on sexual difference. Does this mean that for the tradition in question here it is only for a man that one can say, "Character is fate"? The example from Blanchot would contradict that, though Baudelaire, like Rabelais, seems to have primarily men in mind. But the narrator and protagonist of Blanchot's *L'arrêt de mort* is of course male. The emphasis in that novel is on the way the two women, "J." and "N.," mediate for the narrator an experience of the ultimate loss of death. This death is experienced by the male protagonist as the strange fate of having always already died, or as the impossibility of dying, which, for Blanchot, comes to the same thing. That deep furrow across J.'s palm figures the narrator's fate as well as hers, since his fate is to experience death through her. This relation finds its comic counterpart in Rabelais's claim that the universal male fate is to be a cuckold. For Baudelaire and for Rabelais, there is no guignon for a man, only something missing in the man's character that gives him perpetual bad luck. This absence is written here, there, everywhere, on his hands, in the stars, in the movement of birds, in the bumps on his skull, on his forehead, in almost legible characters. For Blanchot a man's fate is even written on the palm of the woman he loves. What will happen will happen. The man is fated from all time to choose this path or that at each crossroads, so gradually making the configuration of lines which, after the fact, becomes the manifest hieroglyph of his life. Each man is like Prince Almas in the Persian tale "What the Rose Said to the Cypress": "Prince Almas immediately started; he rode till he came to the parting of the ways. He remembered quite well that the right-hand way was short and dangerous, but he bethought himself too that whatever was written on his forehead would happen, and he took the forbidden road."[29]

Meaning is a physiognomy.—Wittgenstein, *Philosophical Investigations*

Interrogating the assumption that the meaning of a sign is its correspondence with something extrasemiotic is one main focus in Wittgenstein's *Philosophical Investigations* and in the antecedent *Blue and Brown Books*.[30] The question of the interpretation of character in the sense of moral nature from character in the sense of physiognomy is one of the topics to which Wittgenstein keeps returning, as to a nagging puzzle that cannot quite be solved.

How can one use Wittgenstein as an example, since his thinking itself proceeds by way of examples among which there is no common essence? Wittgenstein's examples are bound together rather by that strange relationship of "family resemblance," which he compares to the threads woven or twisted to form a single rope, though the threads at opposite ends are not contiguous or intertwined. And how can one describe or summarize or paraphrase or interpret work that has so decisively challenged traditional assumptions about the possibility of doing these things?

Family resemblance is itself a figure from physiognomy. It joins the "image" of the many-stranded rope, the image of language games, the image of interpreting drawings or portraits, the image of the interpretation of a piece of music, and so on, in a long chain of figures in Wittgenstein's thinking. What is the "literal" subject of these figures in the *Investigations* or of the *Investigations* as such? The question cannot be answered, not even by "language" or "the functioning of signs," since one of Wittgenstein's main points is that there is no single operation of signs, but "countless different language games." Each example is literal and concrete. Interpreting faces or portraits is a perfectly real or empirical life situation. At the same time it has been introduced as an example of something else that Wittgenstein has been talking about earlier or will talk about later. The example is not a simple presence, but the displaced representation of something not present or presentable. The distinction between literal and figurative breaks down once more, as it has again and again in my following of Ariadne's thread. All Wittgenstein's "examples" are catachreses, which is perhaps what, without using the word, he was saying, again and again. Wittgenstein's work is one of the most powerful efforts of deconstruction in twentieth-century European philosophy, if "deconstruction" is taken in one of its many meanings, namely, as a putting in question of deeply rooted presuppositions by patiently going over and over the language in which these presuppositions are expressed.

One result of this breakdown of the distinction between literal and figurative language in Wittgenstein's case is that it is extremely difficult to detach any one "example" from the others, since they are inextricably interwoven in one another in his expression of them. As he affirms, in a sentence which recurs in the *Investigations,* it can be said of any detachable unit of his writing that "a multitude of familiar paths lead off from these words in every direction" (PI, 143e). Any passage cited from Wittgenstein puts one in the midst of a familiar labyrinth in which a multitude of other passages, segments, have a tantalizing family resemblance to the passage, passage-way, one is reading or following and are therefore relevant to understanding it. Wherever one goes in this labyrinth one remains within a domestic enclosure. It is "all in the family," so to speak, and wherever one goes, it all seems uncannily familiar. One has been there before.

A careful dismantling of our instinctive assumptions about reading moral character from the character of a face or a portrait is one line woven into the labyrinthine rope-walk of words Wittgenstein made:

Let us now consider a very instructive case of that use of the word "particular" ("bestimmt") in which it does not point to a comparison (einen Vergleich) and yet seems most strongly to do so,—the case when we contemplate the expression (Ausdruck) of a face primitively drawn in this way:

Let this face produce an impression (Eindruck) on you. You may then feel inclined to say: "Surely I don't see mere dashes. I see a face with a *particular* expression." But you don't mean that it has an outstanding expression, nor is it said as an introduction to a description of the expression, though we might give such a description and say, e.g., "It looks like a complacent business man, stupidly supercilious, who though fat, imagines he's a lady killer." But this would only be meant as an approximate description of the expression. "Words can't exactly describe it," one sometimes says. And yet one feels that what one calls the expression of the face is something that can be detached from the drawing of the face. It is as though we could say: "This face has a particular expression: namely this" (pointing to something). But if I had to point to anything in this place it would have to be the drawing I am looking at. (We are, as it were, under an optical delusion which by some sort of reflection makes us think that there are two objects where there is only one. The delusion is assisted by our using the verb "to have," saying "The face *has* a particular expression." Things look different when, instead of this, we say: "This *is* a peculiar (eigenartiges) face." What a thing *is*, we mean, is bound up with it; what it has can be separated from it.

"This face has a particular expression."—I am inclined to say this when I am trying to let it make its full impression upon me.

What goes on here is an act, as it were, of digesting it, getting hold of it, and the phrase (Ausdruck) "getting hold of the expression (Ausdruck) of this face" suggests that we are getting hold of something which is *in* the face and different from it. It seems we are looking for something, but we don't do so in the sense of looking for a model of the expression outside the face we see, but in the sense of sounding the thing without attention (ohne Aufmerksamkeit untersucht). It is, when I let the face make an impression on me, as though there existed a double of its expression, as though the double was the prototype (das Urbild) of the expression and as though seeing the expression of the face was finding the prototype to which it corresponded—as though in our mind there had been a mould and the picture we see had fallen into that mould, fitting it. But it is rather that we let the picture sink into our mind and make a mould there.

When we say, "This is a face, and not mere strokes," we are, of course, distinguishing such a drawing

from such a one

And it is true: If you ask anyone: "What is this?" (pointing to the first drawing) he will certainly say: "It's a face," and he will be able straight away to reply to such questions as, "Is it male or female," "Smiling or sad?," etc. If on the other hand you ask him: "What is this?" (pointing to the second drawing), he will most likely say, "This is nothing at all," or "These are just dashes."[31]

This passage sets against one another two theories of character in all senses of that word. The passage functions as a demolition of the manifest theory of character in Poe's "Autography." For Poe, at least in the theory dominating his essay, a signature is a sign of the preexisting nature or character of the man or woman who wrote it. Its meaning lies in its similarity to what it represents. Just this comparison theory of character is challenged by Wittgenstein here (and in all those familiar adjacent pathways).

A complex set of different language games or family scenes of interpretation are in question simultaneously here, but their relation to one another (this is just the point) is that of adjacent similarity or family resemblance rather than of analogy governed by some central or original prototype on which they are all modeled. Reading a sentence, understanding a portrait or drawing, recognizing and "reading" a face, interpreting a conglomeration of lines as being on the one hand mere squiggles or on the other a meaningful configuration—all are similar. All seem to involve a comparison between some character or sign and something else of which it is the sign, but all, Wittgenstein wants to say, contain their meanings within themselves and in the act whereby we appropriate them or let them appropriate us, make an impression on us, enter intimately within us. What Wittgenstein says depends on a play on the metaphors latent in the English words *expression* and *impression*. The corresponding German words are made of different prefixes added to "druck," meaning "pressure" or "thrust," also "print, printing; impression; type": Ausdruck, Eindruck. This part of the *Brown Book* was not translated by Wittgenstein, but he may have had the play among the various German words in "druck" in mind. In both languages the root figure is the blow or stamp whereby a configuration is transferred from prototype to copy, molded after the original mold. Wittgenstein uses the words to fight against the concept embodied in the figure within the words.

Is the example Wittgenstein uses, that of the primitively drawn face, fortuitous or innocent? Would any other face have done just as well? Is there any significance in the fact that Wittgenstein chooses a drawing that "impresses us" as representing "a complacent business man, stupidly supercilious, who though fat, imagines he's a lady killer"? No example is innocent, certainly not this one. The drawing works like a Rohrschach blot. "We" read into it one of the fundamental figures of patriarchal hegemony, but a satirical version of that figure, one that undercuts its authority. This businessman is fat. He only imagines he is a lady killer. An implicit proposition is asserted by the example rather than by anything Wittgenstein says overtly. The example tells us the assumption that pictures represent something other than themselves, some proto-type, is in complicity with patriarchal, "logocentric," "phallogo-centric" ideology. The phantasm of the fat complacent lady-killing businessman is a grotesque emblem of that ideology.

Playing or understanding a piece of music offers another example of what Wittgenstein is saying:

> Here one is inclined to ask "What is it like to know the tempo in which a piece of music should be played?" And the idea suggests itself that there *must* be a paradigm somewhere in our mind, and that we have adjusted the tempo to conform to that paradigm. But in most cases if someone asked me "How do you think this melody should be played?," I will, as an answer, just whistle it in a particular way, and nothing will have been present to my mind but the tune *actually whistled* (not an image [Vor-stellungsbild] of *that*). (BBB, 166; G, 257)

These passages reveal the paradoxical relation between the no-tion of metaphor and the notion of realistic representation. Though these seem opposite poles—for example, in Jakobson's theory of the two types of aphasia and the two types of literature, meta-phorico-poetic and metonymico-realistic—they are based on the same assumption about the way signs have meaning. To see a primitively drawn face as "having a particular expression" is to see it "as" something else, as a metaphor, image, or simile for that something else, the prototype of that expression. Or it is, alterna-tively (but the alternative is the same thing), to see it as an accurate, "realistic" representation or "image" of that prototype, as a good portrait copies accurately the features and expression of the "orig-inal" of the portrait.

But as Wittgenstein argues again and again by way of different examples patiently explored, the meaning is in the sign, not in its imitation, copying of, or reference to, something other than itself but:

> What we call "understanding a sentence" has, in many cases, a much greater similarity to understanding a musical theme than we might be inclined to think. But I don't mean that understand-ing a musical theme is more like the picture (Bild) which one tends to make oneself of understanding a sentence; but rather that this picture is wrong and that understanding a sentence is

much more like what really happens when we understand a tune than at first sight appears. For understanding a sentence, we say, points to a reality outside the sentence. Whereas one might say "Understanding a sentence means getting hold of its content; and the content of the sentence is *in* the sentence (der Inhalt des Satzes ist im Satz)." (BBB, 167; G, 257)

An even better formulation of this is to say that the meaning is in the use we make of the word or words: "In order not to be deluded we have to ask ourselves: What is the use, say, of the words 'this' and 'that'?—or rather, what are the different uses which we make of them? What we call their meaning is not anything which they have got in them or which is fastened to them irrespective of what use we make of them" (BBB, 170). The reader will remember that the section about the primitively drawn face is in the service of explaining a particularly instructive use of the word "particular."

The meaning of a word is posited by the function of the word, not determined by its true correspondence to something other than itself. Meaning is performative, constitutive, not referential. As a theory of character this means that there is no occult "self" or "consciousness" or "moral character" that manifests itself in face, signature, palm, tea leaves, or whatever. There are only the face, signature, palm, tea leaves, and so on. These constitute that character. They *are* that character. They *are* that character as they are read by the man himself or by his neighbors, that is, when used in a certain way. "We" are under a "strange illusion" when "we seem to seek the something which a face expresses (etwas. . . das von einem Gesicht ausgedrückt wird) whereas, in reality, we are giving ourselves up to the features before us" (BBB, 166; G, 256). It is of extreme importance to see that Wittgenstein, like de Man or Derrida, gives no support to the idea that the meaning of a sign or configuration of signs is freely imported from the outside, for example, by the "response" of a reader or community of readers. Meaning is not "read into" a sign in the sense of projected on something that passively waits for us to lend it meaning. No, the meaning is in the sign, and we give ourselves up to it, let it make a particular impression on us, just as de Man asserts that what happens in reading happens. In reading, he says, freely translating Hölderlin's "es ereignet sich aber das Wahre," "what is true is what is bound to take place."[32]

The relation between the portrait and the man's face, for Wittgenstein, is the same as the relation between that face and the man's moral character. In both cases the mimetic lines are cut. The characters, in the sense of signs, stand alone. They generate their own significance as they make an impression on the one who sees them as signs and not as mere dashes and who uses them in a certain way.

Wittgenstein's expressions of this are slightly peculiar. This peculiarity suggests that the reader is here reaching the borderline on this side of what cannot be thought, said, or written in Wittgenstein's idiom. The word *character* and its cognates play a fundamental role here, but in order to say what he wants to say Wittgenstein has to truncate the range of meanings in the family of words. Rather than being the sign for something else "character" remains for him a particular configuration of lines which creates and maintains its own meaning as it is used by the one who contemplates it. It has a particular character, and its power lies all in that, as when Wittgenstein says, "This sentence has *its own character* (seines eigenen Charakter)" (BBB, 180; G, 275), or when he says the "particular experience" of reading a sentence, "taking it in," is "an experience of an intimate character" in which "the written words themselves which I read don't just look to me like any kind of scribbles" (BBB, 167).

The difficulty is in describing the difference between seeing it as mere scribbles, meaningless lines, and seeing it as a character with a particular character. Here Wittgenstein's expression becomes necessarily tautological, circular, since he has denied himself the possibility of a comparison that would generate a copula. This is like de Man's "what happens must happen." To see a character as a character is to let it sink into one, to let its particular expression make an impression, according to a metaphor which is latent in the play between these words and in the words *character* or *physiognomy*. That is the image of a signet, brand, or stamp that duplicates itself while remaining just itself, or at any rate a mirror image of itself, a pointer, but not pointing beyond itself. Such a stamp is capable of innumerable duplications while remaining itself and not leading to any act of comparison. "We distinguish," says Wittgenstein, "seeing a drawing as a face and seeing it as something else or as 'mere dashes.' . . . And in letting the face impress itself on me and contemplating its 'particular expression,' no two things of the multiplicity of a face are compared with each other; there is only *one* which is laden with emphasis (mit Nachdruck). Absorbing its expression, I don't find a prototype of this expression in my mind; rather, I, as it were, cut a seal from the impression" (BBB, 165; G, 254–255).

Of such an impression or of any of the seals cut from it all that can be said is that it is what it is. It can neither be validated by comparison with any prototype, nor can it be subdivided within itself so that we can say the "particular expression" is caused by this or that feature. It is total and totalizing. It has no meaning at all, if meaning means correspondence of the sign to what it means. It is a physiognomy with no gnomon, a sign which does not point beyond itself: "When I say 'I don't see mere dashes (a mere scribble) but a face (or word) with this particular physiognomy,' I don't wish to assert any general characteristic of what I see, but to assert that I see that particular physiognomy which I do see. And it is obvious that my expression (Ausdruck) is moving in a circle" (BBB, 174; G, 266).

The self-enclosed circularity without escape of the experience of character is given striking expression in a passage using negatively one more figure, that of a jigsaw puzzle:

> And thus also we may think that when we look at our drawing and see it as a face, we compare it with some paradigm, and it agrees with it, or it fits into a mould ready for it in our mind. But no such mould or comparison enters into our experience, there is only this shape, not any other to compare it with, and as it were, say "Of course" to. As when in putting together a jig-saw puzzle, somewhere a small space is left unfilled and I see a piece obviously fitting it and put it in the place saying to myself "Of course." But here we say, "Of course" *because* the piece fits the mould, whereas in our case of seeing the drawing as a face, we have the same attitude for *no* reason (ohne Grund). (BBB, 166; G, 256)

For no reason! The experience of reading any sign—a face, a sentence, a piece of music, or whatever—is illogical, alogical. It has no logos, no reason, ground, or base. It cannot be measured or rationalized, made part of any logical system. It is entirely sui generis, incommensurate with any other experience. It is just this act of reading or of using the character which it is, letting the character here and now make this particular impression on me. That is all there is to it, all that can be said about it.

The trouble with such acts of using, a trouble perhaps even

Wittgenstein does no more than hint at, is that it shares the un-predictability and proneness to error of all performatives. To take a sign as so and so is always to mis-take it, and in each case differently, in a particular way. This mistaking and differentiation can be corrected and regularized by no coercive conventions, col-lectively agreed upon, in spite of Wittgenstein's appeal to a "we" that will always see the drawing as a fat businessman.

Wittgenstein's need to argue so vehemently and persuasively the impossibility of any private language is an uneasy pivot in his thinking.[33] The game of prolonged discrimination he plays is lost the instant he admits that any private language could exist. If any language is private, then all languages might be private or are contaminated by privacy, thereby deprived of regularity and pro-priety. All uses of all signs, all interpretations of character, are, in so far as they are positings, performatives, at the same time nec-essarily to some degree private, bound by no rules, in that partic-ular sense "mistakes." Wittgenstein's use of the word *particular* expresses this individuality. The face has a "particular expression." This disquieting freedom of signs is a necessary consequence of cutting them off from any mimetic function. But it is the whole bent of Wittgenstein's thinking to do that. If this situation is trans-ferred to the representation and interpretation of moral character in novels or in real life, one might say that all readings of character, mine of myself, mine of other persons, those in any novel by the narrator, the characters, the reader, are always necessarily in error. They are in error in the particular sense that they are not verifiable by reference to anything outside the sign that the sign is a sign of and that might validate them as true. Perhaps a better way to put this would be to say that such readings are neither true nor false, since they are not open to either invalidation or validation by any check of their correspondence to a model or prototype. Such read-ings are the private reading of a meaning on the basis of lines taken as a sign, for example, as a face which "has" a "particular expression." The reading is made "for no reason," but we do everything possible to persuade ourselves that the reading has some outside base or authority, for example, in its necessary repeatability every time the reading is performed by any member of the "we." But we must ask, "Who is this 'we'?"

Wittgenstein constantly skirts the conclusion to which his insight leads him, but the continuation of his lifelong meditations depends on not quite taking that last step into the vacant center of his verbal labyrinth. This step would have put him where Nietzsche, in his theory of character, was from the time of the *Philosophen-buch* on. Such a step would not have made it impossible to go on thinking and writing, as the example of Nietzsche's perpetually growing pile of notebooks indicates. It would, however, have changed the rules of the game in such a way that the Wittgenstein-ian meditation as we have it would have been impossible. That meditation is motivated, kept going, by the following aporia: On the one hand, Wittgenstein's essential insight is that "meaning is a physiognomy," that is, that meaning is intrinsic to signs and to the uses we make of them, not generated by the correspondence of the sign and something else. If this is the case, however, all language is private in the particular sense that the meaning of any sign, even its character as a sign, is generated anew and somewhat differently in each use or encounter of it by each person, even though that use is the "impression" the sign makes on its user. On the other hand, as Wittgenstein says, a private language is no language at all. It is incapable of being fixed in that regularity and repeatability necessary to make a sign a sign, part of a systematic code capable of being deciphered with certainty the same way every time and used for communication.

The image of the expression which makes an impression, as a stamp makes a seal, is a remnant of this notion of a fixed repeatable code, present even in the metaphors whereby Wittgenstein disman-tles the paradigm or prototype theory. If all language, to be lan-guage, must be public, then any word in that language, any sign—for example, the primitively drawn face or the face of my beloved—must in one way or another be governed by some paradigm. It must draw its meaning not from its own intrinsic physiognomy, but from its physiognomy in another sense, as an index or pointer, a gnomon, indicating something else which it names, imitates, refers to, is metaphorically similar to, namely, the expression which the drawing "has," the "character" of my beloved or whatever. This metaphorico-mimetic theory of meaning, however, is precisely what Wittgenstein, patiently, over and over again, with a multitude of brilliant examples, is concerned to deconstruct. Meaning is phy-siognomy in the first sense. It is in the sign, not in the reference of the sign to something else. If the meaning of a face is in the face, in the impression its expression makes on me, if the character of my beloved is in my interpretation of the character of her features, then that impression or interpretation is free of any control beyond the features themselves. Whatever of the public, regular, or transmissible it may have is extremely fragile, bounded on every side by the abyss of privacy.

Between these two possibilities, the possibility that all language is private, and the return to some form of the discredited paradigmatic theory, Wittgenstein's thought oscillates. From that oscillation it draws its strength to continue down its familiar pathways, crossing and crisscrossing over that landscape to which he compares it in the preface to the *Investigations*: "For this compels us to travel over a wide field of thought criss-cross in every direction" (PI, vii). Wittgenstein's thought, to vary the metaphor, is like a river that is impelled forward by its zigzag pressure against the banks on either side. The double meaning of the word *physiognomy* and the subtle analysis of what goes on when we read character in a face is one important channel in that torrent of thought.

Character as Apotropaic

The concept of character, as all these examples have shown, reifies a figure. The figure is that peculiar form of synecdoche whereby the sign itself (the engraved mark or "character") is substituted for what it signifies (character in the sense of fixed, incised lines of personality, "character traits" imprinted permanently on the supposed consciousness of the individual and constituting his selfhood). The characteristics of the visible "character" or physiognomy are assumed to be characteristic of the invisible selfhood too, though there is no possibility of verifying that assumption. Access to character in the sense of fixed personality goes only by way of characters in the sense of external signs. Character (in the sense of self) is never present. It is always over there, somewhere else, pointed to by characters (signposts) that cannot be followed to reach an unmediated access to what they indicate. "Wherever we see or divine movement in a body," says Nietzsche, "we learn to conclude that there is a subjective, invisible life appertaining to it. Movement is symbolism for the eye [Bewegung ist eine Symbolik für das Auge]: it indicates that something has been felt, willed, thought" (E, 271; G, 475). If a stone moves, we think it must be alive and thinking its stony thoughts. For Nietzsche's word *movement (Bewegung)*, one can by extension include all those elements of physiognomy and gesture that are taken as signs, as a Symbolik, of a hidden inner character, feeling, willing, thinking. Bewegung:

the word enfolds within it the word for path: *Weg.* To move is to
set forth along the road tracing out the lifeline externalizing a
hidden inner character and constituting in the end the traveler's
"fate."

Nevertheless, in spite of the powerful tradition, best represented
by Nietzsche on the Continent and by Hume in Scotland, dismantling the assumption that self is a substance, there is no novel that
is "really a novel," from *Don Quixote* to *Ulysses, The Waves,* or
even *L'Innomable,* that does not create in two ways the powerful
illusion of characters. One is the character of the narrator. The
narrator seems to be a man or woman speaking to other men and
women. We yield to an almost irresistible temptation and think of
the narrative voice as that of the author. We name the narrator of
Middlemarch "George Eliot," the narrator of *The Warden* "Trollope." The second illusion is that of the characters. They seem men
and women like ourselves. This positing of two forms of character
is a distinguishing feature of the novel as a post-Renaissance genre.
Or perhaps it characterizes narrative as such. Do we not ascribe
character to the narrators and personages, mutatis mutandis, in
fairy tales, Norse sagas, and the *Odyssey*?

The mutatis mutandis works according to a law of parsimony
in the creation of artistic illusion by conventional means. Ernst
Gombrich has made this familiar in his magisterial challenge to
representational realism, "Meditations on a Hobby Horse."[34] The
"impression" of character, to use Wittgenstein's word, is produced
differently within each culture and each "period" of a culture. It
may be produced by the most economical means, since it is reinforced by powerful conventions and presuppositions about character within the public for whom a given novel is intended. As two
sticks and a bit of yarn will do as a gallant horse for a child, so a
few words lightly sketched out at the beginning of a novel create
magically, for the readers within its tradition, the strong impression
of two characters: that of the protagonist, that of the storyteller.
In the case of a first-person novel, the two are of course the same.
Often, it is worth noting, the magic gesture depends unostentatiously on some figure of speech. Examples are the initial presentations of Pip in *Great Expectations,* of Dorothea Brooke in *Middlemarch,* and of Jim in *Lord Jim*:

I called myself Pip.[35]

"How very beautiful these gems are!" said Dorothea.[36]

He was an inch, perhaps two, under six feet, powerfully built, and he advanced straight at you with a slight stoop of the shoulders, head forward, and a fixed from-under stare which made you think of a charging bull.[37]

In *Great Expectations* the figure is "pip" as seed. In *Middlemarch* the image of the gems presents the first parabolic emblem in the novel. The image of Jim as charging bull creates, for me at least, the distinct impression of a personality, an outline the rest of the novel fills in or at least makes more clearly enigmatic.

What is arbitrary, conventional, and parsimonious about this may be experienced by reading a novel in a somewhat different tradition from one's own. There is something slightly odd and almost unconvincing, for an English or American reader, about the presentation of character in French, German, or Russian novels— for example, in *Jacques le fataliste* or *La Chartreuse de Parme,* in *Die Wahlverwandtschaften,* or in *Crime and Punishment*—in spite of the ability such a reader has to yield to the "real illusion" (Walter Pater's phrase)[38] of characters in them. The reader does this by training and by a slight effort of depersonification, a slight alienation from his or her own culture and from his or her accustomed sense of selfhood within it. Courses in "The European Novel" are designed to provide such displacement. Until the reader gets used to the new conventions, however, these slightly alien novels show, for him, their conventions. He sees the two sticks and the bit of yarn behind the noble charger. Cinema seems perhaps the most "realistic" of narrative forms. Is it not photographs of actual people? Nevertheless, a film, as anthropologists have discovered, is difficult for those who have never seen a movie to interpret until they have had appropriate training. They cannot make anything out of the images on the screen or are distracted by all sorts of peripheral details that would scarcely be noticed by a Western moviegoer. They have a different way of looking.

The function of the novel within the community of its readers is circular. Each culture and each period of that culture has its own complex presuppositions about selfhood. An example would be the English assumption that selfhood is relatively fixed. This is perhaps reinforced by certain aspects of Protestantism. Against this can be set the French conception of selfhood as relatively fluid, as it is, for example, in Marivaux or Gide. These complex conventions are, in each community of readers, during the period of the reign of the novel as a major genre, reinforced and partly created by novels. The reader goes to a novel to be reassured, to encounter characters like himself or herself. He or she reads the novel according to ingrained presuppositions about selfhood. Confronted by characters in the sense of letters on the page, letters that have a magic power to generate the impression of characters in the sense of persons, the reader is like the child with a hobbyhorse, not like the preliterate at the cinema. On the other hand, once that interpretation has been made—once the reader has yielded to the real illusion of knowing Pip, Lord Jim, Elizabeth Bennet, or Dorothea Brooke, following their lives through as he or she follows the text through, knowing them better and better, knowing them intimately from within—the reader turns the line around and interprets neighbors and self according to models encountered in novels. The reader peoples the world with Willoughbys, Claras, and Dorotheas. In this way nature imitates art. England after 1836 begins to be filled with Dickensian characters, even with people who feel themselves to be Dickensian characters.

The novel has a powerful, perhaps indispensable, social function during its reign. It sustains and creates the fictions of character and the characteristic lifelines of characters. These form one of the fundamental cohesive forces keeping each community of readers together. A community may be defined as a group of people who live by the same fictions, the same simplifications, the same hypostatized figures posited as substances. The novel helps to make and sustain such communities.

This function of novels seems clear enough, but what is the function of the contrary aspect which I claim is present in each work of fiction, its putting in question of the notions of character on which its benign power to maintain society depends? This disintegrating would seem to be not only antisocial but even self-destructive, since it demolishes the illusion of character on which the novel's power and function depends. This autodeconstruction reduces the readers of a given novel to the state of the child who has outgrown his toy and sees the sticks and yarn behind the hobbyhorse. Why is this dissolution of its own fundamental fiction as constant a feature of realistic fiction as the creation of the fiction of character in the first place?

I suggest that the function is apotropaic. It is a throwing away of what is already thrown away in order to save it. It is a destroying of the already destroyed in order to preserve the illusion that it is

still intact. All men and women living within a culture and accepting a certain notion of character have an uneasy feeling that
their belief in character, even their belief in their own characters,
may be confidence in an illusion. The function of the self-decon-
structive aspect of novels would then be to assuage this covert
suspicion by expressing it overtly, in a safe region of fiction. Character is then triumphantly reaffirmed in the face of its putting in
question, even if that reaffirmation may be no more than the
persistence of that deconstructing voice, the voice of the narrator
who says "I am I," and goes on saying "I am I" even when he has
demonstrated that there is no "I," or the persistence of the character who says, "I have and am no I."

My hypothesis, then: the novel as the perpetual tying and untying
of the knot of selfhood for the purpose, in the psychic economy of
the individual and of the community, of affirming the fiction of
character by putting it fictionally in question and so short-circuiting
a doubt which, left free to act in the real social world, might
destroy both self and community. Belief in the self, in character, is
thereby precariously maintained by the novel over the abyss of its
dismantling. Is not the positing of the self necessary to the positing
of its fictionality, in a perpetual torsion of nay-saying and yea-
saying, of nay-saying which cannot be said without the yea-saying
its saying unsays? The novel demonstrates, in a safe realm where
nothing serious is at stake, the possibility of maintaining the fiction
of selfhood in the teeth of a recognition that it is a fictive projection,
an interpretation not a fact, and so always open to being dissolved
by a contrary interpretation—for example, that of the multiplicity
or the nonentity of the ego. The novel is a production of its society
which has a certain function within the psychic economy of that
society. It is not a mimetic copy of something which could do
perfectly well without the copy. This would make the writing of a
novel no more than the creation of a supplementary, alternative
world with no relation other than of accurate or inaccurate mirroring to the real social world. Nor, on the other hand, does a
novel create an autonomous self-sustaining fictional world with no
relation whatsoever to the real one.

The apotropaic function—warding off the loss by enacting it
safely and recovering what was lost in simulated or fetishistic form,
beyond its loss—is performed better if it is covert. It should be
performed over and over every time *Robinson Crusoe, Great Expectations, Middlemarch,* or *To the Lighthouse* is read, but it

should not be recognized as such. The function of the fiercely maintained and yet manifestly absurd theory of mimetic representation—the most powerful official theory of fiction during all the period of the heyday of the realistic novel, held by authors, critics, and readers alike, and still imperturbably, or almost imperturbably, assumed by many critics and readers today—is to serve as a screen. This screen allows the hidden, repressed function of the novel to be effectively performed. The importance of that function, and the need to keep it secret, even though the novels themselves everywhere betray the secret, is indicated by the energy, both intellectual and moral, with which the mirror theory of the novel is maintained. It is also indicated by the energy of indignation, again both intellectual and moral, with which the alternative theory is denied. The alternative theory is said to be an inappropriate application of "modern" theories to texts which are innocent of everything but a desire to mirror accurately the social and psychological "realities" of their times for the highly moral purpose of teaching us to know our neighbors better and to love them as they are. Chapter 17 of George Eliot's *Adam Bede* is the locus classicus for this theory in the Victorian novel, though few readers seem to have noticed how Eliot pulls the rug out from under her own theory, both in the conceptual analysis toward the end of that chapter and in her practice of so-called realism in the novel itself.

All the texts of classical realism contain in one way or another this double movement of affirmation and subversion of the main tenets of realism, including the notion of character or selfhood. It is only necessary to read those novels carefully in order to see this, though this is extremely difficult to do, since the energy of repression is strong. As much commentary on these novels demonstrates, the passages deconstructing the notion of character in *Middlemarch,* say, or in *Daniel Deronda* (to cite archetypes of realistic fiction in the Victorian period) are commonly passed over in silence as if they were not there. The presuppositions in favor of character in the mind of the critic are so strong that he imposes an interpretation based on those presuppositions willy-nilly, like a network over the text. Any strong community will rightly resist strongly, and name as dissolute, the dissolution of the fictions it lives by, even the revelation of the covert function, as supports of the community, of those entities which it calls "works of fiction." As Friedrich Nietzsche says, "to be able to read off a text as a text without interposing an interpretation is the last-developed form of 'inner experience'—perhaps one that is hardly possible (einen Text *als Text* ablesen können, ohne eine Interpretation dazwischen zu mengen, ist die späteste Form der 'inneren Erfahrung'—veilleicht eine kaum mögliche)" (E, 266; G, 805). If it is hardly possible, it may not even be desirable. In fact, a reading of George Eliot's novels (to continue with that example) which exclusively follows out those passages undoing the notion of character and so on is no less an interpretation than the one which accepts the characters and talks of them as real people. Both are also equally based on judgments of moral utility, though different ones in each case. The "deconstructive" reading of George Eliot is by no means that "hardly possible" reading of a text as a text without interposing an interpretation that Nietzsche names. What would a text without interpretation be? A set of absurd signs not seen as signs but only as material marks without significance. The text of a novel like *Adam Bede* or *Middlemarch* contains the possibility, indeed the necessity, in the words on the page, both of the "realistic" reading and of the contrary "deconstructive" one. The relation between these two interpretations is not that of simple opposition. It is a paradoxical inherence of each in the other. It is a relation of dependence in which each posits the other as the presupposition of its own operation but at the same time makes that presupposition, as well as its own, impossible exclusively to presuppose. If my hypothesis about the double function of realistic fiction, as an affirmation of character and as a putting in question of character, is correct, readings of such novels should try to do justice to both aspects of their presentation of character. Like any hypothesis, the one I have presented here would need to be tested on an appropriate number of examples. The last section of this chapter will explore one example, George Meredith's *Egoist*.

Meredith

Her character was yet liquid in the mold.
—George Meredith, *The Egoist*

Nietzsche, the OED, Poe on signatures, Wittgenstein, Benjamin, Baudelaire, and the rest—these have been arabesques, parafes (encircling ornamentations), around the true signature of this chapter, the use of line imagery to present character in the novel. But it is impossible to tell where signature stops and parafe begins, just as it is impossible to tell where narrative fiction stops, and something else—literary criticism, or philosophy, or some other form of "non-fiction"—starts. A narrative dimension infects even the most abstract thought. Is not Joseph A. to Z. Miller, in Poe's "Autography," a "character"? And are not Wittgenstein's *Investigations* and *The Blue and Brown Books* full of "characters" in various situations confronting enigmatic signs—for example, trying to figure out what is meant by "Bring me a slab!" or interpreting the crudely drawn face as a fat complacent businessman? And surely Wittgenstein himself, as presented in his works, is a character, as when we say "he's a character!"

Novels, however, are a special case of taking an impression of an expression as Wittgenstein describes it. Reading a novel, taking it in, is a large-scale version of one of Wittgenstein's examples—reading a sentence in a familiar language. On the other hand, many novels perform their own internal analyses of interpreting a person's character by the lines on his or her face. They comment indirectly on what the reader is doing. In this, novels are like the *Investigations* or *The Blue and Brown Books*. The fictive characters in a novel and their fictive credences about their own characters and those of others may play the same role in relation to the deconstitutive analysis by the novel's narrator as do Wittgenstein's examples as they embody the ingrained assumption that there must be somewhere a paradigm with which we compare the sign in relation to his deconstructive argument that the meaning is in the sign. The doubled or ironized structure is similar in both cases. A novel, however, can displace this structure many times over. A novel can multiply narrators, place narrators within narrators. Or it can place the drama of disarticulation within the characters' interpretation of themselves. The "character" of Wittgenstein, on the other hand, remains as distinct and sovereign a presence as that of Socrates in the Platonic dialogues. Wittgenstein remains, for the most part, imperturbably aloof from the investigations he carries on so masterfully.

One spectacular example of presentation of character in the Victorian novel is the chapter entitled "Clara's Meditations" in George Meredith's *Egoist* (1879). *The Egoist* presents a strong sense of living characters: Willoughby, Clara, Dr. Middleton, Vernon, and the garrulous narrator whom the reader first encounters in the celebrated "Prelude." The "Prelude" maps egoism "from the Lizard to the last few pulmonary snips and shreds of leagues dancing on their toes for cold, explorers tell us, and catching breath by good luck like dogs at bones about a table, on the edge of the Pole."[39] The goal of *The Egoist,* the "Prelude" tells the reader, is a mapping of this geography. The novel presents the unimaginable complexity of egoism's topography in a schematic outline and according to a reductive code, small scale matching large scale, part for whole. Such synecdoches assume that the grain of the sample corresponds cunningly to the grain of the whole from which it is taken. For this reason "art is the specific," "the inward mirror, the embracing and condensing spirit." It is "specular" or "spectacular" in the sense of reflecting and thereby making visible. Art can "give us those interminable mile-post piles of matter . . . in essence, in chosen samples, digestibly," "so that a fair part of a book outstripping thousands of leagues when unrolled [the great Book of Earth or Book of Egoism, the record of human social intelligence over the generations], may be compassed in one comic sitting" (13:2–3).

Meredith recognizes that a novel is, as a whole, a figure of speech, rather than merely containing "illustrative" figures. But if a novel is in toto a figure, a vast synecdoche, it figures another figure. A novel does not represent a nontextual reality in a textual condensation. It condenses one enormous book, the Book of Earth, in another compendious shorter one. The social world is already a written record or memorial, a huge data base. A comic novel is a précis of that record. It is not a mimesis in language of something nonverbal, but language about language. It is, moreover, not just mimesis but a synecdochic "specific." It is a homeopathic cure of language by language. It cures by administering a little bit of the disease. Its purpose is performative, not constative. Its intent is medicinal.

The image of comedy as a reading of the vast book of egoism is reinforced, within the body of the novel, by many uses of the conventional figure whereby one person's understanding of another is his "reading" of him. This metaphor is more than conventional in *The Egoist.* It defines another person's character as visible in somewhat enigmatic characters. These must be deciphered if that person is to be understood. Willoughby seems to Clara, for example, "an obelisk lettered all over with hieroglyphics, and [she condemned to] everlastingly [hear] him expound them, relishingly [renew] his lectures on them" (13:116). About this obelisk there will be more to say. In another place, a crucial paragraph in the chapter of "Clara's Meditations," the narrator generalizes, apropos

of Clara's "reading" of Colonel De Craye, about the situation of   **103**
unmarried women in Victorian society, in their deciphering of the   Character
characters of men:

> Maidens are commonly reduced to read the masters of their
> destinies by their instincts; and when these have been edged by
> over-activity they must hoodwink their maidenliness to suffer
> themselves to read: and then they must dupe their minds, else
> men would soon see they were gifted to discern. Total ignorance
> being their pledge of purity to men, they have to expunge the
> writing of their perceptives on the tablets of the brain: they have
> to know not when they do know. The instinct of seeking to
> know, crossed by the task of blotting knowledge out, creates
> that conflict of the natural with the artificial creature to which
> their ultimately-revealed double-face, complained of by ever-
> dissatisfied men, is owing. (13:245)

Reading another person leads to knowing, and knowing is a
transformation of the knower. This transformation is here figured,
according to a well-known Victorian ideological construct, as a
loss of virginity. Henry James's *What Maisie Knew* and *The Awkward Age* are dramatizations of the catastrophic effects on the lives
of upper- and middle-class Victorian women of the absurd presupposition that virginity must be of the mind as well as of the body.
Meredith emphasizes the way it leads women to be duplicitous. In
order to protect themselves from men they must learn to "read"
them, but if they are to remain suitable for marriage they must
appear not to be able to read. Meredith here reads Clara's reading
of De Craye. He takes it as a synecdoche for all those pages of the
Book of Earth that record innumerable maidenly decipherings of
men. If Willoughby's face, or De Craye's, is a text for Clara to
read, that reading is in turn a kind of writing "on the tablets of
[Clara's] brain." This writing the narrator reads in his turn. The
discourse of the narrator of *The Egoist* is, so to speak, a marginal
commentary on the main text. It is an interpretation of the Book
of Social Wisdom, working, as all good interpretation must do, by
detailed explication of samples. These, Meredith claims, can be
taken as fair representations of the whole. Whether or not that is
the case must remain, for now, a suspended question, but it can
be said that the validity of *The Egoist* depends on the validity of
synecdoche.

Exactly what form does Meredith's cure of language by language take? It would appear that the metaphor of reading is just that, no more than a metaphor for transactions that are on the literal level those of consciousness with consciousness. Meredith matches any Victorian novelist in conveying to his readers sharply etched configurations for each character. The reader knows each as the presence of a consciousness to itself. Moreover, each is presented as defined by its awareness of itself in relation to other people.[40] For Meredith I am aware of myself, I *am* myself, to the degree that I am aware of the psychic pressure upon me of other people. These other psyches are like breaths disturbing the flame of my self-consciousness. At the same time they feed that flame. They are necessary to its subsistence. I am conscious of myself as conscious of the consciousnesses of others. This is the general law of selfhood for characters in Victorian novels, but Meredith, especially in his remarkable late novels, beginning with *The Egoist* and continuing through *Diana of the Crossways* (1885), *One of Our Conquerors* (1891), *Lord Ormont and His Aminta* (1894), and *The Amazing Marriage* (1895), excels in presenting intimately, from within, the subtle pressures the consciousness of another imposes on the self-presence of a given character. If art is the specific by being an "inward mirror," Meredith's characters are mirrors within that mirror. Each lives by speculation, by its reflection of the lives of others in itself, or by seeing itself reflected in the mirrors of others. This happens according to a speculative law admirably formulated in Shakespeare's *Troilus and Cressida*:

> The beauty that is borne here in the face
> The bearer knows not, but commends itself
> To others' eyes; nor doth the eye itself,
> That most pure spirit of sense, behold itself,
> Not going from itself; but eye to eye opposed
> Salutes each other with each other's form;
> For speculation turns not to itself
> Till it hath travelled and is married there
> Where it may see itself. (3.3.103–11)

Each mirror's need of another mirror is extreme in Willoughby, the primary egoist in *The Egoist*. This need is the ultimate weakness that makes him the slave of others, in spite of his satanic "generalship" in deceiving and dazzling the eyes of others. As the narrator says, "The breath of the world, the world's view of him, was partly his vital breath, his view of himself" (14:456). Equally shrewd is Clara's dependence on others. Her unwitting enslavement of herself to Willoughby and her struggle to free herself honorably make up the main action of *The Egoist*. Many of its admirably subtle notations of the law that self-awareness is awareness of others are made apropos of her exacerbated sensitivity to the effect on her of what might be called Willoughby's psychic aura, the magnetic field around him of a forceful will to appropriation. An example is the scene in which Willoughby tries to embrace his fiancée as they stroll though his estate. Though he has not yet extended his arms, the imminence of his caress affects her as if it were a huge ocean wave about to sweep her away: "The gulf of a caress hove in view like an enormous billow hollowing under the curled ridge. She stooped to a buttercup; the monster swept by" (13:153).

The sharp configurations of character in *The Egoist* are, so it seems, mediated, described, or interpreted by language, not constituted by it. Such figures as are used in these descriptions are expressions of something other than themselves. Key terms in Meredith's psychology of character are *self, mind, feeling, will,* and *nature.* All these terms suggest a prelinguistic fixed character: "She was to do everything for herself, do and dare everything, decide upon everything. He told her flatly that so would she learn to know her own mind" (13:242); "But decide at once. I wish you to have your free will" (14:326); "It's a dispute between a conventional idea of obligation and an injury to her nature. . . . Her feelings guide her best. It's one of the few cases in which nature may be consulted like an oracle" (14:368–69); "She was not pure of nature . . . ; she was pure of will: fire rather than ice" (13:211).

What is Clara's "nature," this perdurable, substantial self she must protect from Willoughby's invasions and appropriations? The answer is given in chapter 21, "Clara's Meditations." This chapter perhaps served as a model for the celebrated chapter of Isabel Archer's midnight vigil in Henry James's *Portrait of a Lady* (1881). Meredith's chapter dramatizes the moment of dissolution, from within, as a "lived experience" (but the notions of "life" and of "experience" are transformed in this moment too), of the assumption that each man or woman has a fixed character with definite hieroglyphic outlines that may be figured truly by signs, for example, in physiognomy or in linguistic tropes. *The Egoist* as a whole, with its vivid presentation of the intersubjective battle of character with character, is based on this assumption. Victorian fiction, or even, mutatis mutandis, the European novel as a whole appears to be based on the same assumption. *The Egoist* undermines its own generic presuppositions. Much is therefore at stake in these pages. Extracts will indicate their main outlines:

> She was in a fever, lying like stone, with her brain burning. Quick natures run out to calamity in any little shadow of it flung before. Terrors of apprehension drive them. They stop not short of the uttermost when they are on the wings of dread. A frown means tempest, a wind wreck; to see fire is to be seized by it. When it is the approach of their loathing that they fear, they are in the tragedy of the embrace at a breath. . . .
>
> The false course she had taken through sophistical cowardice appalled the girl; she was lost. The advantage taken of it by Willoughby put on the form of strength, and made her feel abject, reptilious; she was lost, carried away on the flood of the cataract. . . .
>
> Thank heaven for the chances of a short life! Once in a net, desperation is graceless. . . .
>
> She was now in the luxury of passivity, when we throw our burden on the Powers above, and do not love them. The need to love them drew her out of it, that she might strive with the unbearable, and by sheer striving, even though she were graceless, come to love them humbly. It is here that the seed of good teaching supports a soul; for the condition might be mapped, and where kismet whispers us to shut eyes, and instruction bids us look up, is at a well-marked crossroad of the contest.
>
> Quick of sensation, but not courageously resolved, she perceived how blunderingly she had acted. For a punishment, it seemed to her that she who had not known her mind must learn to conquer her nature, and submit. She had accepted Willoughby; therefore she accepted him. . . .
>
> She was almost imagining she might imitate him [Vernon Whitford, who has submitted to Willoughby], when the clash of a sharp physical thought: "The difference! the difference!" told her she was a woman and never could submit. Can a woman have an inner life apart from him she is yoked to? She tried to nestle deep away in herself: in some corner where the abstract view had comforted her, to flee from thinking as her feminine blood directed. It was a vain effort. The difference, the cruel fate, the defencelessness of women, pursued her, strung her to

wild horses' backs, tossed her on savage wastes. In her case duty was shame: hence, it could not be broadly duty. That intolerable difference proscribed the word.

But the fire of a brain burning high and kindling everything, lit up herself against herself:—Was one so volatile as she a person with a will?—Were they not a multitude of flitting wishes, that she took for a will?—Was she, feather-headed that she was, a person to make a stand on physical pride?—If she could yield her hand without reflection (as she conceived she had done, from incapacity to conceive herself doing it reflectively), was she much better than purchaseable stuff that has nothing to say to the bargain?

Furthermore, said her incandescent reason, she had not suspected such art of cunning in Willoughby. Then might she not be deceived altogether—might she not have misread him? . . .

She reviewed him. It was all in one flash. . . . An undefined agreement to have the same regard for him as his friends and the world had, provided that he kept at the same distance from her, was the termination of this phase, occupying about a minute in time, and reached through a series of intensely vivid pictures. . . .

[For one in her condition] the brain is raging like a pine-torch and the devouring illumination leaves not a spot of our nature covert. The aspect of her weakness was unrelieved, and frightened her back to her loathing. From her loathing, as soon as her sensations had quickened to realize it, she was hurled on her weakness. She was graceless, she was inconsistent, she was volatile, she was unprincipled, she was worse than a prey to wickedness—capable of it; she was only waiting to be misled. Nay, the idea of being misled suffused her with languor; for then the battle would be over and she a happy weed of the sea, no longer suffering those tugs at the roots, but leaving it to the sea to heave and contend. . . .

Issuing out of torture, her young nature eluded the irradiating brain, in search of refreshment, and she luxuriated at a feast in considering him—[Colonel De Craye, who would tempt her to elope]—shower on a parched land that he was! . . .

She would have thought of Vernon, as her instinct of safety prompted, had not his exactions been excessive. He proposed to help her with advice only. She was to do everything for herself, do and dare everything, decide upon everything. He told her flatly that so would she learn to know her own mind. . . .

Her war with Willoughby sprang of a desire to love repelled by distaste. Her cry for freedom was a cry to be free to love: she discovered it, half-shuddering: to love, oh! no—no shape of man, nor impalpable nature either: but to love unselfishness, and helpfulness, and planted strength in something. Then, loving and being loved a little, what strength would be hers! (13:237–44)

In this admirable sequence the procedures of realism undo themselves by being systematically exploited, taken to that limit where they reverse themselves and become something else. That something else undermines the conventions of storytelling on which the passage itself and the novel as a genre depend. This reversal is an example of the way the conventions and assumptions of any mode of writing contain the tools of their own subversion and will undo themselves if they are carried far enough.

How does this occur? Meredith has in this passage accepted one implicit charge made to the realistic novelist: to represent in words what actually goes on from moment to moment within consciousness. The passage succeeds admirably in this. It creates the vivid illusion that there was a person named Clara who went through this experience. The reader is led to reexperience this experience from within, to share it again. The repetition of this renewal is made permanently possible by the words of the narrator as Meredith has invented them and written them down. The reader dwells not only within Clara's thoughts and emotions but even within her intimate bodily feelings and sensations. As Ramon Fernandez long ago recognized, Meredith's "realism" is based on an assumption of the overlapping, if not quite coincidence, in inextricable copresence, of body, "feelings" (in both senses), mind, external physical world, and the bodies and minds of other people.[41] The latter two are apprehended by the former three—mind, feelings, and body working together to "prehend," as Whitehead would say, natural objects and other people. The "incandescent reason" appropriates, often in spite of itself, in "sharp physical thought," both material objects, such as, in this novel, double-blossomed wild cherry trees, and other persons, such as that Vernon Whitford who lies under the tree for Clara to behold. In this feeling for the inextricable inmixing, though not quite identity, as of wine and water, or of oil homogenized in water, of realms kept more strictly separate by some philosophers and novelists, Meredith anticipates such a phenomenological philosopher of our own day as Maurice Merleau-Ponty. A systematic interpretation of Meredith's work both in fiction and in poetry along the lines initiated by Fernandez's brilliant essay would be possible.

Such an analysis, however, would be only half the story. This passage, like Meredith's narration generally, lays bare its machinery of representation. It puts in question the validity, as mimesis, of both its conceptual formulations and its figurative terminology. It even puts in question the validity of the distinction between conceptual and figurative language as well as those phenomenological assumptions Fernandez formulates so brilliantly and ascribes to Meredith.

In her sleepless, all-night meditation, in Willoughby's house, on her plight in having solemnly engaged herself to marry him, Clara discovers, under the pressure of that situation, that the set of assumptions presupposed in that promise to marry was false. Basic to this structure is the presupposition that she has a solid character on the basis of which promises can be made and kept. Clara's "nature," on the contrary, as she discovers, is an anonymous and shapeless energy that cannot be outlined. It must be compared, incoherently, to fire, to liquid, to the formless wind, to a featureless desert, or to unshaped stone. It changes from moment to moment. It has no permanent shape as yet, for "the tempers of the young are liquid fires in isles of quicksand" (13:145). Vernon Whitford is right to see that Clara's "character was yet liquid in the mould, and that she was a creature of only naturally youthful wildness provoked to freakishness by the ordeal of a situation shrewd as any that can happen to her sex in civilized life" (14:365). Of Clara it must be said that "her needs were her nature, her moods her mind" (13:145). Her "nature" is her "currents of feeling" (14:141). "Nature," "character," "mind" are here dissolved, liquified. They cease to be anything solid on which a promise or a commitment might be based. Self becomes evanescent tempers, feelings, needs, moods, currents of water or fire without permanent shape.

Currents? Water? Fire? What is the status of these figures? The entities for which they are figure—mind, character, and so on—have no literal existence as persisting things, but are themselves figures for the unfigurable. To say Clara is liquid fire in isles of quicksand is no more figurative than to say Clara is her moods, her mind, or her character, since she has no characterable character representable by some fixed hieroglyph or seal. "Character" in this case, if it is to have any meaning, must be distorted from its dictionary meaning as a permanent brand impressed on the psyche and mirrored in doubling characters in features, gestures, physiognomy, words. The word *character* here becomes a figure for what Clara is, namely "her whims, variations, inconsistencies, wiles; her tremblings between good and naughty, that might be stamped to noble or to terrible; her sincereness, her duplicity, her courage, cowardice, possibilities for heroism and for treachery" (14:365). Clara's character, in short, is her liquid, fiery, or airy mobility. "Will," "nature," "feelings," "mind," "self," "character" are not names, in this case, for a stable entity or for its faculties. They are, when applied to Clara, figures drawn from an archaic psychology used tropologically to describe what has no proper name, since it flits away from any attempt to pin it down. Clara's character is not to be what she is. The enterprise of the "realistic representation" of human psychology here reaches a point where it overreaches itself, goes beyond its own boundary lines in the attempt to fulfill its project completely. Realism dissolves itself in the multiplicity of its notations and in its recognition of its dependence on a figurative language for which there is no possibility of substituting proper terms. It is dependent, that is, on catachreses. What is there to be named does not have a consistency or permanence compatible with literal names.

Along with the dissolution of "character" goes a corresponding dissolution of the other half of the Benjaminian dichotomy: fate. If character goes, so also vanishes fate or destiny, that Kismet Clara is tempted to believe in and to which she is tempted to yield herself. If there is no fixed character for Clara there is no predetermined fate either, written in the stars or on her palm. She is destined, like all men and women, to create the outlines of her fate in her actions and choices from moment to moment. This "fate" does not preexist. It is only visible retrospectively, after Clara has become the one who promised to marry Willoughby, broke her promise, and then married Vernon Whitford.

That aspect of realism involving the mimesis in language of states of mind makes a double assumption. It assumes that there is a prelinguistic self or character, and it assumes that this self in its changes may be expressed, mirrored, or copied without distortion in language. Walter Pater, for example, praises Rossetti for choosing the right "term" "from many competitors, as the just transcript of that peculiar phase of soul which he alone knew, precisely as he knew it."[42] *The Egoist*, especially in the "transcription" of Clara's meditations, puts this double assumption in question. This is accomplished in part by overt thematic statement: "Was one so volatile as she a person with a will? Were they not a multitude of flitting wishes that she took for a will?" In part it is done by the manifest role of incoherent figures in the transcription.

The theory of figure implicit in the practice of representation here is made explicit elsewhere in Meredith, for example, in a passage in *One of Our Conquerors*: "It is the excelling merit of similes and metaphors to spring us to vault over gaps and thickets and dreary places. . . . Beware, moreover, of examining them too scrupulously: they have a trick of wearing to vapour if closely scanned" (17:189), or in the following striking formulation in *Diana of the Crossways*: "The banished of Eden had to put on metaphors, and the common use of them has helped largely to civilize us" (16:275).[43] Metaphors are peculiar. On the one hand they are an essential covering, a web or integument of language that serves as a bridge over places where the continuity of language would otherwise break and tumble us into a crevasse or into a copse of undergrowth. Metaphors name the unnamable, present the unpresentable, and thereby serve simultaneously as decent covering and as revelation or unveiling. They make continuous a cloth of language that otherwise would be rent, would fail to reach from here to there in a sequential narrative or other web of words. Covering of what? Unveiling of what? The second passage makes explicit what is implicit in the first. Metaphors serve to cover the pudenda of Eve and Adam's progeny. Since the fall, literal, naked language has been impossible, shameful. Certain things, the genitalia, for example, have been proper to name only indirectly, in names displaced from other less shameful places. These figures are fig leaves to cover the gaps and thickets where proper naming is no longer proper.

This metaphorical naming manifests the aporia inherent in all acts of simultaneous unveiling and veiling. Metaphors, when closely scanned, have a trick of wearing to vapor. They are not appropriate names for those gaps and thickets and dreary places. They are not solid enough to vault us over to the other side. But their inappropriateness is appropriate to their function as veils. When they wear to vapor and vanish they then best function as veils, since they have revealed nothing, told no secrets. At the same time, their function as darning threads crisscrossed to hide a gap in the discourse is no longer fulfilled. The gap is revealed, the abyss which disrupts or breaks the smooth texture of the text, for example, the assumption that the characters in a narrative have fixed and proper selves. The cloth of the veil becomes gauze, transparent and insubstantial as vapor, a weaving of clouds. If the metaphors hold, then they have revealed that gap, and the text is once more broken, since what is revealed is the nameless, figured here as the vaginal gap or the phallic thicket. Many passages in *The Egoist* confirm that these biological differences function for Meredith as implicit figures for socially imposed gender differences.

Is the thicket, however, unambiguously phallic? An impenetrable underbrush in a dreary place seems more like an interlaced integument, a weaving or a veil once more, pubic hair that may hide something or may hide an absence. Weaving, psychoanalysts and anthropologists say, is said to have been invented by women. It is said, according to this myth, to have been devised in the plaiting of pubic hair to make a mock phallus. This weaving was the hiding of an absence and a phantasmal pseudo-revelation. At the same time it was a metaphor claiming the existence of what is not there, so covering the fact that the phallus is not there. The inconsistency of the references to presence and absence in apparently unambiguous figures for gender difference indicates the fictitious, ideological nature of the social distinctions these figures sustain.[44] *The Egoist* is a powerful critique of that ideology as it is linked to the assumption that each person, male or female, has, or ought to have, a fixed character. Meredith's goal is to expose and dismantle the phallogocentrism Willoughby embodies in *The Egoist*. Back and forth between revealing and hiding metaphors vibrate, in Meredith's figures for them, fleeing one extreme, total opacity, as revealing but revealing nothing, making a misleading sham revelation claiming substance where there is none, but finding the other extreme, total transparency, coming to the same thing. Far from springing us to vault over gaps and thickets and dreary places or covering the indecent with decency, the improper with propriety, in fallen man or woman, a metaphorical text is made of gaps and thickets. The gaps and thickets are the metaphors.

It is no accident that so many male novelists in the Victorian period, Thackeray, Dickens, Trollope, or Meredith, project into female protagonists the dramatization of that question fundamental to the novel: can we, or should we, believe that human beings, male or female, have fixed selves? The female protagonist has a lesson to teach us men. The assumption that character is fixed cannot be detached from the presuppositions about gender difference that underlie it. The fixed hieroglyphic of character here plays the role of the logos or phallus, the source and guarantee of all the derivative meanings and configurations of the self: moods, feelings, wiles. Only if Clara is indeed the reflex and mirror image, the choric echo, of the phallic and upright Willoughby, that "obelisk lettered all over with hieroglyphics" (13:116), can she be said to have a self: "In walking with her, in drooping to her, the whole man was made conscious of the female image of himself by her exquisite unlikeness. She completed him, added the softer lines wanting to his portrait before the world" (13:48). But Clara discovers in her meditations that not only does she not have a central column of self charactered over with permanent emblems of her character. She is not even the fixed chalice-like female reflex of that. She therefore cannot reflect back to Willoughby his conception of himself as, in promising to marry him, she has tacitly undertaken to do. She is rather a constant flux, nothing that can be counted on to remain constant. She is the flowing, burning, or blowing of her evanescent moods, whims, wiles, and inconsistencies.

This discovery is also an unsettling revelation for Willoughby. He has depended on Clara to give him a stable female image of himself. He finds he must do without such mirroring. He therefore cannot be certain that he is a perdurable column either, since confirmation of that depends on its echoing in reverse by Clara or by some other woman. Clara's revelation about herself is also a discovery for the narrator and for the male novelist behind the narrator. They have peered into the mirror of an invented female character to seek their own images and to put to the test the phallogocentric assumptions presupposed in the notion of character. The reader too, male or female, puts assumptions about his or her own character to the test when reading such a novel. The integument of metaphor in "Clara's Meditations" is a thin covering over of the sexual issue it more or less directly treats, "the difference! the difference!" Clara is unable to bring herself to fulfill her bargain by consenting to submit herself physically to Willoughby's appropriation of her as a "chalice" (13:50), as an "inanimate overwrought polished pure-metal precious vessel" (13:132). She does not have the solidity or consistency to be such a vessel, the reversed image of the obelisk, glove for his hand. Like the obelisk, Clara as chalice is "overwrought" with designs or signs to be read, but she is overwrought also, it may be, in the sense that one says "her nerves are overwrought."

The man—lover, narrator, or reader—who looks into Clara as mirror to find confirmation of his own character finds only unfixable volatility. This volatility is both revealed and hidden by the network of figures the novelist must use to name it. These are a fluid or vaporous parody of the chalice "overwrought" with designs. The chalice is the obelisk turned inside out, the hollow reflex of the Apollonian sun ray turned to stone and carved all over with the secret hieroglyphic speech of the sun fixed in legible characters for those who have the interpretation of them, as Willoughby pretends to read himself. From obelisk to chalice to vaporous integument of metaphors, each model deprives of substantiality the one before, in a movement toward recognition that metaphors are performative rather than constative. They posit what they name.

Though "Clara's Meditations" conveys to its reader a strong sense of having lived through the vacillations of Clara's "physical thinking," from moment to moment, this following through is impossible without the figures of fire, ocean, storm, stone, wild horses on savage wastes, mapped crossroads, brain raging like a pine torch, and so on. Clara exists as these figures, both in the sense that the reader's phantasmal illusion of her real existence is created by Meredith with the indispensable aid of these figures and in the sense that, if the reader moves through the looking glass to take her as a real person being described in elaborate temporalized notation by the narrator, she exists, in herself, not as a substantial character, but as a sequence of figures, fleeting, evanescent, each succeeded by another that cancels it, as an image of fire cancels one of water, an image of wind the other two, and so on. In this flow of figures, the conceptual words (*mind, will, nature,* and so on) and the literal words for parts of the body (*brain, blood, head, hand, face*) are volatilized, vaporized. They become themselves part of the sequence of figures to be read.

In this vaporizing a complex system of presuppositions is unraveled. The self is revealed to be not something fixed but a multitude of fleeting wishes, feelings, thoughts. The distinction between extralinguistic and linguistic domains, on which mimetic realism is based, breaks down. The self and any society of selves exist as the signs for them. These signs, moreover, are governed by no fixed columnar head sense that justifies reading them in a certain way. The distinctions among literal, figurative, and conceptual language collapse. These forms of language turn out all to be different versions of catachresis, words transferred from some other realm to name improperly what has no proper name and comes into existence as the catachreses are read. For the positing power of that reading, as it has inaugural effects in society and history, the reader must take responsibility, as Meredith's novel in its way shows.

The temporal continuity of the self, finally, essential presupposition of the connectedness of storytelling and of the assigning of ethical responsibility, dissolves into the sequence of those pictorial emblems noted so carefully by the narrator: "An undefined agreement to have the same regard for him as his friends and the world had, provided that he kept at the same distance from her, was the termination of this phase, occupying about a minute in time, and reached through a series of intensely vivid pictures" (13:240). Internal time consciousness in *The Egoist* is a dimension of discontinuity between one moment and the next, of the arbitrary relation of mental image and what it images, and of the absence of identifiable origin or end for convictions or decisions, as other notations in *The Egoist* show. The beginning or source of a given thought, conviction, or penchant of feeling can never be certainly identified. Taking as example Clara's physical distaste for Willoughby the narrator generalizes: "Sweeping from sensation to sensation, the young, whom sensations impel and distract, can rarely date their disturbance from a particular one" (13:71). Much later, trying to explain to Mrs. Mountstuart how and when she came to find that she did not love Willoughby, Clara can express herself only in what might be called a temporal oxymoron: "By degrees: unknown to myself; suddenly" (14:430). There was a time when she intended to marry Willoughby. When she came on her visit to Patterne Hall she did so intend. Then, later, there was a time when she did not. As Mrs. Mountstuart sardonically observes: "And *gradually* you *suddenly* discovered, since you came here, that you did not intend it, if you could find a means of avoiding it" (14:435). Though the change was a fact of consciousness, it did not occur at a time when consciousness was distinctly conscious of it as a fact different from the previous fact of a different intent. The intention of her mind changed both suddenly and gradually, in a fashion not compatible with any image of regular temporal continuity. Nor is it compatible with any concept of the mind as a substantial entity that goes on being the same through time and that is present to itself through time. Clara's change of mind did not take place in her conscious mind but "unknown to herself."

Choosing, intending, and promising are performatives that depend on the mind's continuity and on the mind's constant presence to itself for their efficacy. But Clara neither constantly knows her own mind nor is able to keep it constant to itself. The etiology of her choices, intentions, and promises cannot be identified. Their validity is thereby nullified: "And she could vehemently declare that she had not chosen [when she first promised to marry Willoughby]; she was too young, too ignorant to choose. . . . To call consenting the same in fact as choosing [as Vernon has done], was wilfully unjust" (13:181). The chapter of Clara's meditations is her most acute experience of this discontinuity, this failure of the mind to be present to itself, either in the moment or in the moment's awareness of its origins, its connection to some past moment. The moment of Clara's greatest self-clarification is the moment when she most confronts her opacity to herself.

No doubt most readers know perfectly well, or would say they know if asked, that there are no real people in novels, nor even portraits of real people, only words and the cunning simulacra in words of imaginary personages. And no doubt many people look upon the notion of fixed selfhood as a long-exploded myth, a myth exploded, for example, within the British empirical tradition by Hume. On the other hand, almost all readers of novels, including their most sophisticated critics, continue to think and speak of characters in novels as if they were real people. We all go on uttering sentences something like "And then Clara thinks to herself," and so on. The power of novels to make their readers suspend disbelief in spite of all their linguistic sophistication is very great. Nor does it go without saying that it is a mark of incompetence in a reader to yield to what Pater calls this "real illusion."

In spite of the philosophical demolition of the idea of fixed selfhood, by Hume, by Nietzsche, by Wittgenstein, or by Derrida, most of us, even philosophers and linguists, go on acting toward ourselves and others, in both personal and public situations, as if people had continuous and stable selves. For example, we accept or impose today responsibility for something we or others said, did, promised, or contracted to do yesterday. It might be argued that the continuation of civilized social life, at least as we know it in the West, depends on tacitly accepting the myth of selfhood. This supports my claim that much is at stake in the putting in question of selfhood in such a novel as *The Egoist*. The reader of *The Egoist* is put by the text of the novel in a curious double bind, one perhaps characteristic of "realist" novels. The reader who sees the text as merely language is not being a competent reader. To read a novel properly is to allow oneself to be taken in by the characters, to think of them as if they were real persons, and to speak or write of them as such. To do this, however, is to commit again the egoistic crime of Willoughby against Clara, that is, to treat a fluid assemblage of fleeting catachreses as if it were a fixed personality who might by reflection reassure me about the stability of my own selfhood.

The image of the broken line, intersected by crossroads at innumerable junctures, like Ariadne's threaded labyrinth or Arachne's web, punctuates the passage of Clara's meditations. This image figures the disrupted series of catachreses following one another in time into which her selfhood has dissolved: "Once in a net, desperation is graceless"; "the condition might be mapped, and where kismet whispers us to shut eyes, and instruction bids us look up, is at a well-marked cross-road of the contest" (13:238–39). The lines of character, of portraiture, and of realistic temporal continuity, as well as the borders between literal and figurative language, are blurred and vanish. What remains is "a series of intensely vivid pictures." These are not pictures *of* anything. They are rather embodiments of what they signify. Nature, the body, and other people have been appropriated as emblems for the evanescent states of a self that is always other than itself. Such pictures are the substance of what they picture, like the crudely drawn face in Wittgenstein's *Brown Book*. What the pictures show us are themselves. This showing is controlled by no clear consciousness choosing, limiting, and interpreting the pictures.

Take, for example, Clara's image of herself as "a happy weed of the sea no longer suffering those tugs at the roots, but leaving it to the sea to heave and contend." Is this Clara's image for herself or the narrator's image for her? There is no way to be sure. The firm distinction between the language of the narrator and the language of the character is another boundary line that vanishes, along with the line between literal and figural, the line between linguistic and nonlinguistic, the lines of character, and the temporal line. If there is no stable character for Clara or for the narrator, if "she," "he," "hers," "his," name here the language they use, then there are no grounds for distinguishing between them in a passage in which the narrator speaks in figure or in picture of one momentary whim or fleeting state of mind of the character.

None of the expressions, figures, and little pictures strung together in "Clara's Meditations" are mimetic reflections of something other than themselves. They appear to be metaphors, working by likeness, but it might be better to call them synecdoches. They express by way of a particular similitude, flowing water, devouring fire, or whatever, something that always exists as an encompassing totality, Clara's mind. These figures are all manifestly false identities. Subjectivity is not flowing water or fire. It may only be figured as like water or fire. Such figures, however, are not displacements of any "proper" or "literal" language. Only figurative, that is, improper, language can name the movements of the soul. This is as true of the conceptual terms for the faculties of the self and of words for parts of the body as it is of the terms drawn from inanimate nature to describe the self. Character exists only as displacement, not as the solid ground of its various manifestations. Its "nature" is to have no nature, to be what it is not. This makes all the phrases about "Clara's nature" oxymorons: "her needs are her nature, her moods her mind." Clara's nature exists as the figures for it, those "pictures" that fleet or flit through her mind. This undermines her search for a solid ground in her "nature" or in her "will" for her decision not to marry Willoughby. It undermines also the attempt by the author or by his delegate, the narrator, to practice a theory of fiction based on the adequacy of synecdoche, presenting the totality of human social life condensed in chosen samples, digestibly. The part bears no necessarily representative relation to the whole. It is a distorted image in a concave mirror. To totalize it is to falsify the whole of which it is an idiosyncratic part. The fact that there is no proper language for the self, none but figurative characters for character, since there is no character as such, neither in fiction nor in "real life," dismantles, finally, the attempt by the reader to develop an interpretation of the novel of the type proposed by Fernandez, that is, one grounded

on phenomenology, the version of metaphysics that refers everything back to a solid base in subjectivity.

The Egoist exposes the inherence of language in character. If
Clara's self is that anonymous or nameless energy Meredith's narrator calls her will, her nature, fire, flood, and so on, always in
figure, the relation between words and the self is one of constant
displacement. Each is the displacement of the other. Their relation
generates a line of meaning or force extending itself in a loop
around two foci, each focus an absence or impropriety when it is
confronted directly. Neither language nor consciousness is the basis
of the other but is itself dependent on the other for such subsistence
as it has. Insofar as catachresis is intimately linked, in however
complex or contradictory a way, to prosopopoeia, this means that
the undoing, in *The Egoist,* of the assumption that consciousness
precedes language entails a recognition that selfhood is projected
by prosopopoeic catachreses.

This is the obverse of the role of such catachreses in humanizing
the landscape. Meredith's brilliant and difficult nature poetry—for
example, "The Southwester" or "Hymn to Colour"—explores the
way the catachreses in common language, "face of a mountain,"
"headland," "arm of a lake," "brow of a hill," and so on, have
within them the latent power to generate mythological personages
in the landscape. Our vision of such mythical personages presupposes the existence of human selves as the model for language used
to personify elements in the natural scene—woods, sky, clouds,
sea, fields, hills. "The South-Wester," for example, begins with
relatively unostentatious prosopopoeias—a description of the day
as "wedded white and blue" (l. 2), or of clouds moving in "shadow-
sandals" (l. 4)—but soon the whole stormy day is personified as
the sexual union of earth and the sun-god Apollo. The poem ends
with the reflection that the linguistic act of the poem has renewed,
as a kind of memorial or act of memory, the act whereby the Greek
poets saw gods and goddesses in nature. What begins as productive
or performative poetic language ends as credence in the supernatural beings the words have created before the reader's eyes: "We
could believe / A life in orb and brook and tree / And cloud: and
still holds Memory / A morning in the eyes of eve" (ll. 130–33).[45]
It is the excelling merit of Meredith's poetry to display in the open
the linguistic processes whereby such credences are generated. Meredith's novels, on the other hand, explore the opposite and no less

unsettling linguistic fact: the dependence of our sense of selfhood, of our own and that of others, on our naive confidence in catachreses drawn from nonhuman nature.

Clara's character, since it does not exist as an object, keeps any language for it from being other than indirect, inadequate. The incoherence of the narrator's figures for her character shows that it does not exist as a solid column inscribed in hieroglyphs making possible a unified story. Clara's will, her nature, her character, is her freedom, her lack of a fixed form either in herself or in what is outside her to give her inward form. Of such young people as Clara the narrator generalizes: "The tempers of the young are liquid fires in isles of quicksand; the precious metals not yet cooled in a solid earth" (13:145). Clara cannot be the precious vessel Willoughby wants her to be, a possession he can "walk away with hugging, call all his own, drink of, and fill and drink of " (13:132). Clara cannot be possessed as an object because she has no objective form. As she tells Willoughby: "I am unworthy. I am volatile. I love my liberty. I want to be free" (13:126). She has no solidity, neither as container nor as something containable within a constraining mold surrounding her from outside. Her temper is liquid fire, neither fire nor water, but something in between, in language an oxymoron, physically a contradiction or an absurdity. This liquid fire is contained "in isles of quicksand." This is another oxymoron or palpable absurdity, since islands are not containers but things contained, surrounded, embraced, by the circumambient water, whereas this quicksand is supposed to contain the liquid fire. An isle of quicksand is in any case no substantial molding force, like the "unquick" sand used in certain casting processes. If liquid fire is neither fire nor water, quicksand is neither earth nor liquid but something in between, a mimicry of life. Clara's nature, according to this trope, is not only shapeless fiery-watery energy; it has also not yet encountered, neither within itself nor without, a molding force that might give it definite shape when it cools.

Clara's "nature" is her freedom, her spontaneity. This freedom exists as negativity, as her instinctive rebellion against any form of slavery. It comes into perceptible existence only when she is bound, that is, when she has promised to marry Willoughby. It does not exist as a thing in itself but only as a response to pressure from without, though, as the narrator says, it is readable in her features for those who take time to read. Willoughby's error is that he rushes past her face to plunge for possession of her soul: "He dived

below the surface without studying that index-page. . . . Miss
Middleton's features were legible as to the mainspring of her character. He could have seen that she had a spirit with a natural love
of liberty, and required the next thing to liberty, spaciousness, if
she was to own allegiance. Those features, unhappily, instead of
serving for an introduction to the within, were treated as the mirror
of himself. . . . He desired to shape her character to the feminine
of his own" (13:51–52).

Among Clara's features the most legible sign of her love of
freedom is her hair, especially the hair at "the softly dusky nape
of her neck, where this way and that the little lighter-coloured
irreclaimable curls running truant from the comb and the knot—
curls, half-curls, root-curls, vine-ringlets, wedding rings, fledgeling
feathers, tufts of down, blown wisps—waved or fell, waved over
or up or involutedly, or strayed, loose and downward, in the form
of small silken paws, hardly any of them much thicker than a
crayon shading, cunninger than long round locks of gold to trick
the heart" (13:101). Passage of an admirable erotic beauty! If the
banished of Eden had to cover themselves with metaphors, those
metaphors were no doubt woven of thickets of hair, revealing and
hiding, nape-curls a covering already covered again in a cascade
of further metaphors—roots, vines, wedding-rings, feathers, down,
clouds—each another figure for an absence that encircles softly and
imprisons. This metamorphosed hair in one place stands for unnamed hair in another, as in Pope's "Rape of the Lock." That hair
in turn stands for the abyss of an unpossessable freedom,
"truant," "irreclaimable." The outward signs of this freedom trick
the male observer, trap him cunningly, lock him in, though with
hasps like small silken paws, not even crayon thick, no thicker
than the crayon's shading, and dispossess him of his own freedom.
Willoughby learns from his involvement with Clara what it feels
like to be a spider caught in another spider's woof, an Apollonian
Theseus lost in the intricate labyrinthine tangles of Ariadne's
thread, a male spider in mortal danger in Arachne's web: "His
blind sensitiveness felt as we may suppose a spider to feel when
plucked from his own web and set in the centre of another's"
(14:355).

As features of the visible Clara, her curls are echoes producing
further echoes in a chain or net of displacements. These define
Clara as not being what she is, that is, as being her ungraspable
freedom. She is therefore never able to give back to Willoughby

the stable and reassuring image of himself he seeks in her countenance. If Willoughby wants "marriage with a mirror, with an echo; marriage with a shining mirror, a choric echo" (14:464), Clara is, in Vernon's precise image, a "Mountain Echo." She is an echo that does not return accurately the auditory image of what is shouted to it, but disperses that voice irreclaimably. Clara is "the swift wild spirit, Clara by name, sent fleeting on a far half-circle by the voice it is roused to subserve" (13:37).

——

Here a myth or myths, shadowily present as oblique echoes dispersed in fragmentary éclats throughout *The Egoist*, comes almost to the surface. This is the myth of Narcissus as told in Ovid's *Metamorphoses*. That myth is distorted then, in Mountain Echo, in the great passage about Eve in Book 4 of *Paradise Lost*. Both myths, the classical and the Christian, are echoed again in the distorted or broken mirror of *The Egoist*, for which *Paradise Lost* is the great precursor text. In all these works a complex asymmetrical structure is present. This structure is fundamental throughout Western thought and literature. It is "fundamental" in the paradoxical sense that it both affirms and endangers any fundament. The structure involves a mirroring pair then replaced by a triangular relation still remaining precariously balanced. This triangle is then asymmetrically mirrored in another triangle that parodies and undermines it. The sequence is speculative, both in the sense that it involves mirroring and in the sense that it is the mythical correlative of speculative thought. Its model of perfection is the perfect mirroring of one male figure by another. The female, that imperfect male, missing one member, introduces the deconstructive absence. Her presence as absence means there will always be something left over or something short in the male as mirror, a perpetual too little or too much that makes it impossible for the balance ever to come right and so keeps the story going.

The image of the mirroring pair oscillates in this tradition between the mirroring of male by male in perfect match and the mirroring of male by female in another form of perfect matching, concave meeting convex, as in the androgynous couple in Aristophanes' speech in Plato's *Symposium*. The triangle that replaces the pair is stable only so long as it remains all male, as in the Trinity: Father, Son, and Holy Ghost—the one, its image, and the relation between them, or, in another form of this triangle, God, his perfect image, the Son, and the creation which is fabricated by

God in the the image of the Son, so that the world as a whole and every part of it separately has the countenance of God, is signed with his signature. The female opens the triangle beyond any hope of closing it again or of filling the gap she has introduced. Narcissus's attempt to merge himself with his mirrored image, or, in another version of the Narcissus myth, his lovelorn search for his lost twin sister, is broken by the love for him of Echo, who has no voice but that given by Narcissus and yet subverts that voice in her echo of it and so leads Narcissus astray in his vain search for himself. Narcissus is "deceived by the image of the alternate voice (aeternae deceptus imagine vocis)" (*Metamorphoses, 3.385*). In *Paradise Lost,* Eve's Narcissistic admiration of her reflected image endangers the chain of perfect imagings that goes from God the Father to his speculative match, God the Son, to Adam, the man created in God's image by the agency of Christ ("Man/God's latest image"; *Paradise Lost* 4.566), to Eve, who is in turn Adam's softer image:

> There I had fixt
> Mine eyes till now, and pin'd with vain desire,
> Had not a voice thus warnd me, What thou seest,
> What there thou seest fair Creature is thyself,
> With thee it comes and goes: but follow me,
> And I will bring thee where no shadow staies
> Thy coming and thy soft imbraces, hee,
> Whose image thou art, him thou shall enjoy
> Inseparablie thine. (*Paradise Lost* 4.465–73)

Willoughby's satanic arrogation to himself of godlike self-sufficiency echoes this tradition. His narcissism is imaged in his desire to be surrounded by a world, in particular a wife, that will everywhere reflect back to him his own image. Here again the presentation of character intersects with those corridors in the labyrinth of narrative theory marked "Anastomosis, or Interpersonal Relations," overtly the subject of the next chapter here. Willoughby seeks his mirrored image in miniature in Clara's eyes: "and once gained, they are your mirrors for life and far more constant than the glass" (13:192). This ideal is demolished by Clara, the Mountain Echo, who closes her eyes to him and annihilates him: "Clara let her eyes rest on his, and without turning or dropping, shut them" (13:88); "He found himself addressing eyes that regarded him as though he were a small speck, a pin's head, in the circle of their remote contemplation. They were wide; they closed" (13:91). Clara gives back to Willoughby always something other than his own voice or image. She ruins his project by showing him he exists, satanically, only as image, only as doubled in the outward reflection of himself. Far from being self-sufficient, he is dependent on her for his sense of himself. When she refuses to reflect his ideal image of himself back to him, he feels as if he had been annihilated. That Clara is a Mountain Echo means that in her uncharacterizable freedom she has a negative power to turn all things (fire, water, mountains, vases, double-blossomed wild cherry trees, even poor curtailed Willoughby himself) into emblems of her own lack of character. She turns everything she echoes into figures of speech for her own insubstantiality. Like Echo in Ovid's Narcissus story, who becomes a disembodied voice, floating and ungraspable, after her death, Clara, as her name suggests, is transparent purity, empty air, a mirror with no image in it when a man looks there. She returns whatever is cast against her distorted, disguised, transformed. When Vernon imposes it on Clara's "free will" to decide her fate, he defines her lack of ground as the ground of the decisive commitments that will determine her character and her destiny. Just how this can be I shall show later.

That Clara's bid for freedom has political implications as well as implications for gender relations is indicated by several references to the French Revolution in *The Egoist*. Clara's father makes the connection explicit: "This maenad shriek for freedom would happily entitle her to the Republican cap—the Phrygian—in a revolutionary Parisian procession" (14:420). Such allusions indicate Meredith's awareness that Clara's self-discovery of her lack of self, on the night of her meditations, has unsettling social implications. It challenges any structure of society based on conventions presupposing the stability of male or female character, for example, the ability of a man or a woman to make promises and keep them. Clara's self-discovery also threatens the traditional conception of marriage as an institution in which the husband owns his wife, as he owns his horse or his house. Like Henry James's *What Maisie Knew, The Egoist* corresponds to one stage in the gradual breakdown in England since the Renaissance of the old marriage laws and conventions.[46] Or, it would be better to say, *The Egoist* actively contributes to that breakdown. This subversion of Victorian ideals of marriage is analogous to the way Clara's self-discovery disables the narrator's enterprise of writing a novel that will be an authentic synecdoche of human social experience as a whole. It is also analogous to the undermining of the reader's enterprise of understanding *The Egoist* according to traditional aesthetic principles of wholeness, consistency, and the reference of all in a text back to a pervasive ground of meaning that gathers it into one. If Clara cannot maintain her continuity with herself, if she does not remain the same person from moment to moment well enough to be said to have a character or a will, how can the reader be expected to hold together in one coherent interpretation the text that records the discontinuities and intermittences of her heart, always faithless to itself?

Nevertheless, *The Egoist* has a "happy ending." Clara frees herself from her promise to marry Willoughby and gives herself freely to Vernon Whitford in a meeting that takes place outside the boundaries of the book, "between the Swiss and Tyrol Alps over the Lake of Constance" (14:626). Their meeting occurs on the border between Switzerland and Austria, neither quite in one country nor in the other. It occurs in a landscape that is both rock and water, mountain and lake, in the alps but "over the Lake of Constance." How can this happy ending be prospectively believed? How can the narrator plausibly promise that such a meeting and such a betrothal will take place, or has already taken place to his retrospective eye? How can he plausibly promise that the marriage of Vernon and Clara will be a happy one, based on unshakable love and fidelity? What constancy can Clara promise Vernon by the Lake of Constance, if she has no character to underwrite her fulfillment of any promise, no stable signature to allow her to sign her name to a marriage contract, if she exists only as a multitude of fleeting and inconsistent wishes, if her name on a marriage contract would be as if writ on water? The answer lies in an alternative theory of character and of promising that emerges in *The Egoist,* out of the wreckage left by the demolition, in "Clara's Meditations," of traditional theories of character and of promising. Like all great works of deconstructive critique, *The Egoist* affirms as well as dismantles. If it brilliantly demonstrates the destructive potential of false assumptions about selfhood that are basic to the Victorian ideology of gender difference, marriage, property, class relations, as well as to assumptions about the aesthetics and social function of novels at that time, *The Egoist* also proposes and puts in practice alternatives. These alternatives would be the basis of new forms of democracy, new forms of gender politics, new forms of literature. They would also transform our received ideas about literary history, literary theory, and the practice of literary criticism, such as those that must be apparently presumed in this book in order to get on with the business of putting them in question. These presumptions would include the notion that a work of literature is embedded in a particular historical moment, determined by it, reflective of it. In place of that Clara's self-revelations in *The Egoist* would implicitly redefine literature too as performative promise, rather than merely reflective imitation or deconstructive critique. These implications of *The Egoist* have hardly yet, over a hundred years later, been understood, much less institutionalized or politically implemented, though they anticipate radical ideas about gender relations and new social organizations being proposed now, in the "post-colonial" era, the era in which the nationalism that is so fundamental a part of "aesthetic ideology" is undergoing unprecedented transformations.

If Clara's failure to keep her promise to marry Willoughby is the deconstruction of what might be called a referential theory of promising, her commitment to Vernon is a properly performative promise. The first kind of promise, if it existed, would be founded on something that secures it. In this case, the security would be Clara's state of being in love with Willoughby, having spontaneously committed her "self" to him, though the whole surrounding context of family and community approval would also support and confirm that commitment. Her father's willingness to "give" her to Willoughby endorses her commitment of herself to him and makes it possible. The second kind of promising creates its own ground, including the selfhood of the one who promises, in the act of being made. It therefore remains precariously suspended over the abyss of its lack of prior ground. Clara discovers that the first kind of promising is impossible because there are no grounds for it, no preexisting character, in her or by implication in anyone else, solid enough and persistent enough to guarantee its fulfillment: "And she could vehemently declare that she had not chosen" (13:181).

The other kind of promising requires more explanation. A performative is a form of words that brings into existence not so much what it names as the results of the action it performs. A couple are married when a minister or other proper social authority, in the right circumstances (but what exactly are the "right circumstances"?), pronounces the words, "I pronounce you husband and wife."⁴⁷ But what is performed by language, it would seem, can be, if it does not have the divine ground and sanction presumed in a "church wedding," "unperformed" by another contradictory performative later on. A contract may, at least in certain circumstances, be broken by another contract. If Clara is nothing but her whims, wiles, and inconsistencies, what will prevent her from betraying Vernon, however fervently she performs her initial promise to be constant to him? It seems almost inevitable that at some point she will do so. Whoever she is today, she is almost certain to be someone else tomorrow.

The solution to this problem is one of Meredith's chief concerns throughout his fiction. A crucial passage in *The Ordeal of Richard Feverel,* published in 1859, almost twenty years before *The Egoist,* already confronts this apparent impasse. *The Egoist* is a more subtle dramatization of Meredith's theory of the performative promise in the earlier novel. Chapter 33 of the first version of *The Ordeal* (chapter 29 in the revised edition) describes Richard's clandestine marriage to Lucy. The chapter uses the image of Caesar's crossing the Rubicon to posit a specific theory of performative language based on Richard's experience. His falling in love with Lucy was a spontaneous act of his nature. The arrow of sexual fixation leaped from the bow at the conjunction of his physical maturity and his encounter with a desirable object to focus his diffuse passion: "He was an arrow drawn to the head, flying from the bow."⁴⁸ Richard reaches moral maturity only when, in colder blood, he plans his elopement with Lucy and says his vows to her. This ratifies his natural commitment with a moral and verbal one. The preverbal orientation is affirmed, doubled, and thereby made permanent by a speech act, an "I will." Only then is the commitment irrevocable, so that to betray it, as Richard does, is necessarily disastrous. He attempts to change back to limitless possibility what a combination of nature and a performative promise have made fixed for good, just as Caesar could not go back over the Rubicon once he had crossed it. Caesar could not return to the situation of being free to cross or not to cross. When Caesar had crossed, the die was cast, once and for all. When Richard says his "I will," he creates a new self for himself, a self he must be faithful to or betray, but cannot with impunity dismiss. All men and women, for Meredith in *The Ordeal,* are free, but they are free to use that freedom only once, in the decisive commitment of their lives. When they have once crossed the line from freedom to commitment they are qualitatively different, both physically and morally, from what they were before. They are free now only to remain true to the choice they have made or to destroy themselves by betraying it. The passage working this out is a remarkable description not of a passage *along a line,* as in the various examples of the diegetic thread I have retraced, but of a liminal passage, in another region of narrative or critical geography, *over the line,* across a frontier:

> Although it blew hard when Caesar crossed the Rubicon, the passage of that River is commonly calm; calm as Acheron. So long as he gets his fare, the ferryman does not need to be told whom he carries: he pulls with a will, and Heroes may be over in half an hour. Some, by taking an oar themselves, have done it in five minutes: some in two. Only when they stand on the opposite banks, do they see what a leap they have taken. The shores they have relinquished shrink to an infinite remoteness. There they have dreamed: here they must act. There lie youth and irresolution: here manhood and purpose. They are veritably in another land: a moral Acheron divides their life. Their memories scarce seem their own. The PHILOSOPHICAL GEOGRAPHY (about to be published) observes that each man has, one time or other, a little Rubicon—a clear, or a foul, water to cross. It is asked him: "Wilt thou wed this Fate, and give up all behind thee?" And "I will," firmly pronounced, speeds him over. The above-named Manuscript authority informs us that by far the greater number of carcases rolled by this heroic flood to its sister stream below, are those of fellows who have repented their pledge, and have tried to swim back to the banks they have blotted out. . . . Be your Rubicon big or small, clear or foul, it is the same: you shall not return. On—or to Acheron! (330–31)

The model of moral action proposed in *The Ordeal* is complicated, put in question, transgressed, deconstituted, and then reaffirmed in a new form in the teeth of its demonstrated impossibility in *The Egoist.* If Clara has no "nature" of the objectified kind Richard apparently has, how can she ratify it by her promise to marry Willoughby? On what basis can she, having freed herself from her promise to Willoughby, promise now to be faithful to Vernon? What change has occurred in her corresponding to the change in Richard when he falls in love with Lucy and then confirms this with his willingly pronounced, "I will"? What experience can have given her now what she did not have before, a "character" capable of remaining the same long enough to make promises and keep them?

The novel gives a clear answer to these questions. Clara has been radically changed by her ordeal of struggling to free herself from Willoughby's attempt to keep possession of the beautiful object, fair overwrought chalice, he has contracted to buy. This experience has solidified her fluid nature in the mold and has inscribed on it permanent characters destined to remain the same. She becomes, in her own way, what Willoughby was, an obelisk lettered all over with hieroglyphs. "In her own way": this way is a paradoxical one. The character Clara takes is determined negatively by Willoughby's attempt to possess her. The character inscribed on her by her experience is her unwillingness to be bound. She remains a Mountain Echo to the last, as Vernon wishes her to be: "she must rely on herself, do everything herself" (13:210); "She could have accused Vernon of a treacherous cunning for imposing it on her free will to decide her fate" (14:338). Clara can never be a slavish mirror of what or whom is outside her, as Willoughby wishes her to be, but she becomes through her suffering capable of engaging in a free dialogue of love. In such a dialogue each voice sings its own tune in modulated or even distorted echo of the other. Willoughby, on the contrary, is "a melody with which everything was out of tune that did not modestly or mutely accord; and to bear about a melody in your person is incomparably more searching than the best of touchstones and talismans ever invented" (13:164–65). In the proper dialogue of love, on the other hand, each partner flows his or her own way like two mountain streams encountering: "It is a meeting of mountain brooks; not a colloquy but a chasing, impossible to say which flies, which follows, or what the topic, so interlinguistic are they and rapidly counterchanging" (13:207; this admirable figure describes the conversation of Clara and Colonel De Craye). Or, to give yet a third metaphor for love, each partner must be faithful in changeful intercourse, like the sun and earth in Meredith's poems of mythogenesis, for example "The South-Wester" (1888), cited above. An early passage in *The Egoist* describes in the same figure an ideal of love ultimately fulfilled by Clara and Vernon: "In other words, love is an affair of two, and it is only for two that can be as quick, as constant in intercommunication as are sun and earth, through the cloud or face to face. They take their breath of life from one another in signs of affection, proof of faithfulness, incentives to admiration" (13:65).

That Clara has character no one could doubt. She is a hard, resistant object to Willoughby's solicitations. She causes her father, Colonel De Craye, Laetitia, Mrs. Mountstuart, Vernon, all the members of Willoughby's household, great trouble. Clara becomes the center of their fascinated attention, curiosity, and desire. She displaces Willoughby as the Maypole around which the others execute their comic dance. Rather than Maypole, however, she is a hollow center or whirlpool. Her hard resistance, her character, is her ungovernable freedom, her ungraspable absence. This gathers the others into its vortex like a maelstrom or a tornado. "What have I been in this house?" Clara cries toward the end of the book. "I have a sense of whirling through it like a madwoman." Told by Laetitia that Vernon loves her, she says, "To be loved, I see, is to feel our littleness, hollowness—feel shame. We come out in all our spots" (14:606). The image of the hollow chalice covered with signs or marks returns here once more, as an analogue for the whirlpool, whirlwind, or firestorm.

What are these spots? They make Clara legible after all, though readable as the figures provided by the narrator in "Clara's Meditations" are readable, that is, as characters of her absence of character. The spots are, in a figure that runs all through the novel like a red thread, the signs inflicted on Clara, written so to speak on her flesh, by her "torture"— torture by others and self-torture of her reflection on her experience. Her "character" is these indelible marks, difficult as they may be to read correctly. They make her different at the end of the book from what she is at the beginning. They mold and constrain her volatility and give her consistency enough to make promises. In "Clara's Meditations" her thought of Colonel De Craye is shown "issuing out of torture" (13:241). Much later, told by Laetitia that Vernon loves her, she describes her sense of coming out in her "hollowness" and in all her "spots" in violently sadomasochistic terms: "But are you unconscious of the torture you inflict? . . . The miserable little me to be taken up and loved after tearing myself to pieces" (14:606). In her eagerness earlier to escape from the cage her engagement has put her in, "she [is] all marked *urgent*" (13:243), just as her "tortures" impress upon her body and soul the irrevocable fact that she is betrothed to Willoughby, sworn to him: "The fact [stands] out cut in steel on the pitiless daylight" (13:247), outside standing here for inside according to the normal rhetorical strategies of the chapter. In another passage Mrs. Mountstuart tells Clara that if she jilts Willoughby she "will deserve the stigma" (14:439). Clara's "perceptives," in a passage cited earlier, "write" her understanding of men "on the tablets of the brain" (13:245). Clara's night of self-inflicted torture transforms her by marking her for life, so giving her that character she has lacked. Her meditations make her, after this proleptic crisis, no longer fire, fluid, wind, but cold and hard, prepared for apparently sudden acts, acts discontinuous with her "nature." That nature has been made over by pain, molded and then inscribed with inexpungable characters: "She had gone through her crisis in the anticipation of it. That is how quick natures will often be cold and hard, or not much moved, when the positive crisis arrives, and why it is that they are prepared for astonishing leaps over the gradations which should render their conduct comprehensible to us, if not excuseable" (13:244). This new Clara, having freed herself from Willoughby, can make a new kind of promise to Vernon. In order to understand that promise it will be necessary to make another detour through Nietzsche.

Ten years after *The Egoist* was published the second essay of Nietzsche's *On the Genealogy of Morals* followed a similar line of thought and of figuration. Nietzsche distinguishes, as Meredith does, between different forms of promising—the grounded promise and the groundless inaugurative performative promise. For Nietzsche too, as for Meredith, the claims of the former are always unsubstantiated, while the latter only paradoxically maintains itself over the quicksand of its perpetually shifting self-generation and self-denial. It is not a matter of "influence" here, nor even of strict homology, as of hand fitting glove, or figure on tracing paper exactly fitting over original (to borrow a metaphor from Walter Pater's "Style"). To set Nietzsche beside Meredith juxtaposes similar dissimilars in order to bring out more sharply the configurations of each, like one hieroglyph inscribed over another in palimpsest. How exactly does such a juxtaposition function? What is the relation between similars that are not identical and that are not governed by some identifiable archetype of which they are copies? The raising of that question shows I have crossed in my exploration of the labyrinth of narrative terms the corridors labeled "mimesis" and "repetition." I shall encounter them again if I go far enough.[49]

The second essay of the *Genealogy* begins with a question: "To breed an animal *with the right to make promises* (*das versprechen darf*)—is not this the paradoxical task that nature has set itself in the case of man?"[50] And a little later, in section 3: "How can one create a memory (Gedächtnis) for the human animal? How can one impress something upon this partly obtuse, partly flighty mind, attuned only to the passing moment, in such a way that it will stay there?" (E, 60; G, 802). Promising, for Nietzsche, depends as much on forgetting as on remembering. The person who promises must forget all the differences between one moment and the next in order to create a fictitious world in which things become regular and calculable, including the self. That self will then appear to remain the same through time. It can therefore make promises and keep them. Forgetting is for Nietzsche an active and therapeutic exercise, not a passive vanishing: "Forgetting (Vergeßlichkeit) is no mere *vis inertiae* as the superficial imagine; it is rather an active and in the strictest sense positive faculty of repression (positives Hemmungsvermögen)" (E, 57; G, 799). Meredith, too, it will be remembered, in *The Ordeal of Richard Feverel* makes a loss of memory one of the crucial effects of crossing the Rubicon by making a life-determining choice: "Their memories scarce seem their own!" In Meredith's case, however, forgetting is the sign of a decisive break in a person's life, while for Nietzsche forgetting is necessary to create an illusory temporal continuity and regularity.

The relation of Nietzsche's theory of forgetting in the *Genealogy* to the apparently parallel but in fact reversed notion of forgetting in Freud's *Civilization and Its Discontents* and elsewhere would take me into another bypath in the labyrinth I am exploring. Freud's model of remembering and forgetting is discussed in Walter Benjamin's "Über einige Motive bei Baudelaire."[51] For Freud, consciousness is seen as absorbing the shock of immediate experience and so preserving the deeper continuities of memory. Those continuities accommodate the body and the psyche to its environment. For Nietzsche, on the other hand, consciousness is the realm of continuity, of making regular and calculable, therefore the realm of fiction. The paradigm in Nietzsche is the chiasmus of the one in Freud. The same elements have reverse valences.

Forgetting for Nietzsche must actively shut out experience of the incommensurability of each moment with all other moments, so that people can go on living in their dream worlds of regularity, asleep on the back of a tiger, as Nietzsche puts it in a famous phrase from "Über Wahrheit und Lüge im Außermoralischen Sinne." For Nietzsche, the man or woman who cannot forget is ill, surfeited, as Clara is on the night of her meditations, with a barrage of impressions. Such a person is dazed by awareness of the difference of each moment, each sensation, from all others, distracted by the failure of these sensations to organize themselves around any line of continuity in the self. Promises can be made and kept only by the person who can forget all this, who can forget, that is, what is really there. Such a person can substitute for disorderly experience a fictitious continuity both within and without, the fiction of a permanent character within and belief in the exact repetition of impressions from without. This continuity is the result of a willed memory, not a passive inability to rid oneself of an impression but "an active *desire* not to rid oneself (ein aktives Nicht-wieder-los-werden-*wollen*). It is desire for the continuance of something desired once (ein Fort-und-fort-wollen des einmal Gewollten), a real *memory of the will* (ein eigentliches *Gedächtnis des Willens*)" (E, 58; G, 800). This memory of the will gives a man or a woman that continuity with himself or herself that I have been calling character: "Man himself must first of all have become *calculable, regular, necessary (berechenbar, regelmäßig, notwendig*), even in his own image of himself (seine eigene Vorstellung), if he is to be able to stand security for *his own future*, which is what one who promises (ein Versprechender) does!" (E, 58; G, 800).

How can a man (or a woman) become calculable and regular if by nature he (or she) is flighty, inconsistent, a creature of whims, wiles, inconsistencies? The answer for Nietzsche is like that given implicitly by Meredith: through pain, torture, suffering. Only mental and physical suffering will suffice to burn the configurations of permanent character on a person's flesh. This will teach him or her to remember promises and to remember to forget that he (or she) is different every moment and in different circumstances, so has no reason to remain true to a promise made yesterday or even five minutes ago. "The task of breeding an animal with the right to make promises," says Nietzsche, "evidently embraces and presupposes as a preparatory task that one first *makes* men to a certain degree necessary, uniform, like among like, regular, and consequently calculable (notwendig, einförmig, gleich unter Gleichen, regelmäßig und folglich berechenbar)" (E, 58–59; G, 800).

This making calculable is expressed by Nietzsche in violent

terms. Brutal torture, mutilation, flayings alive, castrations—only these will give man a memory, brand it on his body, and make it possible to count on him (or her). Nietzsche's language here is as excessive as Meredith's descriptions of Clara's sense that she has cut herself to pieces or been strung to wild horses' backs, tossed on savage wastes:

> One can well believe that the answers and methods for solving this primeval problem were not precisely gentle; perhaps indeed there was nothing more fearful and uncanny (sogar nichts furcht-barer und unheimlicher) in the whole prehistory of man than his *mnemotechnics*. "If something is to stay in the memory it must be burned in: only that which never ceases to *hurt* (*wehzutun*) stays in the memory"—this is the main clause of the oldest (unhappily also the most enduring) psychology on earth. . . . Man could never do without blood, torture, and sacrifices when he felt the need to create a memory for himself; the most dreadful sacrifices and pledges (sacrifices of the first-born among them), the most repulsive mutilations (castration, for example), the cruelest rites of all the religious cults (and all religions are at the deepest level systems of cruelties) (auf dem untersten Grunde Systeme von Grausamkeiten)—all this has its origin in the in-stinct that realized that pain (Schmerz) is the most powerful aid to mnemonics. (E, 61; G, 802)

Nietszche's notion of the contractual, promissory basis of in-nocence and guilt is that so much guilt or so much failure to keep a promise may be paid for by so much pain inflicted on the body of the guilty one (the "pound of flesh"). This follows from the relation of morality to a mnemotechnics of pain. Morality is a matter of credit and debt. But a fissure just here splits Nietzsche's thought. It is a split like that between sadism and masochism, or like that between Nietzsche and Meredith. This fissure is a fold dividing what nevertheless remains the same. The point of division, the fault, can never be certainly identified. It is like that line-no-line between the two Cressidas in Troilus's speech in Shakespeare's play: "This is, and is not Cressid" (5.2.171).

Nietzsche appears to hold that there is but one kind of morality, one kind of character, one kind of memory, and one kind of ability to make and keep promises—the one burned into the flesh of slaves by immemorial centuries of mnemotechnical cruelty on the part of their masters: "With the aid of such images and procedures (Bilder und Vorgänge) [he lists these in an adjacent sentence as stoning,

breaking on the wheel, piercing with stakes, tearing apart or tram-
pling by horses, boiling in oil or wine, flaying alive, cutting flesh
from the chest, smearing with honey and leaving the wrongdoer in
the blazing sun for the flies] one finally remembers five or six 'I
will not's' ('ich will nicht'), in regard to which one had given one's
promise (sein *Versprechen*) so as to participate in the advantages
of society—and it was indeed with the aid of this kind of memory
that one at last came 'to reason' ('zur Vernunft')!" (E, 62; G, 803).

A little earlier in the *Genealogy*, however, Nietzsche had described as the "fruit" of this "tremendous process," stretching back
far before the beginning of recorded history, the free man, able to
make promises on his own and keep them:

> The ripest fruit is the *sovereign individual* (das *souveräne Indi-
> viduum*) like only to himself (das nur sich selbst gleiche), liber-
> ated again from the morality of custom (der Sittlichkeit der Sitte),
> autonomous and supramoral (for "autonomous" and "moral"
> are mutually exclusive), in short, the man who has his own
> independent, protracted will and the *right to make promises*—
> and in him a proud consciousness, quivering in every muscle, of
> *what* has at length been achieved and become flesh in him (in
> ihm leibhaft geworden ist), a consciousness of his own power
> and freedom, a sensation of mankind come to completion. This
> emancipated individual (Dieser Freigewordne), with the actual
> *right* to make promises, this master of a *free* will, this sovereign
> man (dieser Souverän)—how should he not be aware of his
> superiority over all those who lack the right to make promises
> and stand as their own guarantors (für sich selbst gutsagen
> darf). . . . He is bound to reserve a kick for the feeble windbags
> (die schmächtigen Windhunde) who promise without the right
> to do so, and a rod for the liar who breaks his word even at the
> moment he utters it. (E, 59–60; G, 801)

There seem to be three kinds of people here, in a puzzling relation
to one another. On the one hand there is the man or woman who
can make promises because consistency of character has been tor-
tured into him or her, burned into the flesh. This habitual or
conventional morality, however, what Nietzsche calls "the morality
of mores (die Sittlichkeit der Sitte)," seems for some reason to have
become less possible now. The ordinary person seems to have
escaped the "social straitjacket" by which "man was actually *made*

calculable," and to have become a windbag whose promises are mere air. The man of today does not remain himself long enough to keep his word even a moment beyond the moment he utters it. On the other hand, this same change seems to have made possible a new kind of person, "the emancipated individual." This must be a man, or woman, who knows that the brand of character is superficial and artificial, however deeply it has been burned into the flesh. Such a person takes it upon himself, or herself, arbitrarily to maintain self-consistency enough to make promises and keep them, knowing that there is no "reason," no base or measure, on the ground of which one should keep a promise, having made it. Such a man or woman has an independent protracted will, and the right to make promises.

What is this will? What is its basis, the reason for its continuation? This is parallel to the question asked earlier in a passage on *The Will to Power*. Who is this "I" who says there is no "I?" The will is one of the elements of character. There seems no reason why the will should be any more "protracted," continuous with itself through time, than any of the other elements of character. "Was one so volatile as [Clara] a person with a will?" the narrator of *The Egoist* asks. "But there is no such thing as will," affirms Nietzsche in *The Will to Power,* as the reader will remember. The same assertion is made in a crucial early section of *The Genealogy,* crucial in that it is a basic presupposition for the book's whole argument, including the argument in the second essay I am following through:

> A quantum of force is equivalent to a quantum of drive, will, effect (Trieb, Wille, Wirken)—more, it is nothing other than precisely this very driving, willing, effecting, and only owing to the seduction of language (der Verführung der Sprache) (and of the fundamental errors of reason that are petrified in it [und der in ihr versteinerten Grundirrtümer der Vernunft]) which conceives and misconceives (versteht und mißversteht) all effects as conditioned by something that causes effects, by a "subject," can it appear otherwise. For just as the popular mind (das Volk) separates the lightning from its flash and takes the latter for an *action,* for the operation of a subject called lightning, so popular morality (die Volks-Moral) also separates strength from expressions (Äußerungen) of strength, as if there were a neutral substratum behind the strong man, which was *free* to express

strength or not to do so. But there is no such substratum; there is no "being" behind doing, effecting, becoming; "the doer" is merely a fiction added to the deed (bloß hinzugedichtet)—the deed is everything (das Tun ist alles) The popular mind in fact doubles the deed; when it sees the lightning flash, it is the deed of a deed (das ist ein Tun-Tun: the English loses the onomatopoeia): it posits the same event first as cause (Ursache) and then a second time as its effect (Wirkung). (E, 45; G, 789–90)[52]

For Nietzsche the "Volk" is enslaved by misconceptions that are "petrified" within language. To be a member of the Volk is to allow language to do our thinking for us. One of the most common of such misconceptions is a doubly erroneous anthropomorphism. Nietzsche, it will be remembered, defines "truth," in a famous formulation in "On Truth and Lies in an Extra-moral Sense," as "a mobile army of metaphors, metonymies, and anthropomorphisms." In Nietzsche's analysis here, an erroneous assumption about human beings, coercively codified in language, namely that each person possesses a "subject" substratum that wills to act in such a way, is falsely projected on inanimate nature. The lightning is personified as a "subject" that wills to flash. But in neither case is there such a doubling into a freely willing doer and a deed that follows this willing as effect follows cause. The deed and the doer are in both cases one. The deed is everything. "Will" as the free will of a doer is a linguistic fiction. The word *will* is rather a synonym for "drive" or "effect," that is, for blind force, the kind of blind force that Nietzsche attributes to primeval, prehistoric, premoral man, who did not think before he acted. The power of Nietzsche's analysis here lies in the analogy he draws between the lightning flashing and the man acting. It is easy to accept the deconstruction of our erroneous attribution of subjectivity and will to the lightning. This is then reversed again to deconstruct the literal presupposition that was the basis of the anthropopmorphizing of the lightning, namely, the assumption that doer and deed may be separated in the case of human beings.

For both Nietzsche and Meredith there is no will in the sense of the free will of a subject. "Will" is one traditional metaphysical name for the ground of character, the "subject substratum." Neither Nietzsche nor Meredith believes there is such a ground. On the other hand, there must be will in order for the sovereign man (or woman) to take it upon himself (or herself), against all reason, to remain true to himself (or herself) and to the promises he (or she) has made.[53] This is the strange fissure in the thinking of both Nietzsche and Meredith.

The bridge over this gap where there is no will but must be will is for Nietzsche provided by the word *instinct* (Instinkt). Instinct, the reader will remember, taught those in power in primeval times "that pain is the most powerful aid to mnemonics." The will to cruelty, to sacrifices, mutilations, castrations was an "instinct." Over the gap of all those centuries of pain branding the memory of five or six "I will not's" into the flesh of those subject to the masters, "instinct" now serves to maintain consistency of character in the sovereign individual: "The proud awareness of the extraordinary privilege of *responsibility* (*Verantwortlichkeit*), the consciousness of this rare freedom, this power over oneself and over fate, has in his case penetrated to the profoundest depths (in seine unterste Tiefe hinabgesenkt) and become instinct, the dominating instinct (ist zum Instinkt geworden, zum dominierenden Instinkt). What will he call this dominating instinct, supposing he feels the need to give it a name? The answer is beyond a doubt: this sovereign man calls it his *conscience* (dieser souveräne Mensch heißt ihn sein *Gewissen*)" (E, 60; G, 801).

The logic (or alogic) of Nietzsche's thought here seems to be the following: the power, energy, or will of primeval man was his amorality, his inconsistency, his lack of character, his attunement to the passing moment, his consequent penchant for cruelty. He was like a lightning bolt in that in him there was no gap between doer and deed. In primeval man thinking did not precede doing. The doer and the deed were one. The man of prehistory could be tamed enough to become moral only if he were deprived of that energy by an operation that Nietzsche consistently defines not only as inscription, the stamping of a permanent character where there was none before, but also as mutilation, as castration. Human history is the story of this taming. Morality must be reinforced even now by symbolic reenactments of this history in which the law is written on the flesh of the lawbreaker, as in Kafka's *In the Penal Colony*. The lawbreaker still today must pay the debt of so much pain for so much infringement of the law. After all the centuries and centuries of this labor of extirpation performed by man upon himself the fruit of this process emerges in the form of the *sovereign individual,* the man of protracted will who can make and keep promises, the man in whom will has become instinct once again, conscience.

What is this "will?" The word must mean two different things across the abyss of the primal will's abscission. The will of primeval man was the spontaneous energy that led instantly, without forethought, to action. The moral man, the man of resentment, product of centuries of torture, has no will. He obeys the law out of fear. A few "Thou shalt not's" have been branded into his flesh. The protracted will in the new sovereign individual, postmoral rather than premoral, must be a prosthesis of the now lost will, a new kind of will to replace the excised one. An awareness of the artificiality of conventional morality, inscribed by cruel force from without, leads the sovereign individual, in full consciousness of what is now missing in him after millennia of training, to brand himself with a promise and with the intention to keep that promise, so creating an artificial will to replace the lost one. This new will again becomes flesh and penetrates to the profoundest depths. There it becomes instinct, conscience, scarcely to be distinguished in its solidity and substantiality from what is missing. The cruelty imposed from without, sadistically, becomes in the sovereign individual a cruelty imposed on himself, masochistically, making for himself in pain a "protracted and unbreakable will (eines langen unzerbrechlichen Willens)" (E, 60; G, 801). In spite of its formidable strength, this will is only a substitute or simulacrum for the genuine spontaneous, original will of the primeval men of power. It is only maintained by the utmost unrelenting efforts. The new will must be recreated every moment over the gulf of an absence by a constantly renewed baseless performative promise. The new sovereign individual repeats over and over, "I will do so and so though I have no will but that negative image of one, hieroglyph for anaglyph, I have carved out of myself." The word or the concept of will, though it may be displaced to "instinct" or to "conscience," still oscillates between presence and absence, solidity and vacancy, like a glove constantly turned inside out, or a displacement of figure and ground in a Gestalt diagram.

This is Nietzsche's version of a contradiction present in one way or another in all performative language. Such language must and must not be grounded on something that precedes it. It both presupposes and creates the selfhood of the one who utters the performative. What about Meredith? Is his dramatization of Clara's ordeal congruent with Nietzsche's analysis? Does Clara emerge from that ordeal as an example of Nietzsche's sovereign man, someone who has earned by self-discipline and self-torture the right to make promises and the ability to keep them? It would seem so, and yet there is something more than a little odd about calling Clara an example of Nietzsche's "sovereign man." The line followed by Clara's story puts together in crisscross form the elements in Nietzsche's dramatic fiction of human history. Meredith's formulations function as a proleptic deconstruction of Nietzsche's male oriented or phallogocentric structure. As Jacques Derrida has shown in *Eperons: Les styles de Nietzsche,* Nietzsche also performs this deconstruction on himself, just as he dismantles, in *The Will to Power* and elsewhere, that logocentrism of the will on which his work is often said to be based. One way to see the difference between Nietzsche and Meredith is to ask whether it really makes any difference whether one says "sovereign man" or "sovereign woman" or "sovereign man or woman." It would seem not. My awkward "he or she's," "himself or herself's," and so on, may seem no more than nominal homage to feminist criticism. The patterns in question in both Meredith and Nietzsche seem conceptual, not tied to the physiological or social features of sexual differentiation. That this, however, is not the case, a moment's reflection will show. It matters a great deal whether a man or a woman is taken as the base paradigm for the moral experience of the human race generally.

In Nietzsche's case the beginning is a male figure, equipped with a will, the symbol of which is his possession of a penis. The mutilating cruelty necessary to make him moral involves always his castration, or displaced figures for his castration. The sovereign individual must then give himself a new will, simulacrum of the old, a prosthetic phallus that will serve as a new logos, ratio, a ruler by which he can measure the value of others. "The 'free' man," says Nietzsche, "the possessor of a protracted and unbreakable will, also possesses his *measure of value (Wertmaß):* looking out upon others from himself, he honors or he despises" (E, 60; G, 801).

Clara, on the other hand, begins, from Meredith's traditional male perspective, with something missing, a lack, the lack of the male member, as all the images of Clara as a chalice, as a vase, as an overwrought polished vessel keep reminding the reader. This lack, she fears, may mean she is without character, unable to live up to the traditional morality of making and keeping promises that society has imposed on her and that she has meekly accepted by promising to marry Willoughby. "Was one so volatile as she a person with a will?—Were they not a multitude of flitting wishes that she took for a will?—Was she, feather-headed that she was, a person to make a stand on physical pride?" (13:239–40). Clara's discovery, as I have argued, is that she cannot fit the male model of willing. But this discovery is implicitly generalized to apply equally to males. Penises they may have but not what those stand for, the primal will that might serve as a base for character. The meaning given to the possession or lack of possession of a penis is revealed to be an ideological fiction, instrument of male hegemony.

Clara, however, goes beyond the discovery that she can never have a character in the way the male-dominated society wishes her to have one. The novel also goes beyond the recognition that what is true for her is just as true for Willoughby. Clara learns that she can create a character for herself in a way that is like but not quite like the self-generated power to make and keep promises of Nietzsche's free and sovereign man. In Nietzsche's case the sovereign individual would be impossible without all those centuries of cruel branding of "I will not's." It exists, however, as the autonomous amoral denial of those prohibitions. The development of Clara's character too depends on the "torture" inflicted by her false position. Clara turns that torture into self-torture and so creates a freedom to choose, to promise and keep her promise to Vernon. This freedom is based on free denial of the mold in which society would pour her. The image for her character is the inscription on the hollow vessel, not the hieroglyph on the phallic obelisk. Clara's will is maintained not as a prosthesis of what is missing but in full awareness of its absence for men and women alike. Both paradigms lead to the paradox of a performative vow that has no basis and that both makes something happen and at the same time reveals the groundlessness of that happening. The two paradigms, Nietzsche's and Meredith's, are reverse mirror images of one another. They are like Narcissus confronting his twin sister, not quite congruent image of himself. They are as like one another, as able to turn one into the other, and yet as different, as the phantasm of a column is like a well.

It might be argued, finally, that it is the function of some speech

acts, in particular the performative "I do" of the marriage ceremony, to mark on the flesh of those who say "I do" a promissory
note or contract making the difference between man and woman,
against all reason, an equivalence that can be the basis of an
exchange. I give myself to you, you give yourself to me. We seal
that promise with a kiss. There is no reason, logos, or ratio in the
economy of such performatives, neither in the sense of rationality
nor in the sense of sustaining base or ground, nor in the sense of
a preexisting common "measure." Such a performative creates the
regularity of character that makes promising and the keeping of
promises possible. It transforms by fiat the incommensurability of
what is exchanged into equality. It creates a yardstick of value.
Even so, the contracted exchange has always a plus-value. The
balance never quite comes right. This might be phrased in this case
by saying that though Clara indubitably does love Vernon and
promise herself to him, she will nevertheless no doubt give him
more than he bargains for. She will remain the Mountain Echo to
the last, "[her] mind . . . [her] own married or not." This is the
way Vernon wants her to be or thinks he wants her to be.

Will and language are here once more elliptically related. Each
repairs the absence of the other. The will and the character it creates
come into existence only in a speech act. Without the energy of
the performative will that makes the flesh a sign, there is no effective language. That language affirms the equality of two contracting
parties that remain nevertheless incommensurate. The performative
promise is a revolution around two incompatible focuses, each
denying the priority of the other, each already there before the
other, but each turning out to be a secondary creation when it is
confronted in itself. This constant turning can never be reduced to
a single-centered circle.

Some version of this alogic, it has been my hypothesis in this
chapter, is always at work in the creation of character in the novel.
Without the powerful illusion of the existence of a character named
Clara Middleton the dismantling of the assumption of preexisting
fixed character Meredith performs in *The Egoist* would be impossible. So also would be impossible the reaffirmation, beyond its
deconstitution, of the development through suffering of a character
regular enough and strong enough to keep promises. Only the
testing of further examples would confirm or deny or modify this
hypothesis. I posit nevertheless the claim that one function of

realistic novels is to allow the reader to act out her or his fear that there is no character, while at the same time reaffirming its existence in a new form, beyond its disarticulation. After all, there is Clara, still caught in the pages of *The Egoist,* brought into existence there in words allowing any reader to decipher her character.

3 Anastomosis

The cords of all link back, strandentwining cable of all flesh. That is why mystic monks. Will you be as gods? Gaze in your omphalos. Hello. Kinch here. Put me on to Edenville. Aleph, alpha: nought, nought, one.

—James Joyce, *Ulysses*

Under what aegis should I put those studies presupposing novels are "really about" interpersonal relations? Anastomosis: image of a line joining two vessels or enclosures, in this case the line from person to person, like a telephone line. As Joyce foresaw, Ma Bell's umbilical chord links every man and woman in the world to every other man and woman.[1] This network makes the I-thou relation universal. No other person is further from me than a finger's touch on the right letters or numbers in sequence: AA-001. Linear imagery, not surprisingly, is a frequent resource in the description of intersubjective relations, whether in novels themselves, in criticism of them, or in analysis of these relations in philosophy, in psychology, or in sociology. I list some of these terms from the opening chapter here: *filiation, affiliation, marriage tie, liaison, genetic line, ancestral line.*

John Keats, in a letter to John Hamilton Reynolds dated February 19, 1818, presents a paradigm of such imagery. The passage will serve as a transition from the corridors of character in the previous chapter to the ambages of interpersonal relations in this.[2] The self for Keats spins an elaborate spider's web in its movement through time. This is the soul the self makes to dwell in. The "soul," for Keats, is something gradually made, so this world is a "Vale of Soul-making." Each man's web, however individual and private it may seem, a secret airy citadel, nevertheless overlaps here and there, in fact at innumerable points, with those of others. In constructing his own subjective labyrinth each man also encounters within himself the withinness of others. The letter presents one of Keats's exuberantly cheerful models of the self. It proposes a way of using the solitary imagination as a means of making "contact," as they say, with others. Keats here solves the problem of interpersonal relations through the activity that might seem most solitary or even solipsistic:

> Now it appears to me that almost any Man may like the Spider spin from his own inwards his own airy Citadel—the points of leaves and twigs on which the Spider begins her work are few and she fills the Air with a beautiful circuiting: Man should be content with as few points to tip with the fine Webb of his Soul and weave a tapestry empyrean—full of Symbols for his spiritual eye, of softness for his spiritual touch, of space for his wandering of distinctness for his Luxury—But the Minds of Mortals are so different and bent on such diverse Journeys that it may at first appear impossible for any common taste and fellowship to exist between two or three under these suppositions—It is however quite the contrary—Minds would leave each other in contrary directions, traverse each other in Numberless points, and at last greet each other at the Journeys end.[3]

This chapter will explore the topography of the self in its various modes of intersection with others. What is problematic about the concept of the self, like that of character, the previous chapter has shown. Like Keats, I shall here interrogate the image of the self as making or having made for it a character that can be thought of as a spatial pattern like a spiderweb or a network of pathways.

The "self" is the possibility of doing that. The self comes into existence when it gives itself or is given a "character." The self, this trope assumes, in its journeys traces out lines making a design. Each self is motivated in doing this by the desire to encounter others. In fact it does meet them, or at least it crosses the traces of tracks made by others. Perhaps the others are encountered face-to-face at the journey's end, though where that end is and what the face to face encounter might be are chief issues, ways out of the maze, to be sought for here. Does the self in fact ever meet other selves? Where? How? Always within itself, as Keats suggests? Or "outside"? What does it mean for the self to go outside itself, to meet, be related to, depend on for its own substance, other selves? These questions will be explored in detail by way of Goethe's *Wahlverwandtschaften,* after a preliminary tracking down of "anastomosis" in Joyce and other authors.

The figure of Ariadne's thread already provides a model for interpersonal relations not unlike those given in the passage from Keats or in the epigraph from *Ulysses.* The labyrinth hides the monster, child of Pasiphaë's guilty love for the bull, sign of the bestial in every sexual coupling. This evidence of a gross crime must be suppressed or appeased every nine years by a tribute of seven youths and seven maidens from Athens, untouched yet by that bestiality, unmarked by sexual linkages. These the Minotaur devours. Ariadne's thread, that retraces the labyrinth, is an image of interpersonal connection in its joining of Ariadne and Theseus, as are the finger and ring in the marriage of Dionysus and Ariadne, or as is that dance of Theseus, the "crane dance," celebrating on Delos his escape from Crete. in Its intricate winding, the latter figures not only the material Daedalean labyrinth, but also the labyrinth of interlacings binding man to woman in society and through the generations. This pattern is repeated again in the sequence of love stories in the Ariadne myth and in the adjacent myths of Theseus and Dionysus. The family story proliferates from one generation to the next or laterally from one family to another in inexhaustible permutation. The many ways our culture has represented intersubjectivity are expressed in emblem by that ancient representation of Ariadne with a kind of bobbin at her waist.[4] From that spool unwinds through all the maze's corridors the string held, at the other end, by her soon to be faithless lover. The thread is his link to her and his means of safe rebirth into the light after his murder of the Minotaur. Ariadne's thread is a sign for the sexual linkage between lovers. At the same time it is a symbolic

umbilical cord from mother to son, as when one says, "He is tied to his mother's apron strings." The anastomosis of interpersonal relations is always ambiguously both, as Joyce saw, and as Freud of course also saw in calling all marriages, from the husband's perspective, displacements of the son's yearning to return to his mother.

Ariadne's thread follows the generations in either direction. The reader may remember a passage in *Either/Or* in which Kierkegaard, or "A," observes that the word *Schnur* means both "string" and "daughter-in-law."[5] The genealogical line by way of the son cannot be continued without that particular string, so the different meanings of the word *Schnur* may be more tied together than "A" thinks. Therefore we grandfathers and grandmothers, or potential grandfathers and grandmothers, say, "Blessed be the tie that binds." Linear terminology for interpersonal relations is always implicitly sexual. In one way or another it refers, however obscurely, to the act of coupling or copulation.

An exuberantly bawdy passage in *Le Quart Livre* of Rabelais brings this into the open with characteristic serial hyperbole. Rabelais piles example on example in a way that not only makes the point but goes beyond the point in a kind of riotous overkill to reveal a latent absurdity in the sociolinguistic fact being exploited. Kinship names, which seem so neutral, so rational and objective, could, Rabelais sees, be otherwise in innumerable different ways. All would come in time to seem neutral, rational, and objective. The multiplicity of examples in a passage of this sort in Rabelais is an integral part of its meaning. A longish citation will be necessary to carry that meaning over into my text here. The passage is based on a brilliant exploitation of several features of line imagery in fiction.

Kinship relations are arbitrary. They are created in the names for them. In one sense all men and women are members of one family. If so, all sexual relations are incestuous.[6] In another sense, even the closest relatives are untied from one another. It is a wise father who knows his own child. An unseeing Oedipus does not recognize his father and mother. His crimes are not patricide and incest, since he does not see and name Laius correctly as his father, Jocasta as his mother. His acts only become patricide and incest in retrospect. Then the events of his life are matched to the words of the oracles. The crime does not exist before the words for it. As Jacques Lacan puts this: "This law, therefore, [the incest prohibition] is revealed clearly enough as identical to an order of Language. For without kinship nominations, no power is capable of instituting the order of preferences and taboos which bind and weave the yarn of lineage down through succeeding generations."[7] If kinship names were otherwise they would define a different order of preferences and taboos. They would weave the yarn differently. Moreover, kinship names, like all names, are figurative in origin. All the sons and daughters of Eve are condemned to dress themselves in metaphors to name their relations to one another. The figures, in this case, tend in one way or another to refer to sexual coupling, as Rabelais's inventions indicate. His figures are drawn from all the other (than sexual) realms of domestic and public economy: cooking, eating, dressing, production and exchange, and so forth. The figures call attention to the way sexual linking, the give and take of copulation, has distributed itself figuratively in all sorts of daily activities in the home and in the town. Activities to which our dreams give a sexual meaning are performed all the time in displaced forms and under disguised names, as when I put on my hat or my shoe, or when I take pen in hand and write these words.

The text in *Le Quart Livre* deals with the island of Ennasin, and "des estranges alliances du pays," the strange relationships of the country.[8] These result from the fact that all people on this island are consanguineous, so that ordinary kinship names and taboos are inappropriate. Anyone can marry anyone. "They were all kindred and related to one another, a fact of which they boasted" (E, 468; F, 59). In the name Ennasin and in the extravagant play of fictitious kinship names Rabelais is apparently parodying simultaneously two contradictory sources: the famous celibacy of the Essenes and the "amours d'alliance" of Marot and Anne d'Alençon. Or at any rate that is what the learned scholars say (see F, 60). Rabelais certainly seems to go beyond these sources. On Ennasin, kinship names and connections are indeed odd. For one thing, since all the inhabitants are incestuously related, they do not use, or hardly ever use, and then in paradoxical ways, the ordinary names of mother, father, sister, and so forth:

> Their relationships and degrees of kinship were of a very strange kind. For they were all so related and intermarried with one

another that we found none of them who was a mother or a
father, an uncle or nephew, a son-in-law or a daughter-in-law, a
god-father or a god-mother, to any other; except indeed for one
tall noseless old man, whom I heard calling a little girl of three
or four, Father, while the little girl called him, Daughter. (E,
468; F, 60)

In this topsy-turvy world ordinary kinship appellations are inappropriate. The inhabitants invent new ones for each encounter,
with inexhaustible mutual bawdiness, transferring terms with reck-
less abandon from those abundant anastomoses going on all the
time in the everyday world of cooking, eating, dressing, buying
and selling, in idioms, proverbial expressions, and so on, to the
implicit linkage which in one way or another occurs, in our world
as on the strange island of Ennasin, every time a man meets a
woman. On this island the game people play is a version of "Fill
in the Blank," followed by the explosive laughter of interpretative
recognition. If A and B are known, the genital facts, in this case,
and if A is to B as C is to D, what is D if C is so and so? We shall
encounter this game again in Goethe's *Wahlverwandtschaften*.
"Sprezzatura" depends on being able to think of more and more
unlikely couplings and, for the partner, to be able to think instantly
of the appropriate rejoinder. In Rabelais's version of this "jeu
d'esprit," or rather "jeu de pas d'esprit," a game that might have
come from *Jokes and the Unconscious,* there must always be a
third, the spectator and fully conscious analyst who says what it
means in another witty way, capping the first joke with a second
and getting another burst of laughter of another kind. The first
laugh arises from getting it right and bringing something out in
the open thereby. It is a release of repressed sexual energy through
displacement into figure. The second laugh is the cool analytic one
that watches from a distance. In one sense it exposes more, since
it expresses the meaning openly. It interprets the metaphor. In
another sense, it covers over again, since what is repressed is the
alogic of sexual desire and sexual linkages, the failure of the latter
ever to satisfy the former. This alogic of desire is perpetually foreign
to the attempts by logic to bring it fully into the open.

It may be for this reason that the game has to be played over
and over with different figures. An intrinsic aspect of all these
images of anastomosis for interpersonal relations, whether in Rabelais, in Joyce, or in Goethe, lies in their inexhaustible serial

variability. It is the essence of such a linguistic game, as of so many Rabelais invents, to be repeatable, to require repetition. This variability arises from the fact that no version ever quite "gets it right." Each is one more figure for the unfigurable. It is impossible to bring into the light of reason my relation to the unattainable other person, Ariadne at the end of her thread or Theseus in the heart of the labyrinth. Nor do the examples form an order or make progress. Rabelais presents a more or less random catalogue of cases. At the arbitrary end of the series, the reader is where he or she was at the beginning, no closer to the goal of final clarification. Here are some of Rabelais's versions. I give first an English translation, then the French, for the mouth-filling resonance of Rabelais's language:

> The degrees of relationship between them were such that one man called a woman, dear Octopus, and the woman called him, you old Porpoise. "Those two must feel a hot tide rising," said Friar John, "when they've rubbed their bacon together a little." Another of them called out with a smile to a stylish young baggage: "Good day, young pretty currycomb," and she answered him with, "A grand morning to you, my chestnut steed." "Ha, ha!" cried Panurge, "come and see a steed currying favour. I bet there'll be some fine warm work, for the chestnut steed with the black stripe must have his cock combed good and often." Another man called to his fancy-girl: "God bless you, dear desk," to which she called back: "The same to you, old brief." "By St Trinian," exclaimed Gymnaste. "That brief must often be lying on its desk." Another called his girl, "Old stagger," and she called him, "You worm." "His worm will have given her plenty of fits of the staggers," said Eusthenes. Another saluted a female relative with: "Good day to you, hatchet," and she replied: "The same to you, helve." "God blast my belly," cried Carpalim. "That hatchet's well helved and that helve's well hatcheted. Do you think he's got the big tip the Roman whores are so fond of? Or perhaps he is a Franciscan friar with a good one."
>
> As we went on, I saw a lecherous fellow who greeted his female relative as, "My mattress," and she called him, "Eiderdown," and indeed he looked a downy old bird. One man called his girl: "Sweet dough," to which she answered: "Old Crust." "Shovel" and "poker"; "clog" and "slipper"; "boot" and

"shoe"; "mitten" and "glove," were other names exchanged
between relatives of different sexes. One man in particular called
his woman his rind, to which she replied: "Dear bacon": and
their relationship was that of bacon to rind. (E, 468–469)

La parenté et alliance entre eulx estoit que l'un appelloit une
femme: ma maigre; la femme le appelloit: mon marsouin.
"Ceulx-là, disoit frere Jan, doibvroient bien sentir leur marée,
quand ensemble se sont frottez leur lard." L'un appelloit une
guorgiase bachelette, en soubriant: "Bon jour, mon estrille." Elle
le resalua, disant: "Bonne estreine, mon fauveau.—Hay, hay,
hay! s'escria Panurge, venez veoir une estrille, une fau et un veau.
N'est ce estrille fauveau? Ce fauveau à la raye noire doibt bien
souvent estre estrillé." Un autre salua une sienne mignonne,
disant: "Adieu, mon bureau." Elle luy respondit: "Et vous aussi,
mon procès.—Par sainct Treignant, dict Gymnaste, ce procès
doibt estre soubvent sus ce bureau." L'un appelloit une autre:
mon verd. Elle l'appelloit son coquin. "Il y a bien là, dist Eus-
thenes, du verdcoquin." Un autre salua une sienne alliée, disant:
"Bon di, ma coingnée." Elle respondit: "Et à vous, mon
manche.—Ventre beuf, s'escria Carpalim, comment ceste coingnée est emmanchée? Comment ce manche est encoingné? Mais
seroit ce poinct la grande manche que demandent les courtisanes
Romaines? Ou un cordelier à la grande manche?"
    Passant oultre, je veids un averlant qui, saluant son alliée,
l'appela: mon matraz, elle le appelloit: mon lodier. De faict, il
avoit quelques traictz de lodier lourdault. L'un appelloit une
aultre: ma mie, elle l'appelloit: ma crouste. L'un une aultre
appelloit sa palle, elle l'appelloit son fourgon. L'un une autre
appelloit ma savate, elle le nommoit pantophle. L'un une aultre
nommoit ma botine, elle l'appelloit son estivallet. L'un une aultre
nommoit ma mitaine, elle le nommoit: mon guand. L'un une
aultre nommoit sa couane, elle l'appelloit son lard; et estoit entre
eulx parenté de couane de lard. (F, 60–61)

The reader will have got the point. There is no end to the
possibilities, since language and everyday life are full of synecdochic exchanges, thing contained interpenetrating container and
standing for it, or producing, as in some of Rabelais's examples, a
compound word that is a linguistic anastomosis in itself. Rabelais
(or whoever wrote Le Quart Livre; there is some doubt about this)
continues for three more pages of examples, including the oyster

in its shell, the "Corne" and the "Muse" which, put together, make a "Cornemuse," bagpipe, the "cheville," cork, which may or may not be able to stop the "trou," bunghole, and ending with the case of "un jeune escafignon," a young pump, that is, a kind of shoe, who marries "une vieille pantophle," an old slipper.

Such reference to sexual coupling, however buried or implicit, is often present even when the ostensible subject is the more spiritual question of the I-thou relation, or the question of other minds.[9] My echoes of phrases from Martin Buber and John Wisdom will serve as reminders that the "other minds problem" has developed as a specific topic in twentieth-century philosophy, not only in the religious philosophy of Martin Buber, with its roots in Feuerbach and the Hegelian, Kierkegaardian tradition, but also in the existential philosophy of Jean-Paul Sartre, and in phenomenology proper, most notably in Husserl's discussion of intersubjectivity in the *Cartesian Meditations,* or in Husserl's numerous progeny, for example in the work of Roman Ingarden or Paul Ricoeur. In addition, a specific Anglo-Saxon tradition of philosophical concern with the problem goes back through Hume to Locke. The "other minds problem" is one strand of modern analytic philosophy, of which Wisdom's book is an example. Current British and American analysis is strongly inspired by Wittgenstein's interest in the topic, with its quite different Viennese roots. To mention Vienna is to remember Sigmund Freud. Psychoanalysis is to a large degree a study of interpersonal relations, the presence of the other within my own psyche. In such a contemporary psychonalyst as Jacques Lacan this becomes almost the exclusive focus. Linear imagery already present in Freud's work becomes explicitly thematized, for example, in Lacan's studies, in *Encore,* of Borromean knots as figures for the relation of the "Je" to the "Autre."[10] Within so-called deconstruction the I-Thou relation tends to be seen as a linguistic problem, but it sometimes receives direct attention nevertheless, as in the chapters on Rousseau's *Pygmalion* and *Julie* in *Allegories of Reading* or in Derrida's "Envois" in *La carte post-ale.*[11]

In sociology, there are a multitude of studies of the intersubjective relation, such as Erving Goffman's *Presentation of Self in Everyday Life* or Georg Simmel's "Web of Group Affiliations."[12] The connection between the one-to-one relation of intersubjectivity and the relation of the individual to the group or to "society" is complex. One important field of sociology, small group theory, deals in part with interpersonal relations at the level realistic fiction dramatizes them, namely that of face-to-face encounters. Such encounters are a traditional topic for anthropological research. The more abstract individual to society or individual to history relation forms the basis of a separate criticism of fiction, much practiced just now, sometimes under the name of "ideology critique." For Louis Althusser the "other" as inadvertent spokesperson for a collective unconscious ideology "interpellates" me into being. Ideology is "unconscious" because it is a structure of assumptions we take so much for granted that we are not aware they could be otherwise. They seem natural rather than cultural or linguistic.[13]

Given this complex array of speculation and research, it is not surprising that one mode of the criticism of fiction has singled out intersubjective relations as the topic of most importance in novels. Such criticism has taken a wide variety of distinct forms. It has tended to be methodologically more sophisticated, or at least more overtly concerned with theory, than the more spontaneous assumption that novels primarily present "characters," though the best critics of character in the novel are far from naive. It is possible to talk about characters in novels, however, as simply and easily as one talks about one's neighbors. To talk of "interpersonal relations" already involves some theoretical reflection. Though much of such criticism tends to go on assuming in one way or another that there are solid, given selves, there at the beginning of a novel, which then "relate" to one another, the shift from person to interpersonal relations usually implies the assumption that each self only completes or fulfills itself in its relations to another. If it is not "I *am* the other," it is at least "I become myself or affirm myself in my relations to others," or even "I *am* my relations to others." To identify exactly the emotional or cognitive bond between one person and another in a given novelist's work then becomes a matter of great importance in discriminating criticism of his or her work. Criticism of fiction can also focus on the relation of the narrator to his characters, defining that too as a mode of intersubjectivity. Or it can see criticism itself as an intersubjective relation between the mind of the critic and the mind of the novelist. Or it can make the center of attention the reader's response to the mind of the author as it has embodied itself in the text. Though the "text" in this case may be thought of as merely marks on the page, potentialities for meanings the reader gives them, nevertheless criticism is always, in such cases, implicitly a transaction between mind and mind, even if it is only a transaction between a real reader and imaginary persons, including the narrator and the "implied reader," as well as the characters. Such ways of reading fiction can define criticism as an attempt by the reader to coincide with the "intention" of the author. Each of these procedures focuses on one or another line in the network of anastomoses joining character to character in a novel, or the characters to the narrator, or the author to the narrator to the character to the critic, or the critic, without mediation, to the cogito of the author, or the reader to the web of relations among the imaginary persons in the text.

A wide variety of such criticism exists within similar basic assumptions about the primacy of intersubjective relations as a determiner of selfhood. This variety can be indicated by listing names of critics who fit into one or another of the pigeonholes I have constructed: René Girard, Wayne Booth, Georges Poulet, Jean Rousset, Wolfgang Iser. The list could be extended indefinitely— for example, to include all those studies of the novel that describe themselves as in one way or another phenomenological—but the names of some mountain peaks on the rugged terrain of such criticism indicate the lay of the land. My concern is with the necessary and yet problematic role of line imagery in expressions of the intersubjective relation, whether in novels themselves or in the criticism of them from the perspective of this topic. Through investigation of some examples, according to my strategy here, I intend not only to "read" those examples but to reach a better theoretical understanding of what it means to say novels are about interpersonal relations.

Anastomosis, then. Here is the primary entry in the OED:

[mod.L., a. Gr. anastumosis (ἀναστόμωσις) n. of action f. anastomu-ein (ἀναστομό-ειν) to furnish with a mouth or outlet.] Intercommunication between two vessels, channels, or distinct branches of any kind, by a connecting cross branch. Applied originally to the cross communications between the arteries and veins, or other canals in the animal body; whence to similar cross connexions in the sap-vessels of plants, and between rivers or their branches; and now to any cross connexions between the separate lines of any branching system, as the branches of trees, the veins of leaves, or the wings of insects.

A double contradiction is inscribed in the word *anastomosis*. This contradicted contradiction is especially evident when the word, or the topology it describes, is used, for example by Joyce, as a model for interpersonal relations, in a transfer from the primary anatomical, botanical, or topographical uses.

The first contradiction lies in the fact that an anastomosis may be an intercommunication either between two vessels or between two channels. It makes an important difference whether one thinks of the self as a closed vessel, like a lake, which might communicate by way of a stream with another lake, or whether, on the other hand, one thinks of the self as itself a river, flowing from its sources toward its mouth. In the latter case I think of myself as tied to all the previous generations of my family. I am a momentary channel through which that genealogical heritage flows on to my children and grandchildren. In this case the anastomosis is a branch channel between channels, necessary perhaps to keep the river flowing, as the connection between husband and wife, of different families, is necessary to keep the blood lines of both families going on, though now with a mixture of the two genetic streams.

The root in *anastomosis* contains this double contradictory possibility. The Greek *stomatikis* (*stomatíkis*) means "pertaining to the mouth," but of course stoma, mouth, gives the modern word stomach, by a metonymic transfer, as the OED says: "Stomach . . . a. Gr. stomacos (στόμαχος), orig. the throat, gullet, hence the mouth or orifice of any organ, esp. of the stomach, and later the stomach itself; f. stoma (στόμα), mouth." *Stomach* in modern English derives by displacement from the name for the opening into it. *Ana* means "up, in place or time, back, again, anew." It is a double antithetical prefix signifying both reaffirmation and reversal. If the stomach is thought of as a container, an anastomosis makes an anastomach, an opening or mouth in it, reversing its enclosure. If the stomach is thought of as already a mouth or channel, as it was "originally," an anastomosis makes a new mouth or opening in what is already open, a vessel in the sense of a communicating tube between one container and another.

The second contradiction lies in the fact that an anastomosis may be thought of either as an external link between two vessels or channels, or as entering into the vessel it opens, so that it becomes a version of the figure of container and thing contained. Jacques Derrida has called this version "invagination." Something already sheathlike has another sheath turned into it, like one finger of a glove turned inside out while the rest of the glove remains outside out. What was outside becomes the inside border of the inside, and what was inside becomes an outside container for this new inside, though it is still inside the larger surface of the glove, in an oscillating reversal in place, something like that created by a Möbius strip or a Klein bottle. An anastomosis flows into the vessel it opens, pierces it, and becomes enclosed by it. Anastomosis as the name for a figure of speech, for example, means "insertion of a qualifying word between two parts of another word."[14] The example Joyce gives in the Aeolus section of *Ulysses* is "underdarkneath."[15]

The uses of the word *anastomosis* and its verbal and adjectival forms cited in the OED play back and forth between the external and internal senses of the word, as well as between the alternatives in the first contradiction I named. In the sentence "The African name for a central lake is Tanganyika, signifying an anastomosis, or a meeting-place" (1859), the image is of an opening in a closed vessel. On the other hand, an anastomosis is also an "apertion and opening of two vessels into one another" (1615), where the sense of "vessels" is ambiguous, meaning perhaps channel and perhaps enclosed container. A text of 1858 speaks of "the ribs not straight but irregularly anastomosing, that is, running into and coalescing with each other." Another passage, from 1830, has "the veins of their leaves . . . anastomosing in various ways, so as to form a reticulated plexus of veins of unequal size." Another in *Blackwood's* for 1842 speaks of "a Flemish landscape irrigated by anastomosing ditches." All three of these last clearly mean connecting channels, while two other passages, one early, one late, seem to have in mind the image of invagination, one figure inside another and outside it at once, in a strange embrace (as in the Book of Kells, or in drawings by M. C. Escher, for example his admirable "Reptiles"): "As they through each other glide Make many knots, as if they took a pride In these strange foldings, and themselves did please In those admired Anastomoses" (1630), and finally, "Much of the Celtic ornament . . . consisted of an anastomosis, or network of often grotesque creatures" (1879).

To these examples the OED in a new edition might add the three uses of the word by Joyce, one in *Ulysses*, the others in *Finnegans Wake*. All three passages, and other analogous ones, such as my initial citation from *Ulysses*, play on the complexities inherent in the image of the line between one self and another as a figure for the way the self becomes itself, maintains itself, or grounds itself in the other. Joyce uses the word in a directly sexual sense. Anastomosis has for him a double reference: one to the invagination of the male member in sexual intercourse, I-thou relation par excellence, or as Joyce says, apropos of the lovemaking of HCE and ALP, "O I you O you me!";[16] the other to the twining back from navelcord to navelcord which relates us to all mankind and ultimately to the great mother of all, Eve. In one case the anastomosis is an external line linking one enclosed vessel, the self, to another or to others. In the other case, the self becomes itself by actual entry into the other or by being entered into in an anastomosis of the other sort. In this case the self is the line, not something joined externally to another self by a communicating channel. Taken together, the two forms of anastomosis in their multitudinous proliferations from generation to generation make an image of all men and women joined in an immense network of navelcords and sexual couplings. These taken together make a huge labyrinth or reticulated genealogical tree binding each man or woman to all the others back even to Eve. As the examples in the OED indicate, one anastomosis seems to call for another, and then another, in serial or netted proliferation, until a whole field of such connections is created, like a knitted or crocheted fabric, or like chain mail.

The first use of the word *anastomosis* in *Finnegans Wake* is of copulation, not birth. It comes at the end of the intercourse of HCE and ALP, when the cock crows and dawn comes. It amusingly superimposes images of religious or political union and schism on sexual terms, with an echo of Blake's call to the liberation of desire: "Humperfeldt and Anunska, wedded now evermore in annastomoses by a ground plan of the placehunter, whiskered beau and donahbella. Totumvir and esquimeena, who so shall separate fetters to new desire, repeals an act of union to unite in bonds of shismacy. O yes! O yes! Withdraw your member. Closure. This chamber stands abjourned" (FW, 585).

The other use of the word in *Finnegans Wake* is of great interest for my present exploration of the intersubjective line, though, like almost any passage from *Finnegans Wake,* it has a considerable plus value beyond that, which I shall not reinvest at the moment. To attempt a full exegesis of the passage would take me too far out of my line. The passage refers more to the navelcord than to the male member in anastomosis with the female vessel, though it is not exactly either. The sentence is descended from the single use of the word in *Ulysses*, in the Oxen of the Sun, where Elizabethan prose chronicles are being imitated. There the reference is to Eve, "our grandam, which we are linked up with by successive anastomosis of navelcords" and who "sold us all, seed, breed and generation, for a penny pippin" (U, 389). In *Finnegans Wake* this becomes a much more complex genetic image involving the famous letter dug up by the hen from the dump. The latter here becomes the breakfast egg containing all the genetic code inscribed in chromosomes carrying the message, born of all the sexual couplings since Adam and Eve. This message joins each one of us, link by link, back to the grandsire and grandam of all. It gives each of us in turn the chance to mate with another, to recombine the genetic letters once more, so passing them on to our children. We thereby become momentarily the intercommunicating vessel or anastomosis before we die and "go on to dirt dump" (FW, 615), leaving the immortal message to twine itself onward from generation to generation into the future. The passage itself, in all the games it plays with the combination, recombination, and superimposition of letters and of Greek and Latin roots, is an example of the thing it talks about, since the anastomosical permutation of all the letters of the alphabet, word flowing into word, meeting and mating with it, to produce new words as progeny, is a figure of and figured by the sexual couplings and genealogical transmissions that are the chief topic of the sentence:

> Our wholemole millwheeling vicociclometer, a tetradomational gazebocroticon (the "Mamma Lujah" known to every schoolboy scandaller, be he Matty, Marky, Lukey or John-a-Donk), auto-kinatonetically preprovided with a clappercoupling smelting-works exprogressive process, (for the farmer, his son and their homely codes, known as eggburst, eggblend, eggburial and hatch-as-hatch can) receives through a portal vein the dialytically separated elements of precedent decomposition for the verypet-purpose of subsequent recombination so that the heroticisms, catastrophes and eccentricities transmitted by the ancient legacy of the past, type by tope, letter from litter, word at ward, with sendence of sundance, since the days of Plooney and Columcellas when Giacinta, Pervenche and Margaret swayed over the all-too-ghoulish and illyrical and innumantic in our mutter nation, all, anastomosically assimilated and preteridentified paraidioti-

cally, in fact, the sameold gamebold adomic structure of our
Finnius the old One, as highly charged with electrons as hophaz-
ards can effective it, may be there for you, Cockalooraloora-
loomenos, when cup, platter and pot come piping hot, as sure
as herself pits hen to paper and there's scribings scrawled on
eggs. (FW, 614–15)

The full unraveling of this tightly woven text would be an almost
interminable job, work for the ideal sleepless reader Joyce wanted.
A preliminary net, however, can be easily knit to catch some of it.
A basic grid or groundplan can be laid out as the context for the
word *anastomosis* as Joyce uses it. The "Mamma Lujah" is both
the perpetually circling and regenerating ("vicociclometer") mother
principle, the mama of all, and at the same time the nuclear family
(Joyce said "Mamalujo" stood for Mama [Nora Joyce], Lucia, his
daughter, and Giorgio, his son). At the same time the "four-
housed" ("tetradomational") narrative mastering ("domator" is
Latin for tamer, [animal]-breaker), the ever-repeating family story
as told by Matthew, Mark, Luke and John, that is, all the not quite
synoptic versions of the universal narrative. A "gazebocroticon" is
a plausible (*krotêtikos,* Greek for plausible, from *kritikon,* Greek
for "choice," "picked out," critically) and choice gazebo or open
summer house, but also the place of erotic mixings. It is also a
good place to see these (by way of the fake Latin: gazebo, I shall
gaze) on an analogy with panopticon. A gazebocroticon is where
it all happens, over and over, but where it may all be seen happening, an egg with a view. This mothering power receives through a
portal vein (another anastomosis there) all the genetic material of
all the generations of the past reduced by decomposition to its
elements ("dialytically separated"), all the ancient legacy of the
past in the form of letters, figures, topes (in the sense of topoi,
places, commonplaces, traditional phrases), types (in the sense of
hieroglyphic characters), words, coming down from Roman times
(Pliny and Columnella), when wildflowers (periwinkle [Pervenche],
and daisies [Margaret]) bloomed in an Ireland as provincial and
inarticulate ("mutternation") and as uncanny as Gaul ("ghoulish"),
Illyria ("illyrical") and Numantia ("innumantic"—Numantia was
a city in Hispania Terracouninsis, Roman North Spain). The people
of the mother nation then were ghoulish, without lyrical power,
and lacking in *numen* or spirit, mere mutterers. This egg of all has
an internal or self-moving ("autokinatonetical") ability to join

these elements again in the "anastomosical" mixing of oestration, offering the egg ready for fertilization at Cockcrow ("Cockaloor-alooraloomenos"), as in the copulation of HCE and ALP. This leads to the passing on once more to the new generation of an atomic structure which is Adamic, as old as Adam, and at the same time "adomic," homeless, belonging promiscuously to all, a haphazard rearrangement of the genetic code and yet one more lawful generative message, already given its identity by its heritage ("pre-teridentified") and yet almost private or personal to that one assemblage of letters, like a proper name which is both specific to one person and yet joins that person to a family and a nation, to all humankind ("paraidiotically").[17]

Anastomosis for Joyce is a triple interpersonal linkage making and marking out the three "ecstacies" of time: past, present, future. Anastomosis joins each person to all the previous generations back to Adam and Eve. It joins man and woman in sexual intercourse, type of interpersonal relations in the "now" of present life. It passes the genetic message on to future generations through the new loop in the endless navel-cord, telephone line from alpha to omega. Joyce puts it in an eggshell: "eggburst, eggblend, eggburial and hatch-as-hatch can." As Jacques Derrida says in *Glas,* and as Joyce already knew, human temporality is generated by these family ties and cannot exist without them:

> Family time: there is no time except that of the family. Time passes only in the family. The opposition between already, not yet, already again, all that forms the time of the not being present (not there), all that constitutes time as the *Dasein* of a concept which is (not) there, the being there of the not there (one more not—not not there—or one less), is a family scene.[18]

For Joyce too "being there," human existence as *Dasein,* the presence of the self to itself, is hollowed out by temporality as anastomosis. In anastomosis the self is always outside itself. The presence of the self to itself in the present is the presence within that self not only of the other person who invades the self as the vessel of the body is invaded in sexual intercourse but, by way of that invasion, the presence as absence, "l'être là du pas-là," which that interpersonal relation repeats. For Joyce the self is beside itself, outside itself, and so the self is not a present self-enclosed entity, the "I am I" of self-reflection. It is all those anastomosical family links making HCE, Humphrey Chimpden Earwicker, also "Here Comes Everybody."

This multiplication of the self, its shadowing or inhabitation by ghosts in swarms, would not dissolve the self if the line of repetitions led back to a firm archetype, great granddaddy or grandmama of all. What, for Joyce, is the ground, the head, or source of this multiplied, temporalized self? Can one say that for Joyce the self grounds itself in interpersonal relations? Does the self find a solid base for itself in all those family links binding it to others, reenacting on a hundred stages at once the primal drama of mother, father, daughter, and twin sons? To answer these questions it is necessary to return to my initial epigraph for this chapter, the passage from Stephen's meditations in the "Proteus" section of *Ulysses*. What those "cords of all" are that "link back, strandentwining cable of all flesh," we now know in more detail. They are anastomoses in all their senses. But what, for Joyce, is at the head of the line, to get it started and to tie it down, giving it something to hang from, like the firm loop crossing from the first hole on the left to first hole on the right at the bottom of a shoelace?

At the head of the line must be whatever party is reached by calling Aleph Alpha nought, nought, one, that is, what comes before the first letter and before the first number. But this is, as the telephone number to Edenville indicates, not a positive creative power, not God, the all-making *Logos,* but nothing, a zero, an absence, the navel-lacking belly of Eve, "Heva," *Oheva,* Hebrew for "life," like a blank piece of paper, as Joyce says in the paragraph following my epigraph: "Heva, naked Eve. She had no navel. Gaze. Belly without blemish, bulging big, a buckler of taut vellum" (U, 43). From that doubling of the O ("nought nought") the first navelcord began, the phallus-shaped stick or line in its crisscross multiplication and division into segments, making the first letter of the Hebrew alphabet, the first letter of the Greek alphabet, and the first positive number ("Aleph, Alpha, . . . 1"), starting place of all letters, words, types, topoi, sentences, numbers, enumerations, and accountings. In Joyce's version of Western sexist or phallogocentric ideology not the male member but the female lack of member is the beginning. The "gaze" at that belly without blemish is Joyce's form of the male child's primal look at his mother naked and his discovery that she lacks a penis. The absence of the maternal phallus means the absence of an original ground or logos, measuring stick and giver of substance for all the selves descending in successive anastomoses, one after one, from that first double nought. "Heva, naked Eve" was as Joyce says in the same paragraph "spouse and helpmate of Adam Kadmon," the first man, and until then androgynously self-sufficient, able to mate with himself. As helpmate she broke that self-sufficient self-reflection and self-engendering, turning the circular mirroring into the spiral of all the generations, umbilical cord after umbilical cord. Eve brought the zero into the human equation, the lack of self we have all inherited. She was therefore the "womb of sin" (U, 43).

If Stephen gazes in imagination at the fabulous expanse of Eve's belly without blemish, the blank sheet on which all subsequent human characters were written, "as sure as herself pits hen to paper and there's scribings scrawled on eggs," he has a moment before imagined "mystic monks" gazing not at Eve's belly but each at his own omphalos, name not only for the navel, but for that universal center of the cosmos, the "omphalos" at Delphi. "That is why mystic monks," says Stephen to himself. That is why they contemplate by contemplating their navels. It is a way of becoming self-sufficient, like God, by initiating and maintaining an enclosed circuit of specular speculation, the self looking at itself and grounding itself in itself, like the "I am I" of God. The serpent promised deification to Eve and Adam: "Will you be as gods?" Mystic monks aim at the same goal by self-contemplation, trying to close that universal navelcord back in on itself in an O: "Gaze in your omphalos." Instead, as the rest of the passage indicates, they reach, by following the umbilicus back, not to the ground of themselves in the solid substance of God, but to that perpetual O, womb of sin, source in absence, the bulging belly of naked Eve, alpha, aleph, and omega too, start and finish of the whole human story. This belly lasts for all time. It is shining and perpetually fertile, but also perpetually virgin, uncut, unharvested. It is a principle of ever-renewed "Life," like a smooth heap of white grains of wheat, original seeds of all, as Joyce says in the phrases quoted from Traherne's *Centuries of Meditation* just following the comparison of Eve's belly to a buckler of taut vellum: "No, whiteheaped corn, orient and immortal, standing from everlasting to everlasting" (U, 43). In Traherne's *Centuries* Century 3, section 3, this is: "The Corn was Orient and Immortal Wheat, which never should be reaped, nor was ever sown. I thought it had stood from everlasting to everlasting." This in turn echoes the Bible, *The Song of Solomon* 7:2: "Thy navel *is like* a round goblet, *which* wanteth not liquor:

thy belly *is like* an heap of wheat set about with lilies." The

sequence is itself an anastomosical chain leading from text to text
(including those phrases from the Litany to the Virgin which so
fascinate the Stephen of *A Portrait of the Artist as a Young Man*)
back to the biblical passage where the image of the woman's belly
as like a heap of wheat is associated with a navel which is there,
not absent as in the case of Eve, but there as a hollow container,
the round goblet, figure again of the female. If the woman has or
has not a navel it comes to the same thing, or the same lack of
thing, from everlasting to everlasting. If Eve's belly without blemish
has stood from everlasting to everlasting as orient and immortal
wheat, she must not in any way have been "begotten," but be co-
eternal with God, or even precede and outlast the creator, or even
be herself the creator, ever-virgin and ever-fecund, the O from
which all letters and numbers, A's and 1's, emerge, a double O in
fact, O of the belly and O of the female genitals.

For Joyce, then, "intersubjectivity" is a Narcissistic attempt, like
that of the mystic monks contemplating their navels, to get back
to the beginning, the ground, the substance of oneself or of one's
self in the other. The goal is to recuperate that missing maternal
phallus, to find the 1 before 0 which by multiplying itself becomes
1: nought nought one. The 1 is the basis of all letters and numbers,
as, for example, the word for "letter" in German is *Buchstabe*,
literally "book staff." O and the single line of the staff or stick are
the primary numbers, as the stick is the basic element of all letters
of the alphabet. 0 and 1, female and male in their joining, generate
by anastomosical recirculation all the numbers and letters, as a
digital computer knows only zero and one, no and yes, but can be
programmed to say or to count anything.

The search for this primal one, Joyce's model indicates, is necessarily unsuccessful. At the back of the back the line loops back
on itself in a repeating absence, the double zero. All men and
women come from the zero, not from the one. Therefore each is
without ultimate ground for his or her selfhood. The one, the
straight line, the staff from which the A is made, Aleph or Alpha,
comes from the zero. Nought nought gives you one, and then the
whole chain follows from generation to generation. The letter A is
a basic model for anastomosis, the double line with a single source
at the apex crossed by a line or bar. The straight line, the staff, the
rod, goes back to the nought and is lost in it. Each man thinks he
needs the other, the woman, to be himself, to be securely in pos-

session of his masculine authority, as Willoughby needs Clara in *The Egoist*. This desire can never be satisfied, as Joyce has Stephen experience in that imaginary confrontation, his gaze at the vacant expanse of Eve's belly without blemish. This belly is the womb of sin, the first sin being the first coupling of the 0 and 1, making letters and lines of letters, types, words, sentences, the long looped, interrupted, crisscrossed navelcord taking mankind further and further away from the original 0, the omphalos, belly button of the world, and yet always remaining based on that lack of base, the O enduring from alpha to omega, everlasting to everlasting.

The Elective Affinities has possessed all along a disturbing power (ein trüber Einfluss). In congenial temperaments (verwandten Gemütern) this may rise to rapturous enthusiasm. In those who are alien to the novel the reaction becomes hostile consternation (widerstrebender Verstörtheit). Only an indefectible rationality (die unbestechliche Vernunft) is able to cope with it. Under the protection of such rationality the heart may dare to abandon itself to the prodigious, magical beauty of this work.[19]

To read a work of such power and beauty as Goethe's *Wahlverwandtschaften* takes some courage. My excuse is that I too have been overwhelmed by its beauty. Moreover, perhaps better than any other work of European fiction it dramatizes, within the form of the realistic novel, what is at stake in the use of line imagery to figure interpersonal relations. Whether my calculating exploration of the latter, protected I hope by an indefectible rationality, will allow me to abandon myself safely to the novel's prodigious beauty remains to be seen.[20]

That *The Elective Affinities* is stitched together by figures of lines there can be no doubt. In one passage Goethe (or the narrator) alerts the reader to look for the red thread of a recurrent theme running through Ottilie's diary, as the English king's ropes are indicated as belonging to him by such a thread wound through each: "Just so is there drawn through Ottilie's diary, a thread of attachment and affection (ein Faden der Neigung und Anhänglichkeit) which connects it all together, and characterizes the whole."[21] The nature of that red thread is by no means easy to identify. The narrator says it is there, however, and so it must be. The red thread in Ottilie's diary must have to do with the presence in everything she writes there of her love for Edward. This is said to be an

attachment (Anhänglichkeit), as though she were tied to him. None
of the diary entries, however, has anything directly to do with this love. It is not easy to detect the indirect presence of the red thread making these general reflections and maxims express Ottilie's affinity for Edward. Nevertheless, the red thread is always there, as could be demonstrated for each, and as I shall try to do later for some.

Ottilie uses the figure of the line herself when, near death, she writes, since she is past speaking: "I have stepped out of my course (Bahn), and I cannot recover it again" (E, 258; G, 209). A long catalogue could be given of places in the novel where the relation between one person and another is spoken of as a line, bond, or tie. Here are some examples. The narrator says of Ottilie, when her love for Edward has absorbed her whole life: "It seemed to her as if nothing in the world was disconnected (unzusammenhängend) so long as she thought of the one person whom she loved; and she could not conceive how, without him, anything could be connected (zusammenhängen) at all" (E, 190; G, 155). To Charlotte, on the other hand, her newborn son Otto seems "a new link (Bezug) to connect her with the world and with her property" (E, 204; G, 166). The estate itself is an externalized image of the relations among the people living on it. Newly planted trees and shrubs form a tie binding one part of the landscape to another, just as the characters are bound by kinship or affection: "already the young plantations, which had been made to fill up a few openings, were beginning to look green, and to form an agreeable connecting link (angenehm zu verbinden) between parts which before stood separate" (E, 205; G, 167). To give a final example, Edward, when he is determined to separate himself from his wife, marry her to his friend the Captain (now Major), and marry Ottilie himself, exhorts his friend: "Disentangle and untie the knots, and tie them up again (diese Zustände zu entwirren, aufzulösen, zu verknüpfen)" (E, 229; G, 186).

All those paths, roads, and boundary lines that wind their way through Edward's estate trace out literal lines. Those same lines are retraced in the Captain's carefully detailed scale drawing of the estate. Much attention is given, an attention that may seem excessive or irrelevant, to topographical details of the estate. The changes made in it are described in oddly precise elaboration, as though it somehow matters whether a path goes this way or goes that way, or whether a new summerhouse is put in this place or in that, or whether or not the old gravestones in a country church-yard are moved to make way for a new path.

The most important use of line imagery in *Die Wahlverwandt-schaften* is in the title and in the working out of the title's impli-cations in a passage in chapter 4, as well as in the story as a whole. The novel opens with a passage unostentatiously connecting the theme of estate building with the image contained in the title: "Edward—so we shall call a wealthy nobleman in the prime of life—had been spending several hours of a fine April morning in his nursery-garden, budding the stems of some young trees (junge Stämme) with cuttings (Pfropfreiser) which had been recently sent to him" (E, 1; G, 5). This sentence is a good example of the way everything in this novel counts. Items that function as apparently casual realistic details, put in for mimetic verisimilitude, are at the same time emblematic. In this case the image of grafting, the crossing of one genetic line with another, stands as a proleptic hieroglyph for the novel as a whole. A "Pfropf" is a stopper, cork, bung, or plug, as the abrupt stoppage of the "pf" at the word's start suggests. A "Reis" is a twig, sprig, or shoot. A "Pfropfreis" is a sprig inserted like a stopper into the stem of a growing tree. Grafting is a form of anastomosis. On all its levels—linguistic, topographical, psychological, and interpersonal—*Die Wahlver-wandtschaften* is a novel about such anastomosical crossings.

The image of grafting used as a figure for human relations appears once explicitly much later in the novel, when the Assistant gives his opinion about fathers and sons: "One form of activity may be woven (verweben) into another, but it cannot be pieced (anstückeln) on to it. A young shoot may be readily and easily grafted (verbindet sich) with an old stem, to which no grown branch admits of being fastened (anzufügen)" (E, 195; G, 159). Goethe here opposes weaving to grafting. The former is a super-ficial kind of joining in the sense that the threads remain separate and separable, even though they are woven together. Grafting, on the other hand, is an intimate joining of two lines so that their life continues thenceforth as one. One life flows into the other and draws life from the other. Grafting must be a true anastomosis or crossing, product of an elective affinity or Wahlverwandtschaft between planted stem and inserted new shoot, else they would not grow together.

The customary translation of the title, *Elective Affinities,* is the correct equivalent English idiom, but it does not exactly match the play of metaphor in the German word. The German word says chosen (*Wahl*)—related (*verwandt*)—conditions (*schaften*): conditions of being related that are chosen. The English suffix *ship* is not far from the German *schaft,* as in "relationship." The center of the word *Wahlverwandtschaften* is the image of relationship. The word *Verwandten* is the ordinary German word for relations in the sense of those closely tied by blood or marriage. (Benjamin uses the word as an adjective to describe those who have a special, perhaps dangerous, affinity for *Elective Affinities.*) Goethe too puts a strong emphasis on the notion that related things and persons are drawn to one another by powerful attractions. These lines of force pull things or persons which have an affinity strongly toward one another and make them want to meet, merge, combine, and make a new compound changing each thing from what it is into something else.

What a thing is in itself, for Goethe, is determined initially by its relation to itself. Its affinity for something else changes its self-relation, which is its self-identity. "In all natural objects with which we are acquainted," says the Captain, "we observe immediately that they have a certain relation to themselves (daß sie einen Bezug auf sich selbst haben)" (E, 32; G, 30). The Captain says this fact is "obvious," but it is an odd way to define an entity. It appears to say a given single substance draws its unity and singularity from the fact that it is double. Each entity is divided into at least two parts. Each part has not merely a relation to the other but a strong attraction to it. This makes the singleness and identity of the thing. A Narcissistic self-reflection is there already in the singleness of any thing or person. Goethe uses the word *Bezug,* which means "relation" but which has a root indicating an act of drawing toward. A train engine is in German "ein Zug." Every entity which is really single has as a main feature of its identity a strong tendency to hang together, as a drop of quicksilver will recombine if it is broken into fragments. All the little parts run back together into a single globular whole, best symbol since Parmenides of oneness: "When we were children," says Charlotte, "it was our delight and wonder to play with quicksilver, when we split it into little globules and let them run into one another again" (E, 33; G, 30).

Nevertheless, this oneness in all natural objects, made of self-relatedness, has also, apparently as a feature of its intrinsic power to enter into relation with itself, a tendency to enter into relations with other natural objects. Charlotte, anticipating the direction of the Captain's explanation, perhaps already foreshadowing her elective affinity for him, says: "As everything has a reference (einen Bezug) to itself, so it must have some relation (ein Verhältnis) to others" (E, 33; G, 31). The word translated here as "reference" is *Bezug* again, translated in the previous sentence as "relation." The word translated as "relation" in the second clause of the second sentence is "Verhältnis," perhaps a more neutral word, though it would be the word used to name an adulterous liaison.

Each thing has a potential affinity for many different other things, as a person has many blood relations and in-laws making up a network of connections, of "Verwandtschaften." With only one thing at a time, nevertheless, can it be joined. This bond's human correlative, for Goethe, is marriage and sexual union. Such a joining of objects seems a matter of choice, so strong is the attraction drawing two elements, say sodium and chlorine, together and producing of their merging a new substance, salt. The most interesting case is the one which manifests this power of election by showing an irresistible preference for this over that in a given substance. As Edward puts this: "Affinities (die Verwandtschaften) begin really to interest only when they bring about separations (Scheidungen)" (E, 35; G, 32). The example Goethe gives, or has the Captain give, in this little lesson in early nineteenth-century chemistry, is the power of sulfuric acid to displace the carbonic acid radical in limestone ($CaCO^3 + H^2SO^4 = CaSO^4 + H^2O + CO^2$):

> Thus, what we call limestone is a more or less pure calcareous earth in combination with a delicate acid, which is familiar to us in the form of a gas. Now, if we place a piece of this stone in diluted sulphuric acid, this will take possession of the lime, and appear with it in the form of gypsum, the gaseous acid at the same time going off in vapor. Here is a case of separation (eine Trennung); a combination (Zusammensetzung) arises, and we believe ourselves justified in applying to it the words "Elective Affinity" (Wahlverwandtschaft); it really looks as if one relation (ein Verhältnis) had been deliberately chosen (erwählt) in preference to another. (E, 35; G, 32)

The most interesting cases of all, however, are those where four elements, combined at first in pairs, substitute partners in a criss-cross exchange or chiasmus, each taking a new mate in a simultaneous quadruple manifestation of elective affinities. What was attraction becomes repulsion and is replaced by another irresistible attraction. This merging and flying away seems not only to indicate life and volition in inanimate matter. It also indicates an occult transcendent power at work in, and behind, nature: perhaps chthonic, below, profound; or higher up, hidden above. This universal power is an inner law that manifests itself differently in each particular all-compelling elective affinity but remains the same in its secrecy:

"And those are the cases which are really most important and remarkable—" [says the Captain,] "cases where this attraction (Anziehen), this affinity (Verwandtsein), this separating and combining, can be exhibited, the two pairs severally crossing each other; where four creatures, connected previously, as two and two, are brought into contact, and at once forsake their first combination to form into a second. In this forsaking and embracing, this seeking and flying, we believe that we are indeed observing the effects of some higher determination (eine höhere Bestimmung); we attribute a sort of will and choice (Wollen und Wählen) to such creatures, and feel really justified in using a technical word (Kunstwort), and speaking of 'Elective Affinities' ('Wahlverwandtschaften')." (E, 37; G, 33–34)

The German word translated here as "technical word" is *Kunstwort*. Goethe wrote "das Kunstwort Wahlverwandtschaften," "the technical word elective affinities." The word *Kunstwort* has a special valence in German missing in English. *Kunst* means "art." *Kunstwort* means the word peculiar to a certain "art" in the sense of a special mystery, such as the "art" of chemistry. It suggests also, however, "artistic word" or "aesthetic word," a word casting a beautiful veil of appearance over the substance it names, the veil of Maya, so to speak. An example might be the words Goethe uses to produce that magical beauty of *Die Wahlverwandtschaften* of which Benjamin speaks. Opposed to "Kunstwörter," technical words, are what in the English translation are called "symbols," in the German "Buchstaben," literally "letters," or more literally still, book-staves, from the staff- or stick-like lines used to make letters or runes. *Buchstäblich*, for example, means "literally."

The word *Buchstabe* has a complex resonance in the Germany of Goethe's time, since it is the word used by Martin Luther to translate the biblical "letter" of the law as opposed to its spirit, *Geist*. The question of the interpretation of the Bible or of literature generally—for example, the parables ("Gleichnisse") of Jesus—is also at stake in the term. We should take the Bible as literally true, Luther enjoined. But what would be meant by a literal, buchstäbliches, reading of Christ's parables? Is *Die Wahlverwandtschaften* itself to be read literally or spiritually, parabolically. What, exactly, would it mean to do either of these? One does not read far in *Die Wahlverwandtschaften* without feeling that, as in the Bible, every detail in this text, even seemingly irrelevant details apparently put in for mimetic truthfulness, are charged with significance. Whether these should properly be described as literal or as spiritual remains to be decided. The opposition between Geist and Buchstabe, with its biblical and Protestant overtones, like the opposition between written and spoken language, is fundamental to Romantic linguistic theory, for example, in the speculations about language of Friedrich Schlegel.[22]

A complex network of associations is present in Goethe's use of the word *Buchstabe* to name the opposite of *Kunstwort:*

> "I quite agree," said Edward, "that the strange scientific nomenclature (die seltsamen Kunstwörter), to persons who have not been reconciled to it by a direct acquaintance with or understanding of its object, must seem unpleasant, even ridiculous; but we can easily, just for once, contrive with symbols (Buchstaben) to illustrate the relation we are speaking of." (E, 37, translation slightly altered; G, 34)

The opposition between "Kunstwörter" and "Buchstaben" is analogous to the opposition between figurative language and literal language. This opposition is crucial to *Die Wahlverwandtschaften.* The novel dramatizes interpersonal relations in terms of the exchanges of figure and in terms of the relation between literal and figurative language. Or rather, it might be better to say that it expresses the exchanges of figure and the relation between literal and figurative language in the allegorical mode of interpersonal relations. The peculiarity of the "laws of language" is that one must use language to speak of them. No literal language about language exists. Nor is there an appropriate technical language, stable Kunstwörter, free of the metaphors of art in the sense of the aesthetically beautiful. The story of marriage, passion, and adultery that makes up *Die Wahlverwandtschaften* is an allegory of the laws, powers, and limitations of language. This is expressed literally, buchstäblich, in the bare letter symbols in the passage following the one just cited. In another sense, nothing could be more

figurative than expressing chemical or human relations by bare
symbolic letters. It seems to be difficult, both in the words of the
novel and in the imaginary world those words describe, to name
the literal literally. To that problem I shall return. It is the fundamental issue in *Die Wahlverwandtschaften*, both in Goethe's own
language and in the story he tells. Meanwhile, here is his example,
given in the Captain's speech, of the buchstäbliches, a way of
speaking through reference to letters drawn with straight or curved
lines to make the capitals of the alphabet:

> "Suppose an A connected (verbunden) so closely with a B, that
> all sorts of means, even violence, have been made use of to
> separate them, without effect. Then suppose a C in exactly the
> same position with respect to D (das sich eben so zu einem D
> verhält). Bring the two pairs into contact; A will fling himself
> on D, C on B, without it being possible to say which had first
> left its first connection, or made the first move toward the sec-
> ond." (E, 38; G, 34)

This is just the way the exchanges of metaphor have been defined
in the Western tradition since Aristotle. Every metaphor can be
reduced to a proportional relation: A is to B as C is to D. As in
all ratios, the terms are potentially interchangeable, so that A is to
C as B is to D. A can replace C in relation to D. B and C then
mate. The lines can be redrawn to make a new ratio giving the
same equivalence: A/B = C/D or A/C = B/D. The basic paradigm
of *The Elective Affinities* is the following: human relations are like
the substitutions in metaphorical expressions. Or, to put it the
other way, since these metaphorical analogies are reversible: the
laws of language may be dramatized in human relations. Edward
explicitly makes this application in a passage just following the
one quoted above. The passage comes at the end of the chapter
establishing the universal natural law the novel exemplifies. Edward does not yet know that the irresistible new Bezugen, attractions, he and the others will manifest will not be the ones he
imagines. They will be affinities destroying his marriage by replacing Charlotte with Ottilie in his own love and putting the Captain
in Edward's place in Charlotte's affections. Nevertheless, what he
says allows for that possibility and anticipates it. The formula does
not tell which of the possible combinations will be stronger than

the others, breaking bonds and making them in defiance of any human or divine law, such as the law of faithfulness in marriage:

> "Now then," interposed Edward, "till we see all this with our eyes, we will look upon the formula as an analogy (Gleichnisrede), out of which we can devise a lesson for immediate use. You stand for A, Charlotte, and I am your B; really and truly I cling to you, I depend on you, and follow you, just as B does with A. C is obviously the Captain, who at present is in some degree withdrawing (entzieht) from you. So now it is only just that if you are not to be left to solitude, a D should be found for you, and that is unquestionably the amiable little lady, Ottilie. You will not hesitate any longer to send and fetch her." (E, 38; G, 34–35)

Edward has understood the law but he is unable yet to make the right application of it. The reader in retrospect can do so, however, as the story unfolds recounting Edward's irresistible adulterous passion for Ottilie, hers for him, and the scarcely less powerful attraction of the Captain and Charlotte for one another.

The model of exchange and relationship worked out in this early chapter is exemplified on three levels in the novel: on the level of interpersonal relations, on the level of the language, and on the level of the building of roads, paths, gardens, lakes, and houses on Edward's estate. On all three levels the paradigm seems to be the same. A literal, self-related substance is related to other such substances by lines or channels of force. These make possible transformations of that substance in which it nevertheless retains its identity. It becomes truly itself in those relations to another. This, it will be remembered, is one mode of relationship expressed by the word *anastomosis*. The title of Goethe's novel might be translated as "chosen anastomoses."

On the linguistic level, the concept of figurative language depends on stable referential meaning. Reference gives a substantial virtue to words. They borrow substance from the things they literally name. The power manifested by the exchanges of metaphor depends on carrying over this literal energy of words into the new context. There the words in combination with other words are used in a translated, transposed sense.

In the changes of the landscape effected by Edward and his household, the four lovers project a model of their changing relations on the estate. They draw it out as on a map, giving their

relations external embodiment in the rocks, trees, water, paths, and
houses they have reshaped, as a building is man-made but rests
solidly on the earth below. The phrase "the wedlock of the stone
with the earth (die Verbindung des Steins mit dem Grunde)" (E,
64; G, 55) describes the ritual laying of the cornerstone for the
new house Edward builds on the hilltop. He places it there because
Ottilie has chosen the spot as best. Goethe, or his narrator, reports
in the prose the poem the young mason speaks at the ceremony.
This is in deference, one may suppose, to the prosaic language of
the novel as a genre. The oddness is that this is a prose translation
of a poem that does not exist, as perhaps the novel as a whole
may be said to be. The novel is, it seems, the literal which can give
the affective, the lyrical or spiritual, only in "an imperfect rendering
(unvollkommen wiedergeben)" (E, 63; G, 55), but surely no words
could be more artful than Goethe's in this text.

Interpersonal relations, for which the other two levels function
as parables, obey the same laws. Each person has in Goethe's view,
so it seems, a substantial selfhood. This enters into relations with
others. In doing so it becomes more truly itself. It changes but only
to become what it already is. Like transpositions of language and
estate building, intersubjectivity is securely grounded on a hidden
energy. This energy manifests itself especially in the intrinsic tendency of substances at all three levels to combine preferentially
with certain other substances. These tendencies are stronger than
conventional human laws, such as laws of marriage, even though
the latter may seem to have God as their sanction. Such tendencies
appear to be the Buchstabe that is stronger than any Geist.

———

The ontologically grounded system I have sketched would seem
to be a firm base for a total reading of *Die Wahlverwandtschaften*.
Such a reading would move back and forth among the various
analogies, from the theme of landscape design and estate building
to the crisscross relations among the lovers, to the functioning of
the text's language, in which everything is meaningful, "geistlich"
and "buchstäblich" at once. Like Ottilie's beauty, the novel's dan-
gerously beautiful surface is grounded on metaphysical laws this
surface manifests. Seen from this point of view, the novel is an
admirable demonstration of the relation between European aestheticism and Occidental metaphysics. Far from being incompatible, these are mutually sustaining, as they appear to be, for example, in Hegel's *Ästhetik*. Metaphysics generates aestheticism,

that mode of art in which the highest value is a surface of beauty open to the senses and feelings. In poetic language this is a surface made of figurative transformations and substitutions. Even the seeming glorification of adulterous passion over the obligations of the marriage bond in *Die Wahlverwandtschaften,* troubling to readers of the novel from its first appearance, is, in this reading, only apparent. The divine ground of marriage in God's law and the chthonic ground of the elective affinities that draw Edward to Ottilie, Charlotte to the Captain, are in the end reconciled. God's law is stronger than the law of the elective affinities. Or it may be that the former makes use of the latter. Or perhaps the the latter is no more than another manifestation of the other, mysteriously altered, a figurative version of which God's law is the literal base. It is not only Ottilie's power to resist her love for Edward that makes her saintly. The passion itself touches her with spirituality. It manifests her attunement with powers more than human. The body of Ottilie, dazzlingly beautiful still in death, visible yet through the lid of her glass-covered coffin, has a miraculous healing power. The bodies of the two lovers, Edward and Ottilie, dead of their unfulfilled passion, lie finally side by side in the village church, their fate accomplished:

> Falling asleep as [Edward] did, with his thoughts on one so saintly (die Heilige), he might well be called blessed (selig). Charlotte gave him his place at Ottilie's side, and arranged that thenceforth no other person should be placed with them in the same vault. . . .
>
> So lie the lovers, sleeping side by side. Peace hovers above their resting-place. Fair related images of angels (heitere verwandte Engelsbilder) gaze down upon them from the vaulted ceiling, and what a happy moment that will be when one day they wake again together! (E, 274, translation slightly altered; G, 222)

Goethe himself seems to have given full support to this religious-aesthetic-metaphysical interpretation of the novel in a statement he wrote, using the third person about himself, in explaining its title:

> It seems that this strange title was suggested to the author by the studies he carries on in the realm of physical sciences. No doubt he has noticed that, in the natural sciences, one very

commonly uses ethical comparisons (ethischer Gleichnisse), in order after a fashion to bring nearer to the domain proper to human knowledge matters which are strongly distant from it; so it is possible that in the case of a moral situation (einem sittlichen Falle) he has more willingly taken a chemical image (eine chemische Gleichnisrede) back to its moral sources (sittlichen Ursprunge) because there exists inversely only one single and unique nature and because the kingdom of serene rational freedom (heiteren Vernunftfreiheit) is continually traversed by the indications (die Spuren) of a compulsion of the passions which can only be effaced—and, here below, always in an imperfect way—by a force which comes from higher up (eine höhere Hand: a higher hand).[23]

The ethical realm, the realm of the natural sciences, and the realm of transcendent grace are here distinguished only to be joined in the concept of a single and unique "nature" where all work together, even if not always harmoniously. What Goethe says seems to confirm unequivocally the interpretation of the novel as grounded in a totalizing ontology.

Many details of the novel support the idea that Goethe sees selves as indestructible preexisting substances, securely grounded in some transhuman being. Interpersonal relations are lines of connection drawn between selves so conceived. These lines confirm the selves but do not essentially alter or determine them.

This concept is presupposed, for example, in what the narrator says about the difference between Ottilie's feeling for Edward and her feeling for the Architect: "Her feelings for him [the Architect] remained at the calm unimpassioned level of blood relationship (der ruhigen leidenschaftslosen Oberfläche der Blutverwandtschaft). For in her heart there was no room for more; it was filled to overflowing with love for Edward; only God (die Gottheit), who interpenetrates all things, could share with him the possession of that heart" (E, 162; G, 134). The German word for blood relationship here, *Blutverwandtschaft*, uses the same stem as that in the Wahlverwandtschaften of the title. The word translated as "level," *Oberfläche*, means more properly "surface." *Oberflächlich* means "superficially." Ottilie's relation to the Architect, like blood relations in general, to which it is compared, is a superficial tie that does not involve the depths of her self. It is an anastomosis in the sense of a link between two preexisting vessels of selfhood that does not essentially change those vessels. Even Ottilie's relation to Edward, however, is here spoken of in a figure which suggests that she is such a preexisting container. She is a fixed sheltering reservoir of selfhood filled to overflowing with her love for Edward. Her selfhood is not changed in its shape by that love. What fills her is her love for Edward, not Edward himself. This form of self-reflexive anastomosis, container occupied by thing contained, self overflowing with its dominant feeling, is hardly an intersubjective relation at all. It is, however, interpenetrated and shared, in that sense sustained, grounded, by the ubiquitous "Gottheit," more properly "Godhead" or "divinity" rather than simply God, as the translation has it. This Godhead interpenetrates all things ("alles durchdringt") without filling them and can even be present in the place where Ottilie's love for Edward leaves no room for any thing else.

Another confirmation that this theory of interpersonal relations is present in *Die Wahlverwandtschaften* is the character named Mittler. The word *Mittler* means "mediator," "intermediary." Mittler is a vigorous spokesman for the conventional, religious, biblically grounded view of selfhood and of interpersonal relations. His self-imposed function is to bring peace back to divided families and to preserve the sanctity of the marriage bond. For Mittler, each person as a self-enclosed container connected to another person by some mediating third term—for example, the divine ritual of marriage: "whom God hath joined let no man put asunder." Mittler admirably embodies and speaks for this concept of anastomosis.

Important aspects of *Die Wahlverwandtschaften,* however, are not fully accounted for in this reading. They seem disturbingly at variance with it, even at variance with the interpretation Goethe gave of his novel. These features lead to an entirely different reading of the novel. *Die Wahlverwandtschaften* is an example of the heterogeneity characteristic in canonical works of the Western tradition. An understanding of the alternative paradigm of anastomosis in *Die Wahlverwandtschaften* must be approached slowly, by carefully reading salient passages. The second concept is intertwined throughout the novel with metaphysical notions about intersubjectivity.

An example of this doubleness is Mittler's failure to function as an intermediary keeping the peace in families and keeping married people still married. He fails to persuade Edward to remain faithful to Charlotte. He does not prevent the Count and the Baroness from living happily together outside wedlock. The speech he makes at the baptism of Otto, child of Charlotte and Edward, but in reality "the offspring of a double [imaginary] adultery (aus einem doppelten Ehbruch erzeugt)" (E, 234; G, 191), causes the aged minister to drop dead on the spot. Mittler's passionate speech against adultery and in praise "of that duty which holds man and wife indissolubly bound together (unauflöslich verbindet)" (E, 265; G, 215) is accidentally overheard by Ottilie and is the immediate cause of her death. In order to take Mittler, as he sometimes is taken, as Goethe's spokesman in the novel, the voice of Goethe's own judgment in favor of socially and religiously lawful marriage, Mittler's negative effect on people when he tries to mediate must be suppressed. Whenever Mittler rushes impetuously onto the scene to mediate between its personages in the name of the sacred laws of human relations as expressed in the Ten Commandments he succeeds only in causing them suffering, dividing them further, even killing them in two cases. One might say this represents Goethe's dramatization of God's judgment against these wicked people for their disobedience of his laws. This would, however, hardly apply to the gentle and good minister, unless his acceptance of Charlotte's plan to move all the gravestones in his little church-yard is such a disobedience. Mittler's failure as a *Mittler* indicates that Edward, Ottilie, and the other characters do not exist as persons in a way compatible with the traditional biblical or, more broadly, metaphysical conceptions of selfhood and of interpersonal relations. Far from being a conservative work defending the sanctity of marriage, as Goethe himself sometimes wanted to think it was, *Die Wahlverwandtschaften* is, on one side of its sustained ironic double meaning, a radical questioning of the marriage bond.

The second model of interpersonal relations is present in the motifs of writing and reading that thread their way through *Die Wahlverwandtschaften*. This model is also present in the opposition between spoken language and written language. The importance of the latter opposition was of course fully recognized in Goethe's time, for example in the linguistic speculations of Rousseau and Condillac, or, a little later, in those of Friedrich Schlegel. In Schlegel's thought the distinction between voice and writing, *Laut* and

Schrift, is closely analogous to the distinction between Geist and Buchstabe, since *Buchstabe* means "letter" in the sense of written letter of the alphabet, and *Geist* is "logos" in the sense, among others, of voice, spoken word.

The themes of writing, speaking, and reading are introduced here and there, apparently casually, in the early pages of the novel. One example is a letter from Ottilie's school, before she joins Edward and Charlotte on their estate, informing Charlotte that "there is a complaint of [Ottilie's] handwriting. They say she will not, or cannot, understand how to form her letters (ihre Unfähigkeit die Regeln der Grammatik zu fassen)" (E, 26; G, 25). The translation here is a little loose, but it extrapolates in the right direction. Literally Goethe says "over her unaptness to grasp the rules of grammar." The context indicates that the rules of grammar must here mean the conventions whereby spoken language is recorded on paper in writing. Ottilie's radical strangeness, the impossibility of assimilating her into the ordinary give and take of family or society, is indicated in her inability to accommodate herself to the rules of grammar. She is exorbitant in relation to any rules. But if Ottilie seems maladroit in her writing at school, later on, when she has joined the family at the castle, she is able to imitate Edward's handwriting exactly. It is through this outward sign that Edward knows she loves him. Later still, after her vow of silence, which, as she says, she takes "too literally, perhaps (vielleicht zu buchstäblich)" (E, 258; G, 210), she communicates with other people only in written letters, in Buchstaben. How can she be both unable to write and adept at doing so?

The theme of writing as the graphic representation on paper of something with a different form of existence also appears early in the novel in the Captain's preparation of a "magnetic survey (die Gegend mit der Magnetnadel)" (E, 21; G, 21) of Edward's estate:

> Edward saw his possessions grow out like a new creation upon the paper; and it seemed as if now for the first time he knew what they were, as if they now were properly his own (sie schienen ihm jetzt erst recht zu gehören).
>
> Thus there came occasion to speak of the park, and of the ways of laying it out; a far better disposition of things being made possible after a survey of this kind, than could be arrived at by experimenting on nature, on partial and accidental impressions. (E, 21; G, 21)

To transfer something to a graphic representation is to take possession of it, to make it one's property, proper to oneself. A map takes the outside inside, so to speak. It facilitates further transformations making exterior a model of the interior, the objective landscape a model of subjective feelings. Edward does this later when he redesigns his grounds and builds a new lodge on the hilltop. He makes his estate a schematic map of his relations to Ottilie, to Charlotte, and to the Captain.

The novel itself, with its careful descriptions of the landscape around the castle, is the transfer to paper, in the words of the narration, of an imaginary topography. Within that topography Goethe's story of passion and infidelity enacts or embodies itself. It can thereby be appropriated by each reader. Like Faulkner's *Light in August* or Hardy's *Return of the Native,* Goethe's novel creates an imaginary, internalized landscape. This subjective space could be mapped, though the mapping would reveal anomalies indicating that something unmappable undermines the congruity between landscape and interpersonal relations. Edward's estate is a country of the mind. Within the novel it provides an indispensable means of expressing relationships among the characters. These enact their drama of attraction and repulsion, their dance of desire, within a given set of places with lines between or around—houses, lakes, walls, gardens, woods, roads, paths, streams, bridges, boundaries. What is problematic about this aspect of realistic novels is, however, more properly the property of another chapter in another book.[24] The two corridors of narrative theory here momentarily overlap.

I have used the discussion in the novel of elective affinities to establish the presence of an aesthetic and ontologically grounded interpretation of interpersonal relations in *Die Wahlverwandtschaften.* But this discussion is just preceded by a curious sequence of paragraphs. These, if they are taken literally, at face value, undermine proleptically such an interpretation. The sequence has to do with reading and with reading into. It is part of a line of such passages threading its way through the novel.

One evening Edward reads aloud to the others out of a scientific book. The discussion by Edward, Charlotte, and the Captain of elective affinities arises from this reading. Edward, the narrator tells us, has as "one of his especial peculiarities . . . that he could not bear to have anyone looking over him when he was reading" (E, 30; G, 28). Charlotte casts her eyes on the page as he is reading aloud about chemical affinities. Edward flashes into an anger that seems excessive, though he explains its reasons. It is a passage of great importance for the novel as a whole:

> "When I read aloud to a person," [he says,] "is it not the same as if I was telling him something by word of mouth? The written, the printed word, is in the place of my own thoughts, of my own heart. If a window were broken into my brain or into my heart, and the man to whom I am counting out my thoughts or delivering my sentiments, one by one (meine Gedanken einzeln zuzählen, meine Empfindungen einzeln zureichen), knew beforehand exactly what was to come out of me, should I take the trouble to put them into words? When anybody looks over my book, I always feel as if I were being torn in two." (E, 30–31; G, 29)

This remarkable passage proposes a curious theory of reading aloud. It also offers an odd explanation of the feeling of exasperation each of us has when someone reads over his or her shoulder. Reading aloud is for Edward an inward and self-reflexive activity. It is an activity in which the inward is carefully externalized, over a period of time. It is thereby made available to others, made interpersonal rather than intrapersonal. For Edward the traditional, Platonic relation between written and spoken language is reversed. In Plato, and for the Western tradition generally, speech comes first. Written language is secondary to that. Writing is a supplement. It is an aid to memory and therefore an atrophy of memory, since what is written down does not need to be remembered. For Edward the hierarchy is reversed. It is reversed by a substitution. For him, written or printed language, "stands in place of my own thoughts, of my own heart (tritt an die Stelle meines eigenen Sinnes, meines eigenen Herzens)." In this replacement, what is there first is the words on the page. It is as though the mind and heart were a printed text. Reading aloud is the transfer of written language into the externalizing mode of spoken language. When writing or printing stand in the place of thoughts and feelings, in this reversal of the traditional hierarchy, spoken language is the supplement of writing. This is possible because in the initial "standing in place of" the writing replaces nothing. When I read aloud or silently to myself the words on the page create my thoughts and feelings. They generate ex nihilo my subjective state. Intersubjectivity, in this model, is the transfer of those thoughts and feelings, so generated, to another person by reading aloud as opposed to reading silently.

The narrator expresses this in an economic metaphor. Edward's thoughts and feelings are counted out, or delivered ("zuzählt, zu-reichet") one by one ("einzeln"), parsimoniously, as I might give someone a carefully measured allowance or pay out bit by bit interest calculated at intervals. This reading aloud communicates my state of mind to another. Since this state exists initially in the latent condition of the words on the page of the book I am reading, the trajectory from book to mind to other minds is always vulner-able to being short-circuited. If another person reads over my shoulder she sees what I intend to parcel out "one by one," in a temporal series, already laid out in a simultaneous spatial pan-orama. This anticipates the future state of mind that does not yet exist. It also preserves the one that falls into the past as I finish reading the first words on the page. I then have two different existences, for the overlooker and even for myself. I exist in the temporal form generated by reading aloud. I exist also in the spatial form created by the other's reading over my shoulder. That reading is experienced as though the other person had a little window into my brain and my heart. Therefore he or she knows beforehand exactly what is to come out of me ("immer schon lange vorher wissen könnte, wo es mit mir hinaus wollte"). The result is that Edward feels as if he were being torn in two. He exists twice, in two ways, a temporal way and a spatial way, a spoken way and a written way. This is experienced as a painful violence to the self. This pain explains Edward's flash of unreasoning anger against Charlotte.

This early scene also allows the reader to understand what it means when, later in the novel, Edward does not mind when Ottilie reads over his shoulder as he reads aloud. He reads now not scientific books but love poetry. "Indeed," says the narrator, "he would frequently make longer stops than necessary, that he might not turn over before she had got to the bottom of the page" (E, 60; G, 52). The meaning of this strange change in Edward is made explicit later, shortly before Ottilie dies. While she is obeying her vow of silence and is secretly starving herself to death, Edward returns to his habit of reading aloud: "He seated himself in the same position as he used to do, that she might look over his book; he was uneasy and distracted unless she was doing so, unless he was sure that she was following his words with his eyes" (E, 261;

G, 212). Goethe explains Edward's change in a description of his achieved unity with Ottilie: "To be near was enough; there was no need for them either to look or to speak; they did not seek to touch one another, or make sign or gesture, but merely to be together (nur des reinen Zusammenseins). Then there were not two persons, there was but one person in unconscious and perfect content, at peace with itself and with the world" (E, 260; G, 211). Since Edward and Ottilie are one person, his reading aloud while she looks over his shoulder is a single act performed by a single unified consciousness. They do not need to make any sign to one another in order to communicate, since their communion is already total. Her looking over his shoulder does not tear him in two, since it is performed by another part of himself. Because she is already within his soul, she does not break into his mind and heart when she looks over his book. The reading of Edward and Ottilie projects signs from within a single person toward other people. It is not a mode of communication between them. Since his consciousness is generated by what he reads, his state of mind is ratified by her silent reading as he reads aloud. His existence is substantiated by that other half of himself, his mirror image, Ottilie.

That they are destined to be joined and unified in this way is indicated in another apparently inconsequential but in fact emblematic passage. It is another example of the universal parabolic mode of this book. This makes the text ironic throughout. It is always saying one thing and meaning another, always suspending its own "realistic" discourse, for the knowing reader, in order to say something that subverts the aesthetic, metaphysical, religious, mimetic meaning the narration on the first level seems unequivocally to affirm. In this case, Edward hears, even before Ottilie has joined the others at his castle, that she suffers from headaches on the left side. "It is really very polite," he says, "in this niece to be subject to a slight pain on the left side of her head. I have it frequently on the right. If we happen to be afflicted together, and sit opposite one another—I leaning on my right elbow, and she on her left, and our heads on the opposite sides, resting on our hands, what a pretty pair of facing pictures (Gegenbilder) we shall make" (E, 42–43, slightly altered; G, 38). The importance of the word *Bild* and its variations, here present in the word *Gegenbilder*, facing pictures, will be identified later on. Edward and Ottilie are seen by Edward, even before he has met her, as mirror images of one another, like facing pictures in which it cannot be told which is the original, which the copy. They seem to him two halves of a matching whole, like Narcissus and his image in the water, or like Narcissus and his beloved twin sister, in another version of the myth, or even like Narcissus and that Echo in whom he refuses to recognize his counterpart. When this identity has been accomplished, not just anticipated in a figure, what one performs the other performs too, for example, the double act of reading, he aloud, she silently.

———

The apparently casual motif of reading over one's shoulder, introduced three times at widely spaced intervals in *Die Wahlverwandtschaften*, defines the nature, for Goethe here at least, of both subjectivities and intersubjective relations. To read is to exist. I exist because I read. I come into existence when I read. The act of reading is, for Goethe, the originating moment of subjective life and therefore of whatever relations there may be between subjectivities. This metaphorical extension of reading to cover all human activities, perceptions, and social relations, all acts making sense of the world, changing it, or using it, is made explicit at several points in the novel.

The most important of these follows just after the passage in which Edward flashes out in anger against his wife when she reads over his shoulder. In a tactful attempt to appease his anger she explains that she had lost the thread of what he was reading and had looked over his shoulder to get on the track again. She had been misled by a double meaning latent in language that switched her mind from one line of thought to another. "I heard you reading something about Affinities (Verwandtschaften), and I thought directly of some relations (Verwandten) of mine, of two cousins who are just now occupying me a great deal" (E, 31; G, 29). Edward's response makes a generalization that would lead to a linguistic or rhetorical rather than ontological reading of *Die Wahlverwandtschaften*. Like the ontological reading, the rhetorical one is woven into the text, articulated there like a white thread intertwined with the red one. The novel's lines of self-interpretation contradict one another. The meaning of the novel arises from this contradiction. Each way of reading generates its subversive counterpart and is unable to appear alone.

"It was a comparison (eine Gleichnisrede) which led you wrong and confused you," Edward explains to Charlotte. "The subject is nothing but earths and minerals" (E, 31, altered; G, 29). This might seem to imply that earths and minerals are without ambiguity, something literally there that can be described in literal language, buchstäblich. Charlotte, however, has, as Edward says, been misled by the "comparison." The German word here, *Gleichnisrede,* contains one of the usual words for metaphor, figure, or parable: *Gleichnis.* It is impossible to be sure whether Edward means she has been misled by taking the word *Wahlverwandtschaften* to refer to human relations, whereas actually it is a technical term, a "Kunstwort" referring to chemical affinities, or whether he means, as is perhaps more probable, to call attention to the fact that the "Kunstwort" is actually a metaphor borrowing a term for human relations to describe impersonal chemical reactions. Charlotte has been misled by taking the word literally, as though it were a word used as it might be in ordinary domestic life. Goethe's sexist presumption of a female penchant for taking words literally plays a crucial role in determining the circumstances of Ottilie's death. But the "Kunstwörter" are metaphorical. They are a projection from the human realm to what is outside it. They read inanimate nature as if it were human.

The particular *Gleichnis* in question here is personification, the projection of human qualities into natural objects that are not persons at all. Ruskin was a few years later to condemn this as the pathetic fallacy. The technical rhetorical term for personification is prosopopoeia. This means, literally, giving a human face or a mask to something or someone. By extension it names the figure projecting a name, a face, or a voice into the absent, imaginary, or dead. *Prosopón* is Greek for face, mask, dramatic character, and *poiein* is "to make," the root in "poetry." *Die Wahlverwandtschaften* is an extended allegorical investigation of prosopopoeia in a "realistic story" of marriage and adulterous passion. Such an allegory is an example of what it investigates. It gives human faces or masks to what are impersonal laws of language. The novel is the genre that most systematically and most covertly does this. Personification is any novel's basic presupposition, its founding convention. In indirect discourse, for example, the narrator speaks for the characters, giving a name, face, and voice to imaginary people. One reason for the importance of *Die Wahlverwandtschaften* among major Western novels is the way it brings to the surface this fundamental generic law. This novel foregrounds its own conditions of being.

This law is explicitly formulated in the sentence that follows

Edward's remark to Charlotte. Here is the passage in German: "Es
ist eine Gleichnisrede, die dich verführt und verwirrt hat, sagte
Eduard. Hier wird freilich nur von Erden und Mineralien gehan-
delt, aber der Mensch ist ein wahrer Narziß; er bespiegelt sich
überall gern selbst; er legt sich als Folie der ganzen Welt unter"
(G, 29).

In reading this passage it will be helpful to reflect on another
form of displacement here: translation. I have used primarily the
English translation of Froude and Boylan, with the interpolation
here and there of German words that are particularly important
or difficult to translate. I have not reflected directly about problems
of translation involved in writing an essay in English about this
novel. But Goethe's novel is in part about translation, in an extended sense of that word. Scientists transfer a word that names
human relations to describe transformations among earths and
minerals. Prosopopoeia translates interactions among inanimate
objects into interpersonal relations. The issue of translation, carrying over, transference, displacement, *Bild* in the double sense of
representation in another medium and metaphorical transposition,
is present everywhere in *Die Wahlverwandtschaften*. The novel is
not only difficult to translate. It is also *about* translation. The novel
contains its own oblique commentary, before the fact, on the problems that will be encountered in translating it or commenting on
it, that is, in creating a new text in a different language that will
be grafted on the original and draw its life from that original, while
being as different from it as a grafted tree is from the rootstock
on which it grows.

A list of the diverse examples in *Die Wahlverwandtschaften* of
such insertion would almost be a recapitulation of all the thematic
and linguistic material that makes up the novel. The novel opens
with a scene in which Edward is grafting new shoots on his trees,
carrying the life of the old trunk into the new growth, just as
Ottilie's diary and the interpolated novella are grafted within the
normal third-person narration of the text. They translate its concerns into other languages, as do the two scenes of *tableaux vivants*
that occur at crucial moments in the action. The apparently irrelevant attention to landscape design and to the question of portraits
and gravestones translates into other thematic domains the central
concern of the main action. That action, along with its interpretative figure, the image in the title, has to do with the question of
what is involved in the transfer of affections from one person to

another and with what is involved in the use of the term *Wahl-verwandtschaften* to name such displacements. This word is carried over from the necessitarian realm of the natural sciences (that borrowed it in the first place from the human realm) to personify the irresistible affinities of one person for another as if they were "elective" or willfully "chosen" (*gewählt*).

The passage calling man a true Narcissus is translated by Ryan as follows: "'It is a figure of speech that has distracted and confused you,' said Edward. 'The book is dealing with minerals and different types of earth, but man is a real Narcissus—he finds his own image everywhere and sees the whole world against the backdrop of his own self'" (112). Froude and Boylan translate the passage differently: "'It was the comparison which led you wrong and confused you,' said Edward. 'The subject is nothing but earths and minerals. But man is a true Narcissus; he delights to see his own image everywhere; and he spreads himself underneath the universe, like the amalgam behind the glass'" (31). Hollingdale, finally, renders it this way: "'It is a metaphor which has misled and confused you,' said Edward. 'Here, to be sure, it is only a question of soil and minerals; but man is a true Narcissus: he makes the whole world his mirror'" (50).[25] *Gleichnisrede*, as can be seen, is translated variously in the three versions as "figure of speech," "comparison," and "metaphor." Hollingdale conflates and curtails the last two phrases, though he keeps the image of the mirror. *Folie* is "amalgam" in Froude and Boylan, and "backdrop" in Ryan. Her translation effaces the image of the mirror, obscures the enigmatic precision of Goethe's *Gleichnisrede,* and avoids puzzling aspects of the original by hiding them behind a much blander English transposition.

Goethe, by the way, says "der Mensch," meaning presumably "mankind," all men and women. But the question of gender difference is fundamental in this novel. To put this another way, Ottilie's Narcissism is radically different from Edward's. I shall return to this issue.

Do the nuances of difference among these translations really matter? Well, for one thing, the obliteration in Ryan's translation of Goethe's definition of man as not just like a "backdrop" but like that particular backdrop that makes the silvering of a mirror obscures the relation between this passage and an exceedingly odd one that comes later when the Captain begins his explanation of Wahlverwandtschaften for Charlotte: "An allen Naturwesen, die wir gewahr werden, bermerken wir zuerst, daß sie einen Bezug auf sich selbst haben" (G, 30). "With all natural objects the first thing we notice is their relation to themselves" (Ryan, 113). When this definition is transposed from natural science to man, as the Captain *does* transpose it, it defines "man" as strangely doubled within himself in the sense that the primary or initial definition of man is that he has a relation to himself. This relation is a strong drawing of himself to himself, "ein Bezug." It is another way man is a true Narcissus. "Relation," though it is an entirely appropriate English word, misses the implication of a strong attraction of man to himself in "Bezug." One figure or "Gleichnisrede" proposed by the Captain for this ties this passage to the image of man as the amalgam behind the glass in a mirror: "Und schon als Kinder spielen wir erstaunt mit dem Quecksilber, indem wir es in Kügelchen trennen und es wider zusammenlaufen lassen" (G, 30). "And when we were children we found it fascinating to play with mercury, dividing it into little balls and letting it run together again" (Ryan, 113).

Goethe's word *Folie,* translated by Ryan as "backdrop," by Froude and Boylan as "amalgam," and omitted altogether by Hollingdale, means, according to *Cassell's German Dictionary,* "foil; thin leaf of metal; film, silvering (*of mirrors*); (*fig.*) background, framework, basis of comparison." Mirrors were originally made of polished metal. Such mirrors survived in common use into the nineteenth century at least, as is attested by George Eliot's use of such a mirror, the pier-glass, as the basis of a comparison in a celebrated passage in chapter 27 of *Middlemarch.* Goethe must mean that more modern kind of mirror made by backing a piece of glass with silvering or Folie. *Silvering* means coating with an amalgam made of mercury and tin or silver, so mercury is present both in Goethe's image of each person as the foil of a mirror and in his image of individuals as bits of quicksilver that have a strong attraction bringing them back to a larger globular whole.

Ryan's effacement of the image of the mirror keeps the reader from trying to figure out just what Goethe, or Edward, means by saying man is a true Narcissus. This effacement is achieved by selecting the figurative meaning of Folie, "backdrop," rather than its literal meaning, "silvering." It is impossible to be sure whether we are meant to take what Edward says merely as a reproach to Charlotte for interpreting what he has been reading as applying to her own preoccupations with her troublesome relations, or whether we are to take it, as the context of the rest of the chapter might justify doing, as a reproach to the scientists (and others) who Narcissistically project human qualities such as will or choice into inanimate objects. What Edward says could be taken both ways, though the two ways go in opposite directions.

The scientists use prosopopoeia to construct their Kunstwörter. The metaphors behind these terms are then forgotten. The words come to be taken as literal. *Wahlverwandtschaften,* for example, is the proper technical term for the special "preferential affinities" certain chemical elements have for one another. The literal word is then metaphorically projected again into human relations in a prosopopoeia in reverse that is a regular feature of such a play of figure. Another example is the way George Meredith personifies nature in his poetry but then in his novels borrows terms from that personified nature to define the subjectivities of his characters. In *Die Wahlverwandtschaften,* each of these linguistic operations, that of the scientist, that of Charlotte, appears to be grounded in the literal referentiality of the other, but the other, when examined, turns out to be already a figure drawn from that realm into which it is now being redisplaced. No unambiguous literal reference can be found in the use of language on either side, as Edward's initial definition of the particular way man is a true Narcissus recognizes.

The peculiarity of this definition lies in the way it sees man as an absence, as the neutral and invisible possibility of taking on this or that image, rather than as a preexisting, substantial self. Man is a true Narcissus who loves to see his own face everywhere in the mirror of the world. He "delights to see his own image everywhere," as the Froude and Boylan translation puts it. Goethe's German is "er bespiegelt sich überall gern selbst," literally, "he reflects himself willingly everywhere." *Spiegel* is "mirror" in German. Man does this, however, by spreading himself behind things like the thin layer of "amalgam" behind a sheet of glass that makes it a mirror.

The German word *Folie* not only has the dictionary meanings I have cited. It also may be impossible to keep out shadowy overtones from other languages, as well as the full semantic and figurative range in German. *Folie* in French means "folly" or "madness." A "foil" is a fencing foil. "To foil" is to frustrate or impede, as in "foiled again." A "foil" is a fold or leaf, as in "folio," the fold of a book, or as the leaf put behind a jewel to set it off is its foil, or as the goldleaf used as background in glass mosaic or medieval painting is a foil. The figurative meaning of German *Folie*

as "background, framework, basis of comparison" allows for these
contradictory possibilities. Both a backdrop and a framework are
foils in the sense of contrasting or opposing elements setting off
what is put in front or framed. There is a major difference, however, between setting off by framing and setting off by putting
behind, especially when what is put behind is the invisible foil of
a mirror that never shows itself, but only shows what is reflected
in it. *Folie* as "foil" in the sense of "basis of comparison," finally,
is yet another figurative use. It makes "foil" the vehicle of a metaphorical analogy, as in the comparison here between the silvering
of a mirror and man. "Folie" here is a "Folie" for man; foil is a
foil for man. Once again, as in the cases of "Bild," "Zug," and
"Verwandt," the example is also *about* the figurative displacement
it exemplifies.

Far from being a fixed self that can see its own image in the
water, as Narcissus did, man, in Goethe's definition here, is without
face or figure. Each person is neutral, invisible, without fixed image
or character, like the invisible foil behind a mirror. Each person
puts this nonentity under the whole world, including other people,
as if he were the world's ground, but a ground without substance.
The image of himself he sees everywhere is made of the figurative
transfer to himself of all the objects he confronts. This happens,
for example, in the rest of this chapter. The chemical image is
applied by Charlotte, Edward, and the Captain to the relations
among themselves and to Ottilie. But the objects each person confronts are already in themselves, as they are confronted, examples
of personification. We see them by way of the anthropomorphic
projection of human qualities into inanimate objects.

Edward, Charlotte, and the rest name human relations in a figure
drawn from the behavior of chemicals. Man sees himself in rocks,
trees, and water. But if man reads the world in human terms,
personifies it, in turn he reads himself in terms of those personified
inanimate objects. Man has no images for himself but those generated by his reflecting himself everywhere. He has no terms for
inanimate objects but those illicitly projected from the human
realm. As the Captain says, "That is how man sees everything that
lies outside him: his foolishness and wisdom, the willed random
nature of his own actions (seinen Willen wie seine Willkür)—these
he imputes (leiht er) to animals, plants, the elements and the gods"
(G, 29; Ryan, 112). This passing back and forth is the substitution

of figure for figure in a constant interchange without literal ground on either side. It names objects with figurative transfers of human terms that are already themselves figurative transfers of natural terms, in a ceaseless coming and going.

"Animals, plants, the elements and the gods"—this odd hierarchy moves down only to leap up at the end. Or perhaps the gods are chthonic, beneath the elements. As they exist for man, they may be as much a projection of human qualities on what does not have them, as much prosopopoeias, as are personifications of the elements, as in the term "elective affinities." What is missing in this slightly twisted or fragmented version of the classic chain of being is man himself. Man, in Goethe's (or Edward's) definition of him here, is now no longer higher than the animals and a little lower than the angels. "Der Mensch" is no more than the transparent, colorless, invisible, insubstantial foil (in the duplicitous sense of baseless "base of comparison") that serves as the reflecting background for the whole chain.

———

The novel presents many examples of the projection of human qualities into animals, plants, elements, and gods, but the important case of projection or "reading into" is not named here. It is rather manifested in the passage itself and in the novel as a whole. This is each person's Narcissistic reading of his or her own qualities into other people in "interpersonal relations," for example, in love. The passage describing man as a true Narcissus is a key to the interpretation of the novel, but the key must be displaced metaphorically, turned to fit the reading of one person by another as well as the reading of animals, plants, elements, and gods.

This extension of the motif of "reading into" is made in a number of passages. These function as a chain of allegorical emblems moving from the earth of graveyards to animals, to portraits, to works of art, to tableaux vivants, to living persons. The passages in question are splendid examples of the subtlety of *Die Wahlverwandtschaften*. Apparently casual passages almost always function as signs of something else. These "signs" are cases in which the discreetly anonymous and ironical narrator has put himself as foil under the psychological social details he is apparently only reporting. He makes those details into oblique images of his own face, that is, of his own reading of the world.

In the episode of the country churchyard, Charlotte, as part of her laying out of new paths and walkways around the estate, moves all the old gravestones from the little churchyard. She has them set in a neat row against the church. She does this so she can make the churchyard into a green lawn with a path going through it. This desecration of holy ground is part of the topographical theme of estate planning that runs all through the novel. One family whose members have for generations been buried in the churchyard protests this desecration. They send their lawyer to explain that the family is withdrawing its annual gift to the church. This becomes the occasion of a discussion of the relation between external signs, in this case gravestones with their inscriptions, and the buried reality these signs mark, in this case the bodies of the beloved dead. For the lawyer, a gravestone with its inscription should be the sign of the direct and immediate presence of the body and even of the person of the beloved dead:

> Yet this stone it is not which attracts (anzieht) us; it is that which is contained beneath it, which is entrusted, where it stands, to the earth. It is not the memorial so much of which we speak, as of the person himself; not of what once was, but of what is (nicht von der Erinnerung, sondern von der Gegenwart). Far better, far more closely, can I embrace some dear departed one in the mound which rises over his bed, than in a monumental writing which only tells us that once he was. In itself, indeed, it is but little; but around it, as around a central mark (Markstein), the wife, the husband, the kinsman, the friend, after their departure, shall gather in again. (E, 132; G, 110)

The lawyer here assumes the immediate and living presence of the signified to the sign. In the case of graves, he assumes the presence of the person himself, not just his body, to the central mark that indicates him. This mark is not only the gravestone with its inscription, but the actual mound of earth (Grabhügel).

Charlotte and the Architect, on the other hand, hold to an alternative semiotic theory. For them a sign is a memorial, the indication of an absence. The sign therefore does not need to be in physical proximity to what it signifies. A dead body dissolves into the earth in which it is buried. It is not necessary to remember exactly where it was put. "The pure feeling of an universal equality (Gleichheit) at last, after death," says Charlotte, "seems to me more composing than this hard determined persistence in our personalities, and in the conditions and circumstances of our lives (Anhänglichkeiten und Lebensverhältnisse)" (E, 133; G, 110). Since Charlotte feels this way it has seemed to her no desecration to move all the gravestones of the little churchyard. The Architect supports her in this and articulates the theory of memorial monuments that justifies her action. "It is not from remembrance," he says, "it is from *place* that man should be set free (nicht vom Andenken, nur vom Platze soll man sich lossagen)" (E, 134; G, 111). If this is the case, then the mounds of earth should be allowed to disappear, to be smoothed over. The monuments and inscriptions may be placed anywhere, "not sown up and down by themselves at random, but erected all in a single spot (an einem Orte), where they can promise themselves endurance" (E, 134; G, 111).

In accordance with this theory the Architect redecorates the side chapel of the church with all sorts of earthly and angelic figures taken as he needs them from his copies of such figures. He has also made a collection, neatly compartmentalized, of weapons, implements, and artifacts taken from old Germanic barrow-graves. These have been wrested, like the pictures he paints on the chapel wall, from their proper places and made into purely aesthetic signs: "These solemn old things, in the way he treated them, had a smart dressy appearance, and it was like looking into the box of a trinket merchant" (E, 137; G, 114).

The two theories of inscription here express the two semiotic theories and the two consequent theories of interpersonal relations between which the novel remains poised. In one case the sign is grounded in a nonlinguistic reality, the reality of a physical object or the reality of a person. The sign gives immediate access to this. In the other theory, the sign is free-floating. It has nothing behind it. Therefore it is not tied to any particular place. It creates the reality to which it seems to refer out of its own aesthetic surface, out of its relation to other signs, and out of the activity of reading (or "reading into") by which the spectator interprets it. This reading projects into the sign a ground it does not have. The novel everywhere indicates, most subtly in its central story, that men and women are continually beguiled into living according to the first theory of signs while the human condition is in truth defined by its subjection to the second. The second notion of signs acknowledges that instinctive and universal prosopopoeia whereby man sees his own face in the mirror of the world, while believing he is seeing something objectively there outside himself, earth, minerals, plants, animals, works of art, other persons, gods—something that will found and support his selfhood.

In one episode, Ottilie's headache when she goes near a spot on the estate associated with Edward is interpreted by a visitor as her "affinity" for a deposit of coal in the earth there. Experiments with a pendulum, somewhat like modern methods of "dowsing," are performed. These convince the visitor that Ottilie is in special resonance with earths and minerals. The reader, on the other hand, knows that the headache is a sign of her love for Edward. It is a sign of that mutual Narcissism whereby each reads the other as the mirror image of himself or herself. The mirror as an emblem of man's Narcissism reappears in connection with baby Otto's drowning. Recounting this, the narrator speaks of "the broad mirror (Spiegel)" of the lake (E, 233; G, 190), and, after the catastrophe, of its "glassy water (Wasserfläche)" (E, 237; G, 193). In another episode, Charlotte's daughter Luciana and her fashionable guests look at a book with illustrations of apes. Luciana amuses and somewhat scandalizes the others by her malicious gift for seeing the faces of her acquaintances in the faces of the apes. "The sight of these hideous creatures, so like to men (menschenähnlichen), and with the resemblance even more caricatured by the artist, gave Luciana the greatest delight" (E, 154; G, 127).

As for the gods, an emblem of man's Narcissistic relation to them is Ottilie's interpretation of the drowning of little Otto as the fulfillment of a malign "destiny (Geschick)" (E, 246; G, 200). This, she thinks, has implacably imposed itself on her, while the reader knows, if he or she follows the interpretation given by the text, that this is only Ottilie's way of explaining a "fate" she has imposed on herself through her infatuation with Edward. The narrator, too, in Froude and Boylan's translation, uses the term *destiny,* for example in speaking of the dead child Otto as "the first offering to a destiny full of ominous foreshadowings" (E, 244). The German original, however, says "eines ahnungsvollen Verhängnisses" (G, 198). These events ominously "hang together" for the narrator. But this is because man's "destiny" is his predicament as a "true Narcissus," maker and reader of signs that are always his own face in the mirror of the world. Ottilie's misinterpretation makes her seem to herself a victim of a malign destiny. "[The Assistant] will learn to see in me," she says, "a consecrated person, lying under the shadow of an awful calamity, and only able to support herself and bear up against it by devoting herself to that Holy Being who is invisibly around us, and alone is able to shield us from the dark powers which threaten to overwhelm us" (E, 248; G, 202).

———

Elemental matter, animals, gods—it is as though Goethe were systematically distributing here and there throughout the novel a series of allegorical examples of man's Narcissistic relation to all these. But the most important members of this series show one character reading his or her own image in the countenance of another person. One version of this is the discussion of portraits (Bilden) that grows out of the disagreement between Charlotte and the lawyer about the proper relation of gravestones and monuments to the bodies of the dead. The word *Bild* is crucial to this discussion. The relation between sign and body ("sema" and "soma," in the old Greek play on words) is connected to the function of portraits, particularly portraits of the dead. The Architect says, apropos of his claim that a funeral monument need not be placed next to the corpse of the person it commemorates, that "at all times the fairest memorial of a man remains some likeness (eigenes Bildnis) of himself. This better than anything else, will give a notion of what he was; it is the best text for many or for few notes (er ist der beste Text zu vielen oder wenigen Noten)" (E, 134–35; G, 111). The image here is apparently of a musical score set to a verbal text, another form of translation. Charlotte says this supports her claim that a gravestone does not need to be contiguous to the body it commemorates, but she confesses also that a portrait generates in her an odd sense of guilt. This arises from the absence of the pictured from the picture: "The likeness (Bild) of a man is quite independent (unabhängig); everywhere that it stands, it stands for itself, and we do not require it to mark the site of a particular grave. But I must acknowledge to you to having a strange feeling; even to likenesses (die Bildnisse) I have a kind of disinclination. Whenever I see them they seem to be silently reproaching me. They point to (deuten auf) something far away from us—gone from us; and they remind me how difficult it is to pay right honor to the present (die Gegenwart)" (E, 135; G, 112).

Ottilie in her diary also discusses the function of portraits. This occurs in the first diary entry the narrator gives the reader. The diary is Ottilie's self-portrait, outlined by that red thread of attachment and affection characterizing her. The text manifests the issues it discusses. It presents a portrait, and it identifies the problematic of portraits. Ottilie's diary is strangely impersonal. It is made up of aphorisms, quotations, and general reflections. These

function, the narrator says, as an indirect expression of her love
for Edward and as an analysis of the quality of that love. The diary
is an unwitting self-portrait, a translation of what Ottilie is into a
picture in words.

The diary begins with an entry in which Ottilie imagines how
good it is to think of resting in death beside the body of the one
we love. Her ultimate "destiny" is to lie in death beside Edward
in the little chapel, but Ottilie's thought also tells the reader something about the nature of her love while she is alive. The image of
love's fulfillment in the contiguity of two corpses leads directly to
Ottilie's reflections on pictures. "Of the various memorials and
tokens (Denkmale und Merkzeichen) which bring nearer to us the
distant and the separated," writes Ottilie, "—none is so satisfactory
as a picture (Bildes)" (E, 139; G, 115). Ottilie then suggests what
seems, if one thinks of it, an odd figure for this bringing together
of the distant by means of a figure or picture, a representation.
The German word *Bild* means figure in the sense of figure of speech
as well as figure in the sense of picture. Goethe is unostentatiously
playing on this play in the word in all this section of the novel.
The problem for a translator is that the play disappears in an
accurate and fluent translation. The translation says "picture" or
"portrait," "figure" or "metaphor," while the German says "Bild"
and so connects to one another all the passages in which this word
appears. The associations of "Bild" with the cognate *Bildung* ("education") are altogether lost in translation. The effort to translate
brings these losses into the open, develops it, as a photographic
film is developed, though the finished translation obscures it again
when it is read by someone who does not know German. Froude
and Boylan, for example, translate "Keins ist von der Bedeutung
des Bildes," in the passage just cited, as "none is so satisfactory as
a picture" (E, 139), while Hollingdale translates this as "none is
more meaningful than the portrait" (Hollingdale, 164), and Ryan,
in the most recent translation, renders it by : "None has as much
significance as does a picture" (Ryan, 181). Each translation has a
slightly different nuance of meaning in English, though each is
accurate enough. All lose the association of *Bild* with metaphor,
and "von der Bedeutung" is a German idiom that has no easy
English equivalent, though it seems clear enough in German.

"To sit and talk to a beloved picture (mit einem geliebten Bilde),"
Ottilie writes, "even though it be unlike (unähnlich), has a charm

in it, like the charm which there sometimes is in quarreling with a friend. We feel, in a strange sweet way, that we are divided and yet cannot separate" (E, 139; G, 115). What an odd idea! Few people, I think, sit and talk to a picture, loved or hated. A picture or portrait (which is it?), according to Ottilie, brings together and keeps separate. It is a mediation, like a quarrel, an anastomosical channel that at the same time marks the permanent distinction between the two vessels it joins. All portraits are unlike in the sense that they are not the same thing as what they represent, just as all translations are unlike the original. What Froude and Boylan translate as "to sit and talk to a beloved picture" is given by Hollingdale as "being with a much-loved portrait" (164), and by Ryan as "To converse with the portrait of a loved one" (181). Hollingdale suppresses the strange idea of a conversation with a portrait in favor of the much tamer "being with." Which is correct, or is either rendering an "unlike" portrait of the original?

In the next diary entry Ottilie shifts again, this time to a surprisingly different figure and to a different theory of "Bilder." The actual encounter with "a present person (einem gegenwärtigen Menschen)," without intermediary, is, writes Ottilie, often like an encounter with a picture ("als mit einem Bilde"). In moving from the intermediary to the immediate, we remain still with the intermediate, as if we were confronting a representation. To put this another way, as Charlotte has already put it, a picture stands for itself, as a person's face does. Neither is a representation of anything else. This, the reader will remember, is just what Wittgenstein says about pictures in those passages discussed in the chapter on character here. Our relations to a picture and to a person are the same. They mix presence and absence, the immediate and the mediate, in a way not allowing measurement of the representation's validity by setting it against what it represents. The relation always remains one between spectator and picture, image, figure, Bild. "We look at him [a present person], we feel the relation (Verhältnis) in which we stand to him; such relation can even grow without his doing anything toward it, without his having any feeling of it: he is to us exactly as a picture (ohne daß er etwas davon empfindet, daß er sich eben bloß zu uns wie ein Bild verhält)" (E, 139; G, 115–16).

Ottilie then goes on to observe that the difficulty of portrait painting lies in the fact that the painter must paint not the person but the relation of the spectator to the person, and not just his own relation, but that of everyone else too: "They [portrait paint-ers] must gather up into their picture the relation (Verhältnis) of everybody to its subject, all their likings and all dislikings" (E, 140; G, 116). A person's face is not what it is. It exists as its relations to all who know the person. It is analogous in this to a sign. A sign also is a configuration of matter that is not what it is, since it includes its interpretation as part of itself, as well as its differential relations to all other words in the same code, even its relations to all the languages into which it may be translated.

At the end of this first section from her diary Ottilie returns to the relation between pictures and the dead. If a portrait preserves a person after death, the picture too is mortal. It too eventually will crumble. With its vanishing will vanish also the signified of which it was the sign, since the portrait brings its referent into existence rather than merely pointing to something that could and does exist without it: "We may fancy the life after death to be as a second life, into which a man enters in the figure, or the picture (im Bilde), or the inscription (Überschrift), and lives longer there than when he was really alive (in das man nun im Bilde, in der Überschrift eintritt und länger darin verweilt als in dem eigentlichen lebendigen Leben). But this figure (Bild) also, this second existence, dies out too, sooner or later" (E, 140; G, 116). The phrase "im Bilde" is translated here as "in the figure, or the picture." Froude and Boylan for once acknowledge the fact that *Bild* may mean "figure" as well as "picture." Hollingdale gives this as "which you enter as a portrait or an inscription, and in which you remain longer than you do in your actual living life" (165), while Ryan translates it as "entered into as if into a picture whose inscription lingers longer than in the real life we live" (181). Hollingdale adds an "or" where the German has a comma of apposition, while Ryan produces the odd notion that the picture disappears while its in-scription remains. But surely Goethe is referring here to the funeral portrait with its inscription, both together at once a portrait and a figure of the dead person. Both meanings of *Bild* are required, as Froude and Boylan recognize, though with the reservation of an "or": "in the figure, or the picture." But though no English phrase may render in one noun the significance of "im Bilde" in German, the effort to translate this apparently simple locution brings some-thing important about both languages into the open.

The quietness of Ottilie's diary may obscure the radical nature of what she often says there, as in this case. The afterlife, in her picture of it, is not the dead person's entry into a transcendent realm sustained by God. It is that person's entry into a second existence generated and kept in being by figures—portraits or epitaphs, pictures or writing. These figures other men and women have made as memorials of the dead. Since such signs, support of the person's second life, are made of the same fragile matter as the body when it was alive, they are subject to the same mortality. They too will die. In their death—for example, in the crumbling of a tombstone—the person dies again, this time for good. The spiritual immortality promised in the New Testament is, it seems, only a figure for the transient immortality created by the figure, "das Bild" in all its senses, that universal prosopopoeia whereby someone sees his or her countenance in the face of another and then projects elsewhere figures of that mask.[26]

In the admirable sequence in *Die Wahlverwandtschaften* going from the lawyer's remarks to those of the Architect, to those of Charlotte, to those of Ottilie, Goethe has presented in intertwined complexity several different theories of figure. He has in addition made for the reader an application to interpersonal relations of the notion that man is a true Narcissus. That application is essential to the interpretation of the main story. At least three different notions of figure figure here, with a number of intermediate positions also indicated.

For the lawyer, the value of a sign, a picture, a figure, or an inscription lies in its proximity to what is signified. The gravestone should be above the body because only the presence of that body, dead though it is, gives validity to the sign. This is a mimetic, representational, or phenomenal theory of signs.

For the Architect, Charlotte, and Ottilie, in slightly different ways and in only part of what they say, a sign brings near the distant, the absent. Its functioning depends on the absence of what it signifies. It is free of place. It need not and indeed should not be near what it represents. It makes what it signifies present in its absence, though it still depends for its meaning and function on the existence of that signified.

In what Charlotte says about the picture standing for itself, therefore being free not only of the signified's location but even of its existence, a third theory is presented. The sign is now seen as creating what it signifies, rather than merely pointing to it either close at hand or out of sight. What Ottilie says of our relation to a real person being like our relation to a picture carries this a step further. Our relation to a living person is like our relation to a

sign, but a sign of the odd sort that has no preexisting reference.
The person is created in our response to his or her face or figure.
We read a personality into the face that confronts us. This reading
into is like the interpretation of a Bild as figure of speech, as well
as Bild as likeness, portrait. The Bild in question is, however, that
odd figure of speech encountered so often here in the corridors of
Ariadne's maze. It is another version of catachresis, the figure that
is neither figurative nor literal, since its referent cannot be brought
forth from the unknown to be compared to the sign for it. If a
person's face is like a picture in this sense, interpersonal relations
are necessarily Narcissistic. I always read my own face in the mirror
of other people. We can never encounter another person face-to-
face in that person's otherness or enter into a direct relation with
that otherness, though indirect relations to it may obscurely determine our fate.

These contradictory concepts of Bild are essential to the meaning
of Goethe's novel. But this complexity is obscured by translations
that use different English words for what is expressed in German
by a single word. Or it might be said that the novel is a Bild of its
meaning, while the translation is a Bild of a Bild, in all the senses
of that word. Those senses are both traduced and produced by the
failure of the translation to be adequate to the original. This failure
occurs not through some contingent and remediable error of translation but through an intrinsic recalcitrance of the two languages.
The original text is a catachresis generating a meaning that depends
on the material complexity of the word *Bild,* while the translation
in its inadequacy is like a portrait (Bild) that in its unlikeness to
the original expresses more our relation to the meaning gestured
toward by the original than to that original in itself.

The sequence I have just followed links elemental matter, dead
bodies, funeral monuments and inscriptions, portraits, and the
faces of those we love. All are regions for the exercise of man's
incorrigible Narcissism. All are opportunities for him to display
his propensity to see everything as figure or in figure, to see figuratively. Another episode, that of the tableaux vivants, makes explicit the connection of this Narcissism with the act of reading and
with the interpretation of works of art. The episode also shows
what is involved in interpreting other persons by their appearance,
their mute gestures, figure, face, and posture.

Luciana turns the household upside down to create a series of living emblems for her guests. Each of these imitates the motionless silent intensity of one or another well-known historical painting. The episode of the tableaux vivants may remind the reader that *Elective Affinities* itself is made up of the verbal unrolling along a temporal axis, in action and speech, of a series of such "tableaux." The novel is a sequence of discrete "finished" episodes. Each advances the story one step further toward its catastrophe. At the same time each serves as an allegorical reading of the story or as a model by means of which the reader can make such a reading. Each such episode sticks in the mind as a single image which has been discursively analyzed by the narrator and which the reader further interprets or uses as an instrument of interpretation. Each is like a dead person's picture which, as the reader will remember, "is the best text for many or for few notes." In Luciana's tableaux vivants this basic strategy of Goethe's narrative is brought into the foreground. It is given in silent emblems. The narrator's commentary on these gives the reader hints about how to read *Die Wahlverwandtschaften*.

Luciana is the center of the first set of tableaux. In a later one arranged by the Architect Ottilie is the central figure. All involve in one way or another a woman who is in a relation of paradoxical subordination to and simultaneous superiority over a man who is father, husband, lover, or son—in the perfect case all four. With a sure instinct, an instinct that does not bode well for her future husband's presumably rightful domination over her, Luciana chooses figures of masculine authority who are in one way or another dependent or impotent in relation to the woman they love. The *Belisarius* of Van Dyck (now ascribed to the Genoese painter Luciano Borzone), Poussin's *Ahasuerus and Esther,* the *Father's Admonition* of Terborch—each fits this pattern. In performing the *Belisarius* Luciana plays the young woman in the background of the painting who is counting out alms into the hand of the seated, blind, deposed general. Belisarius was once conqueror for Justinian of the Vandal kingdom of Africa and the Gothic kingdom of Italy. He is now a wandering beggar in Constantinople. In the case of Poussin's *Ahasuerus,* Luciana chooses to play the part of Esther. Esther saves her people by her appeal to the great Persian king who has chosen her beyond all other women and who has made himself subject to her through his love. Luciana then casts herself as the daughter in Terborch's *Father's Admonition.* In that painting the daughter is scolded, but not too severely, by her father, while the mother watches in sly complicity.[27] Luciana stands with her back to the audience, as the daughter does in the picture. She will not turn around even when the spectators cry out to see her from the front. The reference to reading appears at this point. It is one of many apparently casual figures in *Die Wahlverwandtschaften* reminding the reader that the whole novel is an allegory of sign reading, that is, of what the reader is that moment doing: "The spectators could never be satisfied with demanding a repetition of the performance, and the very natural wish to see the face and front (Angesicht) of so lovely a creature, when they had done looking at her from behind, at last became so decided that a merry impatient young wit cried out aloud the words one is accustomed to write at the bottom of a page, 'Tournez, s'il vous plaît,' which was echoed all round the room" (E, 167; G, 137).

To look at another person, this passage implies, is to look at a picture, as Ottilie has said earlier in her diary. To look at a picture, however, is like reading a written text. It is a picture of that activity, a figure for it. The person's figure is not seen as what it is, but as a trope for antecedent literary and pictorial structures. In this case the precursors are not only a specific painting but the more universal episode of family relations that painting represents: father, mother, and daughter at a certain moment in their relation, or the subversive parody of that in client, whore, and whorehouse matron. In spite of the immobility of the tableau, the figure of the person in it, in this case Luciana seen from behind, is a function in a system of signs. These draw their meaning from their relation to one another back and forth along a temporal line. In spite of its stillness the tableau has the intrinsic capacity to be repeated: "The spectators could never be satisfied with demanding a repetition (Wiederverlangen) of the performance." The tableau exists as the perpetual repetition, in the present, of its lack of self-enclosed presence, since it exists as its reference backward and forward to what it stands for, as is the characteristic of signs, such as those in a written text. The spectators' demand for repetition is also a desire to still this oscillation, to get to the bottom of the representation. This is indicated by the way their pleasure in the repetition becomes an impatient desire to see Luciana's front and face. The cry of "Tournez s'il vous plaît," "please turn over," or simply "over" in modern English convention, is a desire to untrope the trope, to turn it back. The spectators want to get to the literal that is the ground of the figure, as one might turn from the emblematic reverse of a coin to the face on the obverse. (*Bild* is the word in German for the face of a coin.) This desire cannot be satisfied. Luciana steadfastly refuses the spectators' desire to see her front. She is a trope without depth or ground, drawing its meaning only from sideways references. There is nothing but bare canvas on the back of Terborch's *Father's Admonition*. To put this another way, if one were to see her face one would only be seeing another figure, another Bild or Bildnis, never a literal ground of the play of tropes. When the reader of a letter obeys the invitation to turn over she confronts not the "real person" who has written the letter, but only more writing. Luciana, who is usually all superficial chatter and mobility, is in the tableaux vivants for once silent and motionless. Her silence and immobility manifest not only the emptiness behind her noisy motion, but also the vacancy behind all the pictures and figures *Die Wahlverwandtschaften* displays. This vacancy is revealed not least in the novel's demonstration that in interpersonal relations no man or woman can ever encounter the "real self" of another person. The "other" is nothing, for himself or herself and for others, but picture, trope, figure.

The function of the belated tableau in which Ottilie appears as the central figure may be identified in the light of what I have said about Luciana's tableaux. This will allow a transition, as a conclusion for this chapter, to a reading, in the context of all that has been said so far here, of the central drama of *Die Wahlverwandtschaften,* of Edward and Ottilie's love. All the emblematic episodes I have discussed so far teach the reader to read that love in a certain way.

After Luciana's departure, the Architect contrives for Charlotte a Christmas Eve representation in real figures of the manger scene. Ottilie takes the part of Mary. First the scene is presented almost in darkness, with the only light proceeding from the Christ-child. Then, after an interval, the whole display is exposed in a blaze of light, a "splendour perfectly infinite (eine ganz unendliche Hellung)" (E, 179; G, 147). The presentation is a motionless tableau. No specific painting is being represented. Rather the whole iconographic tradition of the Nativity is echoed:

> When the curtain rose, Charlotte was taken completely by surprise. The picture (Das Bild) which presented itself to her had been repeated so often in the world, that one could scarcely have

expected any new impression to be produced. But here, the reality as representing the picture (die Wirklichkeit als Bild) had its especial advantages. . . . By good fortune the infant had fallen asleep in the loveliest attitude, so that nothing disturbed the contemplation when the eye rested on the seeming mother (scheinbaren Mutter), who with infinite grace had lifted off a veil to reveal her hidden treasure. At this moment the picture seemed to have been caught, and there to have remained fixed.

. . . Ottilie's figure (Gestalt), expression, attitude, glance, excelled all which any painter has ever represented (dargestellt). (E, 177–78; G, 145–46)

It would be possible to assimilate this passage to a religious interpretation of *Die Wahlverwandtschaften*. The passage could be seen as a proleptic emblem of Ottilie's saintly death. In her death she is victorious through renunciation, with God's help, over the dark powers that have driven her off her track and threaten to overwhelm her. Ottilie's image as Mother of God prepares for the closing description of the dead Ottilie in her glass-lidded coffin. She is able to perform miracles of healing. "Saintly one (die Heilige)" that she is, she can make Edward "blessed (selig)" in death. A moment's reflection, however, will suffice to indicate that this scene can by no means be put simply on the metaphysical side of the ledger. Ottilie herself feels extremely uncomfortable with her role, as if there were something impious about it, as indeed there is. The impiety lies precisely in what makes the tableau so powerful, namely, in "representing the picture" of the holy with something real. To represent the Mother of God in paint or in stone, in dumb matter, which can be entirely transfigured into emblematic significance, is one thing. But if the matter is social and psychological actuality, the representation may gain in power, but the power comes from the clash, the dissonance between the two levels being presented. The incongruity, intrinsic to "realistic fiction," between "human reality" and allegorical meaning here surfaces in a striking example. Ottilie feels particularly uncomfortable in her role as Mary when, in the second half of the presentation, she becomes aware that her old schoolteacher, the Assistant, has joined Charlotte in the audience. The Assistant is the spokesman in the novel for down-to-earth education, "Bildung" in the sense of practical training for living. Seeing him, Ottilie remembers that the "reality" of her life is her all-absorbing love for Edward: "Like a flash of forked lightning the stream of her joys and her sorrow rushed swiftly before her soul, and the questions rose in her heart: Dare you confess, dare you acknowledge it all to him? If not, how little can you deserve to appear before him under this sainted form (unter dieser heiligen Gestalt); and how strange must it not seem to him who has only known you as your natural self to see you now under this disguise (als Maske)?" (E, 179; G, 147).

The Assistant says not one word about the performance he has witnessed, but later he severely criticizes the redecorations of the chapel of which Charlotte, the Architect, and Ottilie are so proud: "This mixing up of the holy with the sensuous . . . is anything but pleasing to my taste; I cannot like men to set apart certain places, consecrate them, and deck them out, that by so doing they may nourish in themselves a temper of piety. No ornaments, not even the very simplest, should disturb in us that sense of the Divine Being which accompanies us wherever we are, and can consecrate every spot into a temple (jede Stätte zu einem Tempel einweihen kann)" (E, 181; G, 149).

The Assistant is spokesman here for a rigorous Protestantism that foregoes all graven images. The Architect, on the other hand, is the performative defender of an aestheticizing of religious experience. He says by doing. He liberates religious pictures and inscriptions from the place where they have a ritual significance and creates a separate artistic realm of icons that signify themselves.[28] The decoration of the chapel is the working out of his theory. The Christmas Eve tableau is the climactic demonstration of it. The Architect's half-conscious motivation for both chapel and tableau is his undeclared love for Ottilie. All the figures of angels, religious figures, and worshipers he paints in the chapel gradually come to have Ottilie's face. His casting of Ottilie as Mary is the fulfillment of this aestheticizing love. Ottilie, on the other hand, is entirely preoccupied with her love for Edward. Goethe makes it clear that her representation of Mary has such bewildering power because it is a displacement of her profane love for Edward: "Indescribable and immeasurable happiness was displayed upon her features (bildete sich in ihren Zügen), expressing as much her own personal emotions as that of the character which she was endeavoring to represent" (E, 178; G, 146). She is only a "seeming mother," and the child in her lap, her "hidden treasure," from which she is motionlessly caught in the act of lifting the veil, is not her own. The hidden treasure is an absence, a simulacrum. She is

destined to remain virgin, as Mary was. Ottilie's child is by anticipation that little Otto whom Edward fathers on Charlotte in an
act of double adultery in which he thinks of Ottilie, Charlotte of
the Captain, while they make love. This is made explicit in Charlotte's response to the beautiful vision of Ottilie as Mary with the
Christ-child on her lap: "Her eyes filled with tears, and her imagination presented to her in the liveliest colors the hope that she
might soon have such another darling creature on her own lap"
(E, 178; G, 146).

When the reader works out the ironic resonances connecting this
tableau to the main action of the novel, a radically different, almost
blasphemous, certainly scandalous, meaning for it emerges. This
meaning runs counter to the apparent affirmation of Ottilie's saint-
liness. Far from cherishing little Otto, the child with her eyes and
the Captain's features (as Mary cherished the Christ-child), Ottilie
is responsible for his drowning. This precipitates her own death
and Edward's. Though Charlotte hopes that Otto will save her
marriage, as the Christ-child was the light and hope of the world,
the baby is in fact the unviable remainder of the crisscross equation
rearranging the four principle characters according to their elective
affinities. Otto is what is left over, the anomalous offspring of the
double adultery. As such he is destined to be canceled, since the
strange equation of interpersonal affinities that has produced him
is without the grounding necessary to lead to a continuation of the
generations or to a maintaining of Edward's line. Otto, with eyes
like Ottilie's and features like the Captain's, is the emblem of the
Narcissistic mirror imaging of Ottilie for Edward and Edward for
Ottilie. Each sees his or her own face in the other, not another
person with whom he or she might enter into relations appropri-
ately to be called "interpersonal" in the sense of "between separate
persons." The death of Otto presages the fated deaths of Ottilie
and Edward, as each melts into his or her mirror image in the
other, just as Narcissus drowns when he tries to embrace his own
image in the pool, and just as Echo, his auditory mirror image of
the other sex, silent unless he speaks, slowly dies of inanition. The
name "Echo" may even be present in the novel as a hidden anagram
of the names of the four main characters: Edward, Charlotte, the
Captain ("der Hauptmann"), and Ottilie.

The myth of Narcissus is present in Die Wahlverwandtschaften
not just in that one early reference to it ("Man is a true Narcissus").
The myth is dispersed in oblique echoes throughout all the main

story. The novel could be seen as a commentary on the Ovidian myth. In this interpretation the symmetry between Narcissus' relation to his own image and his relation to Echo is implicitly recognized. The Narcissistic lover makes the beloved of another sex into another version of himself and will not or cannot recognize the otherness of that other person. Edward and Ottilie, as I have noted, have headaches on opposite sides and make a mirroring pair. Ottilie imitates Edward's handwriting exactly. This version of the relation between Echo and Narcissus significantly substitutes writing for speaking. Ottilie's vow of silence at the end, her refusal to echo back anything Edward says to her, like Echo's disappearance in the myth, precipitates the death of both Ottilie and Edward. Edward wants Ottilie to preexist his encounter with her as the double of the other sex who will serve as a ground of his own selfhood. He wants her to be there already, as his fated double, chosen for him by an elective affinity, but she is in fact the projected Echo who always comes after him. She can only return back to him what he already is, but that is nothing but nothing. He is a Narcissistic foil, a colorless power of figuration that lays itself under each thing and turns it into an image of himself.

In the Christmas Eve tableau, Ottilie's role as Echo or as a female Narcissus clashes with her role as Mary. The relation between the Christian emblem and the Greek one in *Die Wahlverwandtschaften* is something like the relation between the two in *Paradise Lost*. Mary, the second Eve in the Christian story, repairs the disaster wrought by the first Eve. As the Mother of God, she holds the maker and redeemer of all creation, mankind included, as a helpless and speechless infant on her lap. She is the most powerful version of that story already present in all Luciana's tableaux. This is the story of the seemingly mild and meek daughter, sister, wife, or mistress who triumphs over the male—father, son, husband, lover—and masters him, while remaining herself intact, "virgo intacta." As Dante puts it, she is "la figlia del suo figlio," the daughter of her son. But she is also his mother, indispensable medium of the Incarnation and the ensuing redemption of mankind. For a moment the whole history of the world hangs poised on her, turns on her as axis. In the disturbing parody of this enacted by Ottilie in the main story and reinforced by the discreet echoes of the Narcissus myth, Edward has gone to Ottilie because of a lack in himself. He has sought in her as all true Narcissistic lovers do proof of his own existence and confirmation of his manhood.

He has sought not just his own face in the mirror but an image

that will tell him he exists and is a man. Instead, Ottilie lifts the veil to reveal an imitation confirming his lack of substance and power. This dooms both to death.

———

The law of elective affinities as it works in the main story may now be interpreted. Ottilie's role as Mary in its ironic dissonance with Ottilie's covert role as Echo to Edward as Narcissus gives the reader an emblem of this law. According to Goethe's law of elective affinities, each person has as part of his or her nature an attraction toward another person. This attraction is so strong it seems like an irrevocable choice, the will as nature or intrinsic selfhood. The propensity toward this choice of another person is what that person is. It is his selfhood in the same way as it is the nature of sodium to choose fluorine over chlorine if it has the "choice." The apparently indissoluble bond between sodium and chlorine in salt can always be broken if fluorine is brought nearby, just as Ottilie's proximity infallibly destroys the marriage of Edward and Charlotte. Moreover, the selves of the two persons, Edward and Ottilie in this case, are only to be fulfilled in the relation. Union with the other fills an essential gap in the self. Only union with the particularly chosen other will appease the desire of the self for completion, its desire to become altogether what it already is. The gap in the female self may be symbolized by the absence of the phallus, the gap in the male self by doubt that it securely possesses the phallus. The union of the two is desired as a way of assuring both that the solid staff exists, a *Stab* on which the yarn of lineage and meaning may be securely woven, sign following sign. Each goes to the other for assurance about the existence of a literal, substantial ground for the self and all its transactions. Edward is irresistibly drawn to Ottilie as to his matching mirror image. To Ottilie it seems the world exists and makes sense as an integrated whole only if Edward exists and loves her. Rarely in a novel has the power of erotic desire been expressed more powerfully than in *Die Wahlverwandtschaften*. The novel also shows, however, that this desire can never by any means be assuaged. It is desire for an unattainable completeness for the self, a ground for the self in the other.

Goethe's awareness of the symbolism of the Stab, indication that he did not need Freud or Lacan to tell him what woman wants from man, man from woman, is indicated by a curious episode near the beginning of the novel when Ottilie has just joined the others at the castle. It is an example of Goethe's extraordinary gift for reconciling allegorical emblem with obedience to the stylistic decorums of realism. It is also an example of an interlude that momentarily suspends the forward movement of the story with another story, picture, or event that is tipped in or grafted on. The episode is also an emblem of the desired function of such interpolations: to be a supplement filling a lack.

Charlotte tells Ottilie that it is indecorous for her always to pick things up for people. It may especially be misunderstood by the men for whom she performs these services: "it is not becoming in a young lady (einem Frauenzimmer) to do them for men" (E, 46; G, 41). The Froude and Boylan translation is elided a bit. A more complete version would say: "only it is not fitting for a lady to submit herself to men and to express herself as subservient in this way (nur will es einem Frauenzimmer nich wohl geziemen, sich Männern auf diese Wiese ergeben und dienstbar zu bezeigen)." The Hollingdale translation has "only it is not quite seemly for a woman to display service and submission of this sort to a man" (65), while the Ryan translation says "it is not proper for a woman to show such humble servitude towards a man" (122). Ottilie explains her behavior by a little story from history. This story, she says, has made a deep impression on her: "When Charles the First of England was standing before his so-called judges, the gold top (Knopf) came off the stick which he had in his hand and fell down. Accustomed as he had been on such occasions to have everything done for him, he seemed to look around and expect that this time too some one would do this little service. No one stirred, and he stooped down for it himself (er bückte sich selbst, um den Knopf aufzuheben). It struck me as so piteous (schmerzlich), I know not whether rightly, that from that moment I have never been able to see any one let a thing fall (aus den Händen fallen) without myself picking it up (ohne mich darnach zu bücken)" (E, 47, slightly altered; G, 41–42).

The little anecdote was proleptic of the beheading of Charles. Decapitation is perhaps the most powerful displaced symbol of that castration all men, we are told, most fear. Ottilie's habit of picking up all fallen objects is indeed especially related to men. It is indeed unbecoming in a young lady, since it is, at a triple remove—from fallen object to the gold knob in the story, to the beheading of Charles, to the fear of castration at the head of the chain, the fear of beheading at the head—an attempt to perform

for men that service they most want and need. It is an attempt to
reerect the stick, to give it a head, to reassure men and reassure
herself that there is indeed a literal staff, "ein buchstäblich Stab,"
at the start of the line. The picking up and reinstalling of the gold
knob also functions as an allegorical emblem of the interpolations
throughout *Die Wahlverwandtschaften*: Ottilie's diary, the inserted
novella, the tableaux vivants, the seemingly irrelevant attention to
gravestones and portraits, as well as to questions of landscape
gardening. The function of these interludes is to fill a gap, to
supplement an absence, to make something incomplete whole, for
example by giving the reader a solid ground on the basis of which
he can read the novel proper and its main story.

The anecdote about Charles I indicates that this function cannot
be fulfilled. No one picks up the gold knob. Charles is beheaded.
The novel, moreover, shows Ottilie to be pathetically unable to
make up for this piteous lack in others. Her fate shows to Edward,
to herself, and to the reader that the literal at the head of the line
of letters is not the straight line of the runic inscription, but an O,
an absence, a silence about which nothing can be said. This is the
same pattern as that identified earlier in this chapter in the "nought
nought one" of Joyce. In *Die Wahlverwandtschaften* this lack of
originating ground is dramatized simultaneously on the level of
signs, on the level of interpersonal relations, on the level of the
interrupted and heterogeneous structure of the text, and on the
level of the design of the estate, in the building of the summer
house to supplement the main house. In the area of interpersonal
relations this antimetaphysical or alogocentric dimension defines
another person as an impenetrable mystery, an unbreakable silence,
nothing on which one can securely ground one's selfhood. On the
level of language this is expressed as the breakdown of the Aris-
totelian ratio of metaphor and literal language: A is to B as C is
to D, therefore C can substitute metaphorically for A, D for B. The
ratio breaks down because one element at least of the four cannot
be identified as either literal or metaphorical. In this failure of the
distinction on which the model for interpretation presented by the
title is founded, the secure grounding of the substitutions seemingly
authorized by the ratio also vanishes. Edward's choice of Ottilie,
hers of him, can no longer be justified as submission to irresistible
laws. On the level of the text's stylistic decorum, the apparently
secure distinction between realism and allegorical emblem, "Buch-

stabe" and "Kunstwort," on which my analysis of the novel has depended, collapses in the breakdown of the other patterns. The reader is left confronting a text that has become unreadable, silent, since the means used to unravel it has itself unraveled. Every detail of the novel is at once realistic and allegorical. No section—for example, those interpolations I have identified—can be segregated and then interpreted as the external key on the basis of which the main action can be read. Moreover, the allegorical reading is not so much authorized as freely posited and at the same time undermined by the pervasive irony of the narration. This irony leaves the reader without firm ground to stand on in interpreting the novel.

This lack of a secure ground for reading does not mean that the text is not read. Far from it. But it means that the reading of *Die Wahlverwandtschaften* is neither exegesis, the extraction of a hidden meaning buried within the text, nor diegesis, the narrative unfolding of a clear meaning from beginning through middle to inevitable end in a "recognition," "anagnorisis." Any reading is rather an eisegesis, the imposition of a meaning over a substratum that can never be encountered face-to-face, in the presence of the present. The rhetorical name for this act of reading is "performative catachresis." What the characters, including the narrator, do in the novel, the reader must perforce again do in reading the novel.

An emblem of this act of positing is the function of the interpolated novella, "Die wunderlichen Nachbarskinder," "The Strange Neighbor Children." The novella is sometimes interpreted (for example, by Walter Benjamin, with whom a later critic disagrees at his peril) as the most overt statement of the metaphysical laws of interpersonal relations on the grounds of which the novel proper is to be measured and judged.[29] Benjamin's account of the novella is subtle, complex, and to some degree contradictory. He stresses the differences between the novella and the novel, while at the same time recognizing that the novel began as a novella and still retains traces of the stylization characteristic of that genre. Benjamin identifies the difference in mode and stylistic decorums between the two genres. In the novella, with its fabulous and overtly supernatural elements, the lovers live in direct proximity to the mysterious laws their relation exemplifies. They therefore remain at an inscrutable distance from the reader. The novel, on the other hand, manifests these laws only indirectly, by way of a more inward presentation of character. The novel therefore has as its theme the tragic incompatibility between "real life" and those laws. In the novel these laws manifest themselves as mythic fate, in the novella as liberation. The novella is antithesis to the novel as thesis.[30] Goethe's strong sense of genre and his particular interest in the novella as a specific form with its own firm rules would seem to give support to Benjamin's reading. In a conversation with Eckermann, Goethe defined the novella as "a short prose narrative organized around a single 'unheard-of event' (unerhörte Begebenheit)."[31]

All the main story's crucial elements are present in the interpolated novella: the magic affinity between the lovers, the use of drowning or near drowning as a symbolic entry into a realm of elemental powers, the breaking of a marriage promise when a new irresistible bond supervenes. But everything that comes out badly in the novel comes out happily in the novella. It seems as though the novella were inserted to indicate this possibility. It is a possibility that exceeds common sense. We know "real life is not like that": "To have found themselves brought from the water to dry land, from death into life, from the circle of their families into a wilderness, from despair into rapture, from indifference to affection and to love, all in a moment: the head was not strong enough to bear it" (E, 219; G, 178). The novella, if read in this way, would have somewhat the same function in relation to the whole as the emblematic meanings of particular episodes would have in relation to their "realistic" meanings. This would be especially true if the emblematic meanings in question are those affirming what I have called the metaphysical reading of the novel. The novella would tell the reader how to read the main novel. Or the reader might think of the novella as having the same relation to the novel proper as Ottilie does to Edward, taking her, as Edward does, as a messenger from a transcendent realm who will complete him, who will create and support his selfhood. The interpolated tale, in short, is in a relation of anastomosis to the main text. Anastomosis would have here its most positive meaning. It would name a channel between two independent entities allowing one to support and vivify the other.

It is tempting to accept this reading of "The Strange Neighbor Children," but the interpretation will not hold up under scrutiny. It is dispersed both by study of analogies with the novel's homologous structures and by study of the tale itself in its context. The style of the tale does not differ markedly from that of the novel, as Benjamin recognized. Though one ends happily, the other in death, the same incompatible copresence of realistic and fabulous elements is present in both. Both have the same rapid pace and marked stylization, along with representational details from bourgeois life. *Die Wahlverwandtschaften,* like the novella, culminates in a fabulous event: Ottilie's death and the miraculous cure of Nanny. The novella is fed with the same stylistic and thematic streams as the main story. "The Strange Neighbor Children" functions more to call attention to what is enigmatic about the main story than to give a measure by which that enigma can be solved.

The effect of the telling of the novella on those who hear it is not at all reassuring. That effect is a little like what Mittler's speech brings about at the baptism of Otto. The speech causes the old clergyman to drop dead. The novella is told by the companion of the visiting English lord. Its aim is to amuse Charlotte and Ottilie, to make up for an earlier unintentional faux pas. Instead, it makes matters worse. Both Charlotte and Ottilie leave the room in great distress at the end of the tale. The "principal incident" in the story, we are told, "had really taken place with the Captain and a neighbor of [Charlotte's] own; not exactly, indeed, as the Englishman had related it. But the main features of it were the same" (E, 220). Far from reassuring them, as Benjamin's reading suggests it might, the novella reinforces their anxiety in relation to Edward and the Captain. Far from being an escape into the utopian never-neverland assumed in the generic definition of the novella, "The Strange Neighbor Children" is the incursion of material history. This incursion is the return of something repressed that reveals the hard conditions of the present. The happiness of the "strange neighbor children," after all, brings about the unhappiness of the man whom the girl has promised to marry, just as the union of Edward and Ottilie would break the marriage bond of Edward and Charlotte. The tale is in a relation of anastomosis to the main novel all right, but it is an anastomosis of another sort, a flowing from the same to the same rather than from other to same. To put this in another way, the relation between the two is like the actual relation between Edward and Ottilie. It is a Narcissistic imaging with right and left reversed. In this mirroring the meaning given to the other by its reflection is posited over an unknown and unknowable substratum. This relation is not like that between two separate persons in which I might know and possess the other, so finding a ground for my own selfhood. Nor is it an allegory of the happy exchanges of

metaphor confirming knowledge. Instead, it is an allegory of catachresis, that is, of a performative rather than a cognitive trope.
The relation of the novel and the novella is an emblem of the
relation of representation to actual, material history, rather than
to ideologically concocted history.

If the drama of elective affinities among the four principal characters is now read in the light of the passages I have been accounting for, a quite different understanding of that drama emerges. The
relation among the four can be taken as an allegory of the crisscross
substitutions in a metaphorical ratio, and vice versa. Ottilie, the
last added fourth term, ruins the ratio. She is an unidentifiable final
term, silent or absent. She is neither literal nor figurative, therefore
not properly nameable. She is the "O" or "0," both the first letter
of her name and the zero that undoes the equation. The O or zero
deprives the proportion of its reasonable ground in the distinction between literal and figurative and therefore takes it outside the
safe confines of Occidental metaphysics. Ottilie's silence and unap-
proachability make the relations among the four principal persons like the incomplete metaphorical equations Aristotle allows
for in the *Poetics*. This is that figurative proportion in which one
of the four terms is missing. The examples Aristotle gives involve
the sun, traditional symbol of the logos, ground of all metaphorical
substitutions. The sun is the basic means of transfer, as in those
figures for man—for example, the Sphinx's riddle—that describe
the human life journey as being like the diurnal trajectory of the
sun. Since the sun cannot be looked in the eye, its radiance cannot
be named properly, literally. Literal naming depends on seeing what
is named in the presence of the present, out in the sunlight. Any
name for the radiance of the sun is therefore a catachresis, neither
figurative nor literal. It is, for example, something drawn from the
natural world of engendering and applied figuratively to the pater-
nal engenderer of all metaphors, what Wallace Stevens calls "the
furiously burning father-fire."[32] Aristotle's example is "the poet's
expression," "sowing a god-created flame." The sun is the base of
any metaphorical equation into which it enters. At the same time
it always subverts that equation, since though it is the basis of
seeing it cannot be directly seen itself.[33]

Ottilie plays the same role in the proportion among the four
characters of *Die Wahlverwandtschaften* as the missing term for
the sun's act of casting forth its flame does in Aristotle's example.

She is the blind spot in the novel, invisible from excess of light. She is a kind of black hole into which everything disappears. Edward, dazzled by Ottilie's beauty, imagines that she is his missing other half, to whom he is drawn by a special elective affinity justifying the substitution of her for Charlotte, his lawfully wedded wife. Ottilie is the D substituting for his Charlotte as his B. She is his counterpart in a changed sex who matches him exactly. She will complete what is lacking in him and make him whole. Does she not have headaches on the left side, as he on the right? Does she not imitate his handwriting exactly? And does not the magic goblet that does not break at the dedication of the new house have their initials, E and O, intertwined on it as a prophetic emblem of their indissoluble unity? Edward sees their union written prophetically everywhere.

Edward presents Mittler with a series of figures for his sense of his unity with Ottilie when Mittler comes, in another case of his failure as a mediator, to persuade Edward to give up his "foolish frantic passion" for Ottilie. "And so she is present," says Edward, "in every dream I have. In whatever happens to me with her, we are woven in and in together. Now we are subscribing a contract together. There is her hand, and there is mine; there is her name, and there is mine; and they move one into the other, and seem to devour each other" (E, 124; G, 102). Translated more literally Goethe's German says, "And so her image (Bild) mixes itself in each of my dreams." Edward's relation to Ottilie is the relation of an object to an image, for example, his own face in the mirror, or the relation of dreamer to a figure in a dream. His relation to Ottilie is like the weaving together of two strands to make a single rope or fabric, or it is like the drawing together of two hands, names, and signatures in a written contract. The "contracting" of two persons when they underwrite a joint document, in a performative promise to act as one, substitutes for the naturally and supernaturally based attraction (Bezug) described in the chapter on the elective affinities. Goethe's German (unlike the English translation) plays the double meaning of the word *Hand* as part of the body and as handwriting. Just as one meaning of the word slips into the other, so Edward's hand and Ottilie's hand become their names. The names are then superimposed, merge, and devour one another: "da ist ihre Hand und die meinige, ihr Name und der meinige, beide löschen einander aus, beide verschlingen sich" (G,

102). The relation between the two is mutually sustaining and
mutually destructive, like the drowning of Narcissus.

But Edward's prophetic dream has a different meaning for the
reader from the meaning he gives it. The dream echoes similar
images elsewhere in the novel, the matching hands matching, for
example, the matching headaches. The motif of handwriting here
reminds the reader again that what is involved in interpersonal
relations for Goethe is not persons as such, but signs, images, forms
of writing. Edward and Ottilie exist, both for themselves and for
each other, as images or as writing. Edward is haunted by the
image of Ottilie that hovers always before him. Ottilie is presented
most intimately, most from the inside, in the selections from her
diary. Far from having the inward quality one might expect from
a young woman's diary, these entries are surprisingly impersonal.
They are made up of quotations, citations, maxims, and reflections
such as Goethe composed and published elsewhere under his own
name. If the lovers' "selves" are images, handwriting, or names,
these names have the capacity to move into one another, overlap,
merge, and, in an ominous figure, devour one another like particle
and antiparticle, leaving nothing behind, the "O" their names share
(his name is Edward Otto) and which it is their destiny to become.

This is worked out most fully in the figure of the drinking glass:
"My fate and Ottilie's [Edward tells Mittler] cannot be divided,
and shall not be shipwrecked. Look at this glass; our initials are
engraved upon it. A gay reveller flung it into the air, that no one
should drink of it more. It was to fall on the rock and be dashed
to pieces; but it did not fall; it was caught. At a high price I bought
it back, and now I drink out of it daily—to convince myself that
the connection (alle Verhältnisse) between us cannot be broken;
that destiny (das Schicksal) has decided" (E, 126; G, 104). The
glass is accidentally broken after Ottilie's death by Edward's ser-
vant, who substitutes a nearly identical one, to Edward's dismay.
The reader may see his dismay as a momentary recognition that
the meaning of the first glass was a matter of metaphorical transfer,
another case of "reading into," rather than a literal reading of
what is really there. As the novel everywhere indicates, all reading
is figurative, projective. Or rather, the only true literal reading is a
confrontation with a materiality of the letter figured in the blank
silence or deathlike sleep of Ottilie. Edward reads Ottilie's image
as the reflex of his own, just as he reads the letters E and O, his
own initials, as though they joined his first name with Ottilie's

name. The passage quoted above begins and ends with the notion of a destiny (Schicksal) that binds Edward and Ottilie together and makes them one. That destiny, however, the narration indicates, is posited rather than imposed. It is a baseless projection by Edward, not something objectively there in the world.

All four of the principal characters have the same name or a variant of it: Edward Otto, Otto, Charlotte, Ottilie. The Captain's name is also Otto, and Charlotte contains the name of course as part of itself. All the names stress the hollow O or 0 of absence. There seem not enough names to go around in this novel. All the characters are already undermined by the zero or absence Ottilie brings into the fourfold proportion, making it not A is to B as C is to D, but A is to B as C is to 0. The 0 works back to cancel all the others and make it a null equation: 0 is to 0 as 0 is to 0. When the Captain sees in the drowned body of little Otto "the stiffened image of himself (sein erstarrtes Ebenbild)" (E, 239; G, 194), he is also seeing the "image" of Charlotte, of Ottilie, of Edward, of all four in their strange relation of double adultery or double crisscross canceled figuration. Little Otto is the extension of Edward's genealogical line, which Ottilie has tried to pick up and save, as Mary cherished the Christ-child in the Christmas pageant Ottilie enacts. Instead Ottilie loses the child, ending the line in silence and death.

Ottilie is the odd person out in the system of substitutions among the four. As such, she undoes that system, making the "little circle of three," Charlotte, Edward, and the Captain, into a square with a missing fourth side, thereby disintegrating the figure. Ottilie is neither the literal nor the figurative, or rather she is an impossible embodiment of both. She is an incarnation of catachresis. She is the beautiful unattainable aesthetic surface that spreads a powerful erotic glow over the whole novel. This glow has been projected as a veil over what she "really is" by Edward's Narcissistic love for her as his metaphorical "image." He cannot possess her pleasure as his own. That pleasure remains discrete, elsewhere, unattainable, occurring always too early or too late, somewhere and sometime else. Ottilie is the mute letter, not the aesthetic spirit. She is the "Buchstabe" that undoes Edward's projected love. As the material literal, Ottilie is unattainable, the silent, unnameable, unapproachable letter, embodied sign of the darkness of death, about which nothing can be literally said.

This double existence of Ottilie, as beauty and as death's darkness, is admirably figured in the description of her beautiful corpse beneath the glass-covered lid of her coffin. As the incarnation of the literal, Ottilie cannot enter into relations, not even relations with herself. She expresses the literal in the sense of the senseless matter, marks or lines, of which written language is made. At the same time she personifies the absence of any ground in matter or beneath such marks for the meaning which is spread over them by a process of substitution and sideways superficial transfer. In this she is not the Stab or staff of the Buchstabe, but the 0 of death. The death she represents is not transcendence or sublimation, but death as absence, as the literal "thing" behind all language of which nothing can be said except in metaphor. Such metaphors are veils over an "X ignotum" left untouched by any signs thrown out toward it. Or rather, since absence implies presence, Ottilie is that which never was or could be present. She is neither present nor absent, but simply the blank, the unapproachable, the zero about which nothing can be said except in the Narcissistic falsehoods of figure.

Ottilie's vow of silence, presaging her death, comes, as she writes to her friends, from taking "too literally, perhaps (vielleicht zu buchstäblich)" (E, 258; G, 210), her promise not to speak to Edward. Ottilie writes: "Against his own will he stood before me. Too literally, perhaps, I have observed my promise never to admit him into conversation with me. My conscience and the feelings of the moment kept me silent toward him at the time, and now I have nothing more to say. . . . Do not call in anyone to mediate; do not insist upon my speaking; do not urge me to eat or to drink more than I absolutely must. . . . Leave me to my own inward self " (E, 258–59; G, 210). Ottilie allows herself to write, but no longer to speak. This makes clear the alignment of writing with silence and with the absence of what is implied by speaking, namely conscious-ness, personality, selfhood, the presence of the ego to itself. This opposition functions throughout the novel—for example, in the striking impersonality of Ottilie's diary.

The best emblems of Ottilie's identification with silence, how-ever, even before she lies silent in death within her glass-lidded coffin, are the two times when she appears to be asleep but can hear though not speak. One of these episodes occurred in her childhood, before the novel begins, as she lay, apparently asleep, but actually in a kind of speechless trance, listening to Charlotte describe the unfortunate circumstances of her orphan life. The second time repeats the first. It occurs on the night after she has caused the drowning of little Otto. The passage is one of the most important to an understanding of the novel:

> "This is the second time that the same thing has happened to me" [says Ottilie to Charlotte]. "You once said to me that similar things often befall people more than once in their lives in a similar way, and if they do, it is always at important moments. . . . Shortly after my mother's death, when I was a very little child, I was sitting one day on a footstool close to you. You were on a sofa, as you are at this moment, and my head rested on your knees. I was not asleep, I was not awake: I was in a trance. I knew everything which was passing about me. I heard every word which was said with the greatest distinctness, and yet I could not stir, I could not speak; and if I had wished it, I could not have given a hint that I was conscious. On that occasion you were speaking about me to one of your friends; you were commiserating my fate (mein Schicksal), left as I was a poor orphan in the world. . . . I made rules (Gesetze) to myself, according to such limited insight as I had, and by these I have long lived. . . .
>
> But I have wandered out of my course (Aber ich bin aus meiner Bahn geschritten); I have broken my rules; I have lost the very power of feeling them. And now, after a dreadful occurrence, you have again made clear to me my situation, which is more pitiable than the first. While lying in a half torpor on your lap, I have again, as if out of another world, heard every syllable which you uttered. I know from you how all is with me. I shudder at the thought of myself; but again, as I did then, in my half sleep of death, I have marked out my new path for myself (mir meine neue Bahn vorgezeichnet)." (E, 242–43; G, 197)

When Ottilie writes the letter explaining her vow of silence, she speaks again of the chosen course of her life, but this time with a difference. The rules she made for herself in her first trancelike state were a willed or elected plotting of the course of her life. They were not a destiny imposed on her by either malign or benign spiritual powers, though she may have chosen a course that seemed justified by the Christian values of renunciation and quiet, obedient, devoted work for women in which she has been brought up. Now once again she is making rules that will, it seems, put her back on her track after the detour of her passion for Edward. In her letter, however, after her renewed encounter with Edward, and after her discovery that her passion seems irresistible, a true elective affinity, she recognizes that she can never again recover her path: "I have stepped out of my course, and I cannot recover it again. A malignant spirit which has gained power over me seems to hinder me from without, even if within I could again become at one with myself" (E, 258). "Ich bin aus meiner Bahn geschritten und ich soll nicht wieder hinein. Ein feindseliger Dämon, der Macht über mich gewonnen, scheint mich von außen zu hindern, hätte ich mich auch mit mir selbst wieder zur Einigkeit gefunden" (G, 209–10) Ottilie has stepped out of the destined line of her life. This gives that life a double line. This exorbitance also makes Ottilie herself double. She is divided within herself, unable ever to return to herself and become one with herself, reach unity, "Einigkeit."

That "malignant spirit" is, the reader knows, Ottilie's metaphysical personification of her projection of herself into Edward, reflex of his Narcissistic love for her. Beneath any rules she makes for herself, any course she lays out, beneath even the red thread of her love for Edward, Ottilie is a trancelike silence, a half-sleep of death. This silence cannot love or be loved. It cannot relate itself to anything or to anyone. It cannot speak. It cannot trace a visible trajectory or line. Therefore it cannot be understood by another person or, in its representation, by the reader of the novel. It remains mute, discrete, effaced. It fulfills itself in the final impenetrable silence of her death. In death she becomes what she has been all along: hidden, untouched, mute, mere body, the letter, but therefore all the more desirable in her unattainable beauty. Goethe recognizes that beauty—what Hegel called "the sensible shining of the idea"—is the sign for an unreachable referent. In the same way the novel, clothed in that extraordinary beauty of which Benjamin speaks, can never be penetrated, possessed, and made transparent in any interpretation. It always exceeds and escapes any reading of it.

———

In the presentation of interpersonal relations in narrative, and in the analysis of narrative on the assumption that interpersonal relations are essential in it, two incompatible paradigms persist in our tradition. One sees selves as fixed entities basing themselves on their relations to other selves. The other model of interpersonal relations sees selves as nothing but a locus traversed by fleeting signs. Such selves seek to ground themselves in others by drawing others to themselves, but each such self succeeds only in experiencing its solitude and nonentity. The model narrative in our tradition expressing this self-emptying relation of the self to itself is Ovid's melancholy story of Narcissus. Trapped within his prison house of language, Narcissus is able to see and love only himself. He can hear only echoes of his own voice. He is in dialogue always with himself. For Goethe, however, the solitude of the human condition results from an encounter, if that is the right word, with an unattainable otherness in the other. The solitude of each self is an alternative form of anastomosis in interpersonal relations, not just a relation of the self to itself.

Novels in our tradition often dramatize the interference of these two assumptions about interpersonal relations. Readings presupposing one or the other prejudge the text and are likely to miss something essential. Moreover, interpersonal relations as such can never be the adequate ground, the beginning and end, in reading fictions. Relations between people are always grounded on something else, in one direction by ontological issues that belong to metaphysical rather than to ethical considerations, in the other direction by linguistic problems that stories allegorically represent. This is another manifestation of the law of displacement I have encountered repeatedly in the labyrinth of narrative theory. Each mode of criticizing fiction presupposes the others. Each leads to the others, the others to it.

Die Wahlverwandtschaften admirably shows the way the two forms of anastomosis interfere with one another. The lack of organic unity in our great literary texts is an important manifestation of that tradition's equivocity. This heterogeneity is present in the languages used for self-expression in that tradition, as well as in the lives led in terms of those languages. Life incarnates language, for man the sign-making animal. Ottilie, Edward, Charlotte and the Captain embody laws of language expressed most starkly and literally in the ratios of the elective affinities.

In all the thematic realms the novel touches—in estate planning, portraits, gravestones, tableaux vivants, and so on, as well as in interpersonal relations—two asymmetrical readings of transfers, translations, graftings, or interpolations of one thing or person on another in anastomosic connection are intertwined in Goethe's language. That intertwining forbids a choice between one or the other, though they cannot be reconciled, put in a hierarchy, dialectically organized, or made the themes of a coherent narrative moving from one to the other. In one reading the transfers are grounded, whether in the authority of one of the elements (as the original text may seem to have indubitable authority over the translation) or in the supervision of the transfers by some hidden law or power presiding over the exchanges (as the attraction of Edward and Ottilie for one another may seem governed by irresistible chthonic forces that are like laws of nature). In the other reading there is no such originating or presiding authority. The exchanges themselves posit the phantasm of such an authority over the abyss of its lack in their movements of displacement. Edward, on this reading, Narcissistically projects on the silence and lack of self-presence of Ottilie the other half of himself that will complete him and satisfy his desire. The figure for the first of these readings is the transparent substitutions of proportional metaphor, governed by the presupposition of literal language: A is to B as C is to D. If Edward is to Charlotte as the Captain is to Ottilie, then Ottilie can substitute for Charlotte, linking Edward and Ottilie, Charlotte and the Captain. This exchange would manifest a law that is at once chemical, psychological, and spiritual. The model for the other reading is catachresis: A is to B as C is to 0, taking the zero as an unknown and unknowable quantity that can be named only by a blind positing of a word brought in from another realm that does not substitute for any literal word. In *Die Wahlverwandtschaften* Ottilie is that unknown quantity, unknown even to herself. She cannot be worked into a logical and transparent system of substitutions and displacements.

Die Wahlverwandtschaften seems at first to invite a reading assuming intersubjectivity is a relation between two independent selves, each of which, in his or her love for the other, can function as the ground of that other. This notion of interpersonal relations, the novel shows, is tied to a tightly knit system of philosophical and linguistic notions. This system weaves the fabric of Western metaphysics. One principle grounding this system is the distinction between metaphorical and literal language. The novel dramatizes these metaphysical assumptions in a text of masterly beauty. That beauty, as the sensible shining of the idea, is part of metaphysics. At the same time, the novel also unravels the system in its indirect encounter with something unpresentable, beyond beauty. This is the silence of Ottilie. She is the missing fourth term in the crisscross of elective affinities. This undoing of the line, the breaking of the red thread by the black that cannot be outlined, is always woven within the metaphysical system itself, not least in that part of it involving notions of selfhood and interpersonal relations. This *Die Wahlverwandtschaften* admirably exemplifies. It is a characteristic of realistic fiction as a genre, however, both to show selfhood as dependent on intersubjective lines and at the same time to show that it is impossible to found a self on the bond to another self. This is the end point reached by following Ariadne's thread through the corridor of the labyrinth labeled "Anastomosis."

4 Figure

Toute bonne mémoire est escriture. Elle retient sa figure.—Montaigne

I have now explored three corridors of the labyrinth of narrative theory, after an initial description of seven paths that might be followed. Each has to do with the internal forms of storytelling, as opposed to the relations of a story to what is apparently outside it, perhaps as its base. The latter relations are another story, reserved for another book. In this present book, beginning with the word, concept, figure, or thing named *line,* in all its capability of being used in various ways to talk about narrative, I have included discussion of the line as curved back on itself to form the literality of the *letter.* A letter is a figure in the sense of a linear configuration making a sign that has meaning because it can be differentiated from other signs. From there I have followed the line as *character* and as *anastomosis.* In each case, in a different way each time, the reading has come eventually, by way of the textual intricacies of one novel or another, to a blind alley the tropological name for which is *catachresis*.

"In a different way each time" is as important here as "in each case." The way to each aporia is irreversible in the sense that it cannot be traversed again. When you have followed that particular line you are in a different place and cannot return to where you were, just as the hero of *The Ordeal of Richard Feverel* cannot go back over his Rubicon once he has crossed it. Each theoretical reading (to use an oxymoron) is irreversible in the paradoxical sense that it is productive. On the one hand, it is impossible to go beyond it. It is a blank wall. That is what aporia means: impasse, the absence, in a sequential argument, of a way out or a way beyond. Each reading culminates in an experience of the unreadability of the text at hand. That text hovers between two or more logically incompatible readings. Each may be rigorously demonstrated in its possibility. It is therefore impossible to decide unequivocally for either. The contradictory readings cannot be put into a hierarchy nor can the reader move dialectically through one to the other toward a synthesis in the far off distance or close at hand. On the other hand, each such reading is unrepeatable in the sense that it leaves the reader in a different place from where she or he was before, unable ever to go back to the starting point or ever to be the same as a reader again. Though there is no reason why any one reading has to precede another—why *character,* for example, has to come before *anastomosis*—once the order is arbitrarily chosen, *anastomosis* is different from what it would have been if it had preceded *character*. Each such reading is generative, even though it culminates in an apparent dead end. Each reading produces new readings of other texts, readings that are different from what they would have been if the first reading had not been performed. Each of these new readings is generative in its turn, in unexpected and unpredictable ways. The reading of a single text may make the leap from aporia to aporia, or the movement from text to text may be a series of such leaps.

The temporality of reading and the accompanying theoretical reflection, it can be seen, is radically different from the ordinary continuous time in which we sometimes think we dwell. The latter is a time in which one moment leads to the next by a complex but unavoidable causal determinism. The time of reading, on the other hand, is discontinuous but irreversible. It is irreversible because each reading is performative. Things are different for the reader and for the readers of the reading after it has happened. In the

time of reading the relation between one moment and another is
a sign to sign relation of similarity in difference rather than one of
causal determinism. Human time or historical time, it may be, is
the time of reading, and that other conventional idea of time is an
ideological error confusing the natural and the linguistic.

Reading is an act, a performative use of language. It is a happening that makes something else happen, though never anything
that can be named ahead of time, promised or foreseen. Another
way to put is to say that though I have given the name *catachresis*
to the culminating points of my diverse readings, each catachresis
is different from all the others and reached by different paths.
Catachresis is not what it is. It is a genus of which each species is
a monster, sui generis, incommensurate with any of its fellows.

It might seem that the bent of my argument, nevertheless, as I
have moved here and there through the labyrinth of narrative
theory, has been toward suggesting that recognition of figure's role
in narrative will provide a means of mastery in the analysis of
fiction. A rhetoric of fiction, not in Wayne Booth's sense of rhetoric
as persuasion, but in the sense of a science of tropes, a tropology,
will, it might seem, give command of narrative. Understanding
figures will provide an escape beyond any aporia, a theatrical
bird's-eye view of the whole labyrinth, as none of the other strategies of interpretation do. A chapter named "Figure" might then
be the triumphant happy ending, an escape from the labyrinth at
last. The only way to find out whether or not this is the case is to
try it, once more in terms of a specific example dictating or demanding its own trajectory of reading. But first, what about the
word, concept, or figure of figure itself?

In looking at the configuration of meanings in this word I by no
means presume that the word prescribes and limits its uses, much
less that the etymological root of the word determines all its meanings. The history of a word is the history of the uses to which that
word has been put. That history is full of discontinuous leaps and
displacements. These nonsequential changes do not ever end, even
though the word's meanings come to be embalmed in the OED,
inscribed there according to certain ideological presuppositions
about the priority of literal meanings over figurative ones. If the
word at its origin was already a metaphor, as Rousseau and others
have argued, the later jumps and sideways transformations making
up the history of the word's uses are always themselves figurative,

in manifold ways. They are products of the mind's power to make analogies and to move a word into a new region where it covers a gap in the web of language we spread over what is "out there." Nevertheless, study of the history of a word, with all its shifts, establishes a constellation of the ways the word has been used. This forms a context for new uses we may make of the word. The word *figure* is curious and instructive, since in one way or another it names the process of performative or catachrestic word use that study of any word reveals. We need the word itself to describe its own history.

The word *figure* contains, in the manifold of sentences in which it has been or might be used, the program for reading narratives by way of a science of tropes. The word comes from the short stem of Latin *fingere,* to make, confect, shape (also the root of *feign*). Latin *figura* was the normal translation for the whole range of meanings in the Greek word σχῆμα ("schema"). Nevertheless, the OED gives as the first and primary meaning of *figure* not something made or schematic at all but "the form of anything as determined by the outline; shape generally." Figure is the outline or shape something already has, on its own. Most often, but not always, that "something" is the human body. Putting this first, as I have suggested, may be an ideological rather than a historical or scientific move. Among examples given by the OED of this "first" meaning is one from 1477: "A man that is in a derke kaue may not see his propre figure." Another from 1878: "In addition to this change of size . . . the figure of the ship suffers change." A range of secondary, figurative meanings, such as "cut a figure" or "man of figure," is included by the OED in this category. Only ninth in the list of twenty-six distinct meanings comes the major shift to *figure* not as outline already possessed by some object but as "represented form, image, likeness," as in Shakespeare's *Pericles,* 5.2.92–93: "in Helicanus may you well descry / A figure of truth, of faith, of loyalty" (1608), or in North's Plutarch: "His Cabinet, furnished with many Pourtraitures and Figures of those who had been Travellers" (1676). From this use there is another category shift to *figure* in the sense of a man-made design or pattern, a diagram or illustration, as in Milton's *Lycidas* (l. 105): "His brow with sedge, / Inwrought with figures dim" (1637), or in Tennyson's "Brook" (l.103): "Sketching with her slender pointed foot / Some figure . . . On garden gravel" (1855). James's "figure in the carpet" belongs in this category. Next comes *figure* in the sense of written character, letter of the alphabet, numerical symbol, amount of money. Only as the final displacement from the "literal" meaning comes figure as trope, figure of speech, rhetorical figure, along with analogous meanings as figure of grammar, logic, and music, as in "figured bass." *Figure* as figure of speech is exemplified in Puttenham: "Figures be the instruments of ornament in every language" (1589); Boyle: "That noble Figure of Rhetorick called Hyperbole" (1665); and L. Murray: "Figures of Speech imply some departure from the simplicity of expression" (1824).

From the intrinsic outline something, especially a person, already has, to the mimetic representation of such an outline, to a design that has meaning without being a picture of the thing it stands for, and then finally to figure of speech, trope, the capability of the word *figure* to enter into phrases and sentences shifts in ways that are by no means continuous or logically predictable. Nevertheless, the basis of the shifts, one may dare to guess, is that mysterious propensity, source of all sign making and sign reading, of distinct arrangements of matter, marks on matter, or marks made by matter—for example, the outline of the human body or lines traced on sand—to be taken as standing for something more or other than themselves, the outline of the person for the person, the number five for the concept of fiveness, and so on. *Figure* in the sense of the outline of a human body is already figurative, a "standing for," as in Pliny's story of the daughter of Butades, a potter of Sicyon, at Corinth. She traced the outline of her beloved's shadow on a rock and so invented drawing, made then by her potter father into the first relief.[1]

The OED phrases this act of sign making in the seventh usage of a word related to figure, *scheme*: "a complex unity in which the component elements co-operate and interact according to a definite plan." This formulation leaves open, as no doubt it should, the question of whose plan it is. Who did the planning, the spectator-schemer, or some hidden plotter behind the manifest figure whose design the spectator reads? Or was the design there already, ready to be read, product of no plan at all, as we see Orion in a random configuration of stars? In the case of a figure of speech what seems to be implicit in the borrowed use of the word *figure* for tropes generally and as an equivalent of Greek σχῆμα is the way a certain configuration of words (not just a single word by itself) takes on a power of meaning more than itself or more than any of its elements or than their grammatical sum. A word becomes figurative only when it is twisted from its normal use by its placement in a sentence, usually as a substitute for some more obvious word. This power of signification is analogous to the way an arrangement of lines becomes a number or a written character. In the case of a figure of speech words rather than lines become the constitutive elements of the new "figure" in the sense of meaningful configuration organized according to a unified plan.

The shifts in meaning in *figure,* as given by the OED, are apparently arranged in a logical, chronological, or genetic order, or in all three in combination. First *figure* is intrinsic outline, then *figure* is displaced to name the man-made representation of such an outline, and so on. In fact, such an assumption of order is probably one of those convenient feignings by which we make sense of the world. This is just what the word *figure* names in one way or another. The series of meanings is reversible and simultaneous, not sequential. Any design, outline, or configuration encountered in the world—for example, random marks scratched by a glacier on a rock—is likely to be taken as a representation of something, or as an "abstract" design, or even as a letter or hieroglyph. In the other direction, even the most refined and conventional figure, for example, a printed letter of the alphabet or the figure five, is liable, seen in a certain light, to appear to be what in a certain sense it is, a senseless configuration that just happens to be there or that has escaped all the schemes made to give it meaning. The same thing can happen to that special sort of figure made of words, a figure of speech. The links binding the words may be obscure. The words may therefore have for a given reader a dismaying opacity or even senselessness. Any word said over and over will ultimately be drained of meaning. We all dwell on the borders of aphasia. In one way or another, in one proportion or another, any figure is always seen as figurative in all the senses of *figure* at once. The various senses filtered out by the OED in particular examples are only a matter of emphasis in a specific usage, not a matter of exclusion. Any use of "figure" shimmers figuratively with all its possible meanings.

In what combinations of its senses can one speak of figures in a work of fiction, for example, in Jorge Luis Borges's story of 1942, "Death and the Compass" ("La muerte y la brújula")?[2] The example may seem too artificial to be representative of the main-

stream of realistic fiction. The latter, we tend to assume, is rooted
in the history and in the mimesis of social, psychological, and cultural forms. Realistic fiction is penetrated through and through by history, fundamentally shaped by it, while Borges's stories are ostentatiously *ficciones,* fabricated artifices, *artificios,* that everywhere show the cunning hand of the artificer. Borges's stories are only bound indirectly to particular historical or cultural forms. To this it may be answered that there is always a beguiling verisimilar aspect even in Borges's most concocted fabrications, for example, the circumstantial description of weather, landscape, and cityscape, or the use of apparently realistic place names and proper names. By "realistic" I mean, at least at first glance, just the sorts of names people and places might happen to have: Lönnrot, Triste-le-Roy, Scharlach. In the prologue to *Artifices (Artificios),* the volume of 1944 in which "Death and the Compass" is collected, Borges says this story, "despite the German or Scandinavian names, occurs in a Buenos Aires of dreams: the twisted Rue de Toulon is the Paseo de Juleo; Triste-le-Roy is the hotel where Herbert Ashe received, and probably did not read, the eleventh volume of an illusory encyclopedia" (E, 105). Though Herbert Ashe is another imaginary figure, a character in "Tlön, Uqbar, Orbis Tertius,"[3] it appears that Borges had a real hotel in Buenos Aires in mind in both cases, though it is certainly a Buenos Aires of dreams. And even Triste-le-Roy was not Borges's invention. On the other hand, as every student of fiction these days knows, even the most realistic story shows everywhere the marks of the maker's hand, in shapings and orderings, in names that are apparently arbitrary but in fact are "motivated," and in other such evidences of artifice. "Death and the Compass" is no exception to that.

In any case, "Death and the Compass" is "about" the relation between reality, things as they are, on the one hand, and shapely figurative patterns, such as an ostentatiously artificial work of fiction, on the other. It is therefore an appropriate text by means of which to explore the assumption that a command of figure is the major skill necessary in the interpretation of narrative. Such skill, it might be, is the true Ariadne's thread to be followed out of the labyrinth into the light of day. Manifold images of lines and labyrinths are threaded through "Death and the Compass," so it is an appropriate text with which to conclude a book investigating the image of the line in novels and in narrative theory. Figures appear in "Death and the Compass" in all the senses of the word—

for example, in the figure of the rhomb. This shape is outlined on the map of the city by the master detective Lönnrot. It corresponds to the tetragrammaton spelling out the secret name of God. Figures also appear as local figures of speech strewn as clues within a text in which the wise reader will assume that everything counts and means more than itself, even the most realistic and seemingly irrelevant details. The text as a whole, finally, makes a figure or configuration. One detail follows another in the process of reading until finally an overall meaning emerges as a triumphant solution of the enigma by the detective-reader, the recognition of a figure in the carpet.

"Death and the Compass," as previous readers have noted, is an ironic, self-conscious parody of the detective story. It is a detective story to the second power in which the laws of the genre are brought into the open and made themselves the object of detective work. In that sense, "Death and the the Compass" is cultural criticism. It is an assessment of a major popular art form, a form through which our culture has in part understood itself and created itself. The parodic and ironic aspects of "Death and the Compass" involve an explicit paralleling of the work of reading with the work of the detective. The reader not only doubles the master-detective's work but is expected to go beyond that work and read clues of which Lönnrot is apparently unaware, for example, the meaning of his own name. The chain of detective-readers goes from Commissioner Treviranus, the representative of the "dumb" policeman who always gets it wrong, to Lönnrot the master detective, explicitly a reincarnation of Poe's Dupin, to Scharlach, who outguesses Lönnrot, to the narrator, to me as reader-critic, to whoever reads these pages. The narrator is perhaps Borges, in any case someone who must have survived Lönnrot's death, or how else could his story have been told? The reader of my reading, as reader-detective in her or his turn, has access to "Death and the Compass" at second remove.

The association of Lönnrot with Dupin is made explicitly at the beginning of the story. Lönnrot is a detective of "daring perspicacity (temeraria perspicacia)" (E, 129; S, 147). He "thought of himself as a pure thinker (un puro razonador), an Auguste Dupin, but there was something of the adventurer in him, and even of the gamester" (E, 129; S, 148). There was also something of the gamester in Poe's Dupin too, as readers of "The Murders in the Rue Morgue" will remember. There the work of detection is compared to the game of odd and even, in which the trick is to follow by intuition the reasoning of one's antagonist and to calculate his calculation of one's own perspicacity. Lönnrot fails at the game of odd and even with Red Scharlach and pays with his life.

The ending in the death of the detective goes back not only to Conan Doyle's *Final Problem,* in which Holmes kills Moriarty but only (apparently) at the cost of his own life, as they plunge together into the Reichenbach Falls, but also to that great-grandfather of all detective stories, *Oedipus the King.* Like Sophocles' play, "Death and the Compass" blurs the normally strict boundaries in the usual detective story between detective, criminal, and victim. Borges's story, however, significantly alters the overlapping. In *Oedipus the King,* the detective and the criminal are the same person. The culprit Oedipus hunts down is himself. In "Death and the Compass" the detective is the victim. The more successful Lönnrot is as master sleuth the more certainly he makes his own death inevitable. Rather than beginning with the corpse, this detective story ends with one, the corpse of the detective.

How do lines, labyrinths, and figures made of lines function in this narrative of the detective's self-destruction through his own perspicacity? As I have said, there are many explicit lines making figures in the text, for example those lines making a diamond shape Lönnrot draws on the map joining the murders committed north, west, and east to the correctly predicted point in the south, the villa of Triste-le-Roy where the fourth murder will be committed. This large-scale rhomb echoes the diamond shapes associated with each of the murders, the rhombs of the paint-shop sign in the second murder, the diamonds on the harlequin costume in the third murder, the "rhomboid diamonds" of the windows which "were yellow, red and green" (E, 138) in the observatory of the villa of Triste-le-Roy, where Lönnrot is captured and presumably shot. To Red Scharlach, as he lay for nine days and nights in the villa of Triste-le-Roy with a police bullet in his chest, it seemed that "the world was a labyrinth," and he speaks of the clues he has planted as a "labyrinth" that he has "woven" around Lönnrot in his plan of revenge (E, 139): "I have woven it, and it holds: the materials are a dead writer on heresies, a compass, an eighteenth-century sect, a Greek word, a dagger, the rhombs of a paint shop" (E, 139). In this case Ariadne's thread is itself a maze. Far from being a way to escape from a maze, as in the case of Ariadne's thread, Borges's villain weaves lines into a net that catches and kills its victim. The clues make a figure, a story, a text or textile that becomes a shroud, more like Penelope's web than like Ariadne's liberating thread.

"Death and the Compass" ends, or almost ends, with a curious passage in which Lönnrot, knowing he confronts death, picks up Red Scharlach's image of the labyrinth woven as a net and opposes to that labyrinth of multiple lines a strange nonlabyrinthine labyrinth, a "labyrinth without labyrinth," as Blanchot might say. Lönnrot imagines a labyrinth made of a single straight line, a line not curved back on itself to make a figure, a figure without figure. That labyrinth made of a single straight line first turned my attention to this story and led me to choose it as the concluding figure in my exploration of narrative theory.

Whether there is any temerity in this meditation, any danger to the reader who wants to get all the way to the bottom or to the end of the line is another question. What could be simpler and more conclusive than the reduction of all the complexity of a labyrinth to a single straight line, "infinite and unceasing," followed by a shot presumably bringing the death of the protagonist, the end of the story? If the line curved back on itself to form a figure is a stimulus to thought, perhaps to endless meditation, there is apparently nothing to think about in a single straight line. It is the death of life and thought, like a straight line on a heart-monitoring oscilloscope.

What can this figure of the single-line labyrinth mean? It hardly seems motivated or prepared for by anything that has come earlier in the story, nor does it seem in any obvious way a proper conclusion for the line of themes and figures the story has followed. Probably many readers think of it as another piece of more or less irrelevant cleverness on Borges's part. I shall read my way through the story to see what expectations the one-line labyrinth may fulfill or what implicit lines of thought it may complete.

"Death and the Compass," as Michael Holquist has affirmed in a lecture, uses the cliché of the detective story opposing the dumb policeman to the clever detective to set various theories of interpretation against one another. Treviranus, the police commissioner, assumes that things have a more or less manifest meaning. Borges has borrowed his name from the author of a seventeenth-century treatise on Rosicrucianism. Exactly why that should be so is not immediately evident. It may have something to do with the obscure association of his name with the Trinity. Treviranus: three-manned? Treviranus represents those whom Red Scharlach so hates. He is a man who thinks all roads lead to Rome, someone who believes in a revealed code, without mystery to those who know it, for example, those initiated into the symbolic system of Rosicrucianism. Treviranus is a trinitarian. He is satisfied with the triangle made by lines drawn between the points of the first three murders. These points make "the perfect vertices of a mystic equilateral triangle" (E2, 82). The letter signed "Baruch Spinoza" to Commissioner Treviranus confirms this and so persuades him that the third murder will be the last. Spinoza was no trinitarian, so the signature should have warned Treviranus that he was making a mistake. The name Spinoza adds to the line of Jewish clues in the story. His philosophy provides another possible way of interpreting the story.

Lönnrot is another matter. He intuits from the letter that there will be a fourth murder making the equilateral triangle double, a diamond shape or rhomb. He goes to that fourth point, the villa of Triste-le-Roy, to meet his death. If Treviranus, as he says of himself, is "only a poor Christian" who does not have "time to lose in Jewish superstitions" (E, 131), Lönnrot, as Scharlach correctly calculates, would "prefer a purely rabbinical explanation" for the murder of a rabbi (E, 130). Borges has borrowed Lönnrot's name from the Finnish philologist, Elias Lönnrot (1802–84). That Lönnrot devoted his life to gathering fragments from all around Finland of the lost Finnish epic, the *Kalevala*. He then reconstructed them into a no-doubt factitious whole. The historical Lönnrot was in a manner of speaking the Homer of Finland, but of course only in a manner of speaking. Like a detective, he stitched together detached pieces to reconstruct a lost whole rather than being a master reweaver of formulaic elements as Homer was, or at least as we imagine Homer to have been. Borges's Lönnrot shares with his namesake the propensity for putting fragmentary clues together to make a whole figure. This accompanies his implicit assumption that the figure is already out there in the world, ready to be deciphered. Such a figure would be written on things as they are, like that name hidden by being completely out in the open on the map Dupin refers to in Poe's "Purloined Letter."

"Death and the Compass" parodies, among other conventions of detective stories, this correspondence between a figure of one sort or another made on a map and the solution of a mystery or crime. Examples would include Poe's "Gold Bug" and Conan

Doyle's "Musgrave Ritual," among many others. The relation of landscape or map of landscape to the story enacted on that scene is another corridor within the labyrinth of narrative theory. I shall explore it in another place. Here my interest is in the way the design on a map or on the real surface of a city may be made a figure having meaning, standing for something other than itself, in one or another meaning of the word *figure*. In this case the equilateral triangle on the map is set against the rhomb. Both are then opposed to the "world [as] a labyrinth from which it was impossible to flee, for all paths, whether they seemed to lead north or south, actually led to Rome" (E, 139). All three finally are displaced once more by the labyrinth made of a single line on a map along which a sequence of narrative events might take place. In fact, all four of these figures are not only signs in themselves. They are also configurations of loci tracing out a series of occurrences making a story with a parabolic meaning.

Each of these figures may be abstracted from its material base and made to cover more space and time without losing its figurative significance. This is affirmed by an odd possibility Borges suggests in the prologue to *Artificios*. The elements of "Death and the Compass," he says, might be vastly expanded in spatial and temporal scope without ceasing to outline the same figure and presumably therefore having the same meaning: "After composing this narrative, I have come to consider the soundness of amplifying the time and space in which it occurs: vengeance could be inherited; the periods of time might be computed in years, perhaps in centuries; the first letter of the Name might be spoken in Iceland; the second, in Mexico; the third, in Hindustan" (E, 105).

Lönnrot's hermeneutical assumptions, in their difference from Treviranus's triangular certainties, present alternative possibilities of the way figures may have meaning. It is not easy to decide among these on the basis of the text. Lönnrot tells Treviranus that "reality may avoid the obligation to be interesting, but . . . hypotheses may not" (E, 130). He goes on to say that the trouble with Treviranus's explanation of the murder of Yarmolinsky is that it assumes things happen without rhyme or reason, without governance by any figure: "In the hypothesis you have postulated, chance intervenes largely. Here lies a dead rabbi; I should prefer a purely rabbinical explanation; not the imaginary mischances of an imaginary robber" (E, 130). Lönnrot assumes that apparently random events are going to hang together and make sense. There is a secret meaning inscribed in the figures made by what happens out there in the world. Readers of Borges's story tend to make a similar assumption. They assume every detail in the text is motivated. The reader's complicity in the sort of hermeneutical presuppositions that get Lönnrot killed is of course part of the point of the story. But exactly what sort of meaning does Lönnrot assume is out there in the world, and according to whose plan?

The Hasidim believe that God has a secret name, presumably based on the tetragrammaton of four consonants: JHVH. Possession of the name would give divine knowledge, that is, "eternity—that is to say, the immediate knowledge of everything that will exist, and has existed in the universe" (E, 131). Hasidim believe, according to the "fantasy dictated by the form of [the] story" (E, 105) (for which Borges apologizes in the prologue), that the secret name might be obtained by human sacrifices. The secret name must not only be obtained but "spoken" in order for its power to be acquired. It cannot be spoken as an ordinary word, any more than those four consonants of the Hebrew tetragrammaton can be spoken as such. A consonant without a vowel is voiceless, unspeakable. If one knew the vowel points one could perhaps speak the name, as it has been corrupted by Christian tradition into Jehovah. The imaginary sect of Hasidim Borges invents proposes to speak the name by way of a series of four sacrificial murders. The events themselves will speak. Ultimately four of them will accumulate to form a figure uttering the unutterable. This utterance of the unutterable will be figurable by that rhomb Lönnrot draws with a set of calipers and a compass on the map of the city. Hence the message left written in one way or another at the scenes of the first three murders: *"The first letter of the Name has been spoken"; "The second letter of the Name has been spoken"; "The third letter of the Name has been spoken."*

What, exactly, is Lönnrot's attitude toward this figuration? What is Borges's attitude? What should the reader's attitude be? One interpretation would be a purely sociological, cultural, or historical one. The Hasidim are superstitious enough to believe in the existence of a secret name of God and fanatical enough to commit murder to try to obtain it. The detective who reads dusty books on Hebrew lore, as Lönnrot does, will be able to understand the human and cultural motives of the murderers and so to solve the crime. This would correspond to an interpretation according to ideology, as in most present-day cultural criticism. Another possibility is that Lönnrot too, perhaps also Borges, believes in the existence of the Secret Name and follows the Hasidim in their search. When Lönnrot is captured by Red Scharlach his first words to his captor are, "Are you looking for the Secret Name, Scharlach?" (E, 138). Lönnrot's question seems to presuppose that only this shared motive could have brought them to the same place at the same time, though Lönnrot's question may be no more than irony. Other hermeneutic assumptions would be variations on this last one: the notion that nature in itself is a secret code making configurations readable by a master detective or hermeneut, or the notion that God himself has staged the whole sequence, perhaps to mislead Lönnrot into thinking he is about to obtain the ineffable name of God. It is not entirely certain, on the basis of the text, which of these hermeneutical hypotheses the reader is meant to take seriously and adopt in his or her own interpretation. It might be better to say that the text of the story presents the possibility of all these theories of figure and dramatizes the conflict among them. The end of the story, however, allows the exegete to say more than that.

To reach that end the reader must recognize and account for yet another hermeneutical theory, that embodied in the third figure (in the sense of "character") in the story, the murderer of Lönnrot. This is Red Scharlach, Scharlach the Dandy, "the most illustrious gunman of the south (el más ilustre de los pistoleros del Sur)" (E2, 81; S, 155). Scharlach's motive is to avenge his honor against Lönnrot for the latter's imprisonment of his brother and nearly mortal wounding of Scharlach himself. His revenge is also against the theories of interpretation represented by the other two main characters, their belief that in one way or another events in the world are not merely random and fortuitous. While he lay wounded in the villa of Triste-le-Roy, Scharlach tells Lönnrot after he has captured him, "An Irishman tried to convert me to the faith of Jesus; he repeated to me the phrase of the *goyim*: All roads lead to Rome (Un irlandés trató de convertirme a la fe de Jesús; me repetía la sentencia de los *góim*: Todos los caminos llevan a Roma)" (E2, 85; S, 159). Scharlach is apparently Jewish, but he must be a Jew of a very different sort from those Hasidim who believe God has a secret name and that finding that name will give knowledge of the whole universe and the power over it such knowledge would give. Scharlach is enlightened, faithless, a believer in neither the superficial triangular certitudes of the "poor Christian" Treviranus, nor in the rhomb of the tetragrammaton that fascinates Lönnrot, nor in the labyrinthine assumption that everything has an intrinsic meaning centered on Rome, so that events are organized into roads, narrative sequences making figures leading to that commanding center. Scharlach appears to be a radical skeptic. For him the universe has no meaning whatsoever beyond those projected into it by man. In his voice Lönnrot can hear "a fatigued triumph, a hatred the size of the universe, a sadness not less than that hatred (una fatigada victoria, un odio del tamaño del universo, una tristeza no menor que aquel odio)" (E2, 84; S, 159).

Scharlach's triumph is to have trapped Lönnrot, to have won a game of odd and even with him. Scharlach has taken advantage of the pure chance of the first murder to weave a fictive labyrinth that nets Lönnrot: "I knew that you would make the conjecture that the Hasidim had sacrificed the rabbi: I set myself the task of justifying that conjecture. . . . I sent the equilateral triangle to Treviranus. I foresaw that you would add the missing point. The point which would form a perfect rhomb, the point which fixes in advance where a punctual death awaits you (el punto que prefija el lugar donde una exacta muerte lo espera). I have premeditated everything, Erik Lönnrot, in order to attract you to the solitudes of Triste-le-Roy" (E2, 85, 86; S, 161, 162).

Scharlach hates Lönnrot for nearly killing him and for imprisoning his brother. He hates him also as a representative of fatuous belief in law and order—the belief, for example, that there will be a rabbinical explanation for a rabbinical murder, that events form a configuration that can be read as the signs of a secret meaning inscribed within them. Scharlach's sadness is the sadness of the radical skeptic or disbeliever. For such a person nothing in the universe has any intrinsic meaning. Lönnrot comes to share that sadness when he recognizes that Scharlach has tricked him, that the hypothesis of a rabbinical explanation for the murders is false. They have only a feigned configuration planned for them by Scharlach by taking advantage of the pure chance of the first murder. Scharlach makes a correct calculation of the hermeneutical credulity of Lönnrot. It is a credulity not too different from that of his namesake, who thought the *Kalevala* could be accurately reconstructed from dispersed fragments. This effort of reconstruction was something like putting geographically scattered letters together to spell out the secret name of God. The sadness Lönnrot feels just before Scharlach fires, the reader may guess, is as much the sadness of an ultimate disillusionment as sadness at his own imminent death: "He felt faintly cold, and he felt, too, an impersonal—almost anonymous—sadness. It was already night; from the dusty garden came the futile cry of a bird (Sintió un poco de frío y una tristeza impersonal, casi anónima. Ya era de noche; desde el polvoriento jardín subió el grito inútil de un pájaro)" (E2, 86; S, 162). The bird's cry is futile or useless because it has no meaning and therefore no performative force. It is like everything else in Scharlach's universe and in the universe he has brought Lönnrot (and perhaps the reader) to inhabit for a moment before he fires his gun and ends the story. It neither says anything nor makes anything happen. You cannot do anything with it. It is useless, "inútil."

The figure for Scharlach's hermeneutics of skeptical disbelief is neither the triangle nor the perfect rhomb, nor the labyrinth, but the futility of a mirroring symmetry. Scharlach means "scarlet" in German. It is also a kind of red flower. *Scharlachfieber* is scarlet fever. Red Scharlach's name mirrors itself. It means "Red Red." Scharlach's brother (unnamed in the story) is a kind of double of himself. As Scharlach lay "dying" of fever in the villa of Triste-le-Roy he thought of the world as a labyrinthine prison, "from which it was impossible to flee (del cual era imposible huir), for all roads, though they pretend to lead to the north or south, actually lead to Rome, which was also the quadrilateral jail (la cárcel cuadrangular) where my brother was dying and the villa of Triste-le-Roy" (E2, 85; S, 159–60). The villa doubles the jail that doubles Rome, the prison that incarcerates by lying at the end of any path we take.

Triste-le-Roy, Scharlach's locus and the point of his triumph over Lönnrot, is itself also a labyrinth, but of a peculiar kind. It is the sort of labyrinth that amazes its victims by bewildering symmetric doublings, something like those strange architectural nightmares concocted by Escher:

> Viewed from anear, the house of the villa of Triste-le-Roy abounded in pointless symmetries and in maniacal repetitions (inútiles simetrías y en repeticiones maniáticas): to one Diana in a murky niche corresponded a second Diana in another niche; one balcony was reflected in another balcony; double stairways led to double balustrades. A two-faced Hermes projected a monstrous shadow. . . .

Lönnrot explored the house. Through anterooms and galleries he passed to duplicate patios, and time after time to the same patio. He ascended the dusty stairs to circular antechambers; he was multiplied infinitely in opposing mirrors (infinitamente se multiplicó en espejos opuestos); he grew tired of opening or half-opening windows which revealed outside the same desolate garden from various heights and various angles. . . . On the second floor, on the top floor, the house seemed infinite and expanding. *The house is not this large,* he thought. *Other things are making it seem larger: the dim light, the symmetry, the mirrors, so many years, my unfamiliarity, the loneliness.* (E2, 83–84; S, 157–58)

The villa of Triste-le-Roy creates through various forms of doubling an artificial infinity. The one who becomes lost in it is imprisoned within the sad uselessness of a pointless mirroring. Hence its odd name, or rather hence Borges's borrowing of the "beautiful name invented by Amanda Molina Vedia" on an imaginary map she had drawn.[4] The story is dedicated to her. This is an indication of that name's importance in Borges's conception of the story. In this villa sadness or "Sad" is king because there one can never encounter anything more than one's own face in the mirror. The meaning of each new element is that it is the futile duplicate of another element, neither of which has any priority or grounding authority over the other. The villa's heraldic emblems are a glacial and unattractive Diana, senselessly doubled, and a two-faced Hermes. This Hermes is not the messenger of the gods and the bearer of arcane knowledge. This Hermes is the incarnation of a hermeneutics of suspicion presupposing that the activity of interpretation is a narcissistic self-mirroring. The reader, according to this sad hermeneutics, never gets anything out of a text that he or she has not first put into it or that someone (perhaps an "interpretative community") has projected into it as a trap for the reader. Scharlach has woven a trap for Lönnrot out of cunningly placed signs that do not have the resonant hermeneutic meaning they appear to have. For Scharlach in his feverish dreams the two-faced Hermes turns into a detestable two-faced Janus, god of doorways and thresholds. This Janus is neither on the one side nor on the other, neither inside nor out, dark nor day. He is a god of the in-between, of a twilight that may be dawn and may be dusk. This Janus presides over self-enclosed, self-regarding doubling. He supervises sign making and sign reading as a "monstrous" prison house of language in which you never encounter anything but yourself and in which "Sad" is therefore indeed king:

> Nine days and nine nights [Scharlach tells Lönnrot] I lay in agony in this desolate, symmetrical villa; fever was demolishing me, and the odious two-faced Janus who watches the twilights and the dawns (el odioso Jano bifronte que mira los ocasos y las auroras) lent horror to my dreams and to my waking. I came to abominate my body, I came to sense that two eyes, two hands, two lungs are as monstrous as two faces. . . . On those nights I swore by the God who sees with two faces (el dios que ve con dos caras) and by all the gods of fever and of the mirrors to weave a labyrinth around the man who had imprisoned my brother. (E2, 84–85; S, 159, 160)

With the reading of Scharlach as the personification of a certain theory of reading I seem to have reached a full interpretation of "Death and the Compass." I have read it as a battle of figures in which the prosopopoeia of the threshold, the Janus or Hermes facing both ways, is used to dismantle the figures of the triangle, the rhomb, and the centered labyrinth, along with all the mystified hermeneutical assumptions that correspond to these figures. I have read the story as a use of figure to deconstruct faith in the power of figures to give knowledge, to decipher either a hidden meaning in the world or a hidden meaning in a narrative. In place of that, according to the reading of Scharlach I have proposed, is put a disillusioned recognition that all figures are duplicitous. They are a reading of one's own face in the mirror. Figures give back only what has been put into them. Far from being a reliable means of reaching epistemological certitude they only tell their readers something about the one who has concocted them or who reads them.

This use of a final figure to deconstruct misplaced confidence in figures is so reassuring as to make one a little uneasy. For one thing it appears to replace mystified epistemological assumptions about figures (that the right figure, for example, would spell out the secret name of God and give total knowledge of the universe) not with epistemological uncertainty but with an ultimate epistemological certainty. The reader reaches the certain knowledge that figures do not give epistemological knowledge. This in turn is based on another presumed epistemological certainty. We can know for certain that the world has no secret meaning. It is a passive and meaningless chaos waiting harmlessly to have meaning cast over it like a net, as Scharlach catches Lönnrot in a netlike labyrinth of feigned signs. Or, to vary the figure, meaning can be projected into the world like a figure cast from a magic lantern on a blank wall, as Dibutade's lover's shadow, in Pliny's story, was cast on the stone, in a reversal of Plato's cave. This final presumed epistemological certainty corresponds to a now widely influential theory of reading that sees any text as an innocent absence of meaning into which a reader or community of readers freely and safely projects meanings, whatever meanings are desired or ideologically favored. The use of figure to deconstruct figure still remains within the assumption that a text is a system of tropological substitutions. It still assumes that a mastery of figures is the key to the interpretation of narrative. It assumes that there is at least one reliable figure, namely the one used to deconstruct all the others. Moreover, it turns reading into a reassuringly continuous narrative going from a series of successively demystified mystifications to ultimate disillusioned knowledge, in a familiar totalizing sequence.

To put this another way, the reliable knowledge figures give is shifted in this reading away from the outside world. It is shifted first to knowledge of the way language works as a tool of man and then to the psychology of the one who invents the figures. If Lönnrot does not learn the secret name of God through his interpretation of figures, he, and the reader with him, do learn about the motivations and mental makeup of Scharlach. With this knowledge he solves the murders, including proleptically his own. He dies knowing with certainty why he is being killed.

The reader is put by the story as Borges's "fiction" or "artifice" in the same position as Lönnrot is put in by Scharlach. The reader is presented with a large assemblage of data, data that all seem interpretable. Each detail seems to have some covert meaning, the odd names of the characters, for example, or the various geometrical figures. Some hidden and difficult knowledge is tacitly promised, perhaps even knowledge of the secret name, if the reader can interpret the signs right, put all the data together, draw the right lines between the points, and identify the figure in the carpet. Eventually, at the denouement, when Lönnrot's folly is revealed, the reader may come to feel that he or she has been duped, as Lönnrot by Scharlach. All those clues and meanings, it seems, have factitiously and with malice aforethought been cunningly put in the text by Borges in order to make it a netlike labyrinth to catch the reader. The reader is Lönnrot to Borges as Scharlach. At this point the reader seems left with nothing in hand but an artifice, a dead figure. This artifice gives the reader no knowledge of history or of mankind such as the great realist novelists, George Eliot or Leo Tolstoi, for example, are said to give. Reading "Death and the Compass" we gain only knowledge of Borges as a maker of artificial fictions. These are superficial self-reflecting and self-destroying mechanisms of words that fall to pieces in the reader's hands. Any reader of any work may experience this loss of faith in printed words, this recognition that the text is only marks on paper. The reader has been duped into taking the dead letter as a sort of Galatea come to life. He or she has mistakenly taken that dead letter as a warm simulacrum of real bodies and persons, has taken it as a reliable means of access to other people, to society, and to history. The reader of Borges may feel cheated, the victim of a trick, and cast down *Ficciones* in disgust, in spite of the certain knowledge about Borges himself its stories seem to provide. The reader can feel at least that there is one thing he or she knows for certain, namely, that Borges is a sly fellow who plays with words the same sort of tricks on his reader Escher plays with visible figures.

This apparent endpoint of my reading is, as I have suggested, just a little too reassuringly certain. If the paradigm for all texts consists of a figure or a system of figures and its deconstruction,[5] I have certainly been able to show that for "Death and the Compass." But it is also always possible to go beyond any apparent stopping place or ultimate point in a reading, even one that seems to be a culmination in some elegantly formulated and hermetically sealed aporia. The good reader will learn to distrust interpretations that claim to give reliable knowledge, even bracingly negative knowledge. "Watch out when you think you have 'got it,' for you are then most likely to be duped, the victim of an illusory clarity": that might be the canny reader's motto.

In "Death and the Compass" clues for going beyond the apparent closure I have reached are given by the story itself. It is a little puzzling to conclude that Borges has embodied his own hermeneutical skepticism in the villain of his story, even though this would be a possible irony. Moreover, there is an aspect of the figure of the line as threshold that I have not yet taken into account. The doubling within this figure is redoubled. On the one hand is the figure of a man or woman looking in the mirror, two faces facing one another narcissistically. This gave me the image of someone confronting his or her own face in a text or in the world, finding in either only what has been put into it. Such a mirror is empty until I project my own face into it. Double opposing mirrors may create an artificial infinity duplicating my face and figure ad infinitum in an endlessly receding series. On the other hand, Borges's final figure is of a two-faced Janus or Hermes standing in the midnight or at high noon and facing *outward* from that liminal boundary toward two symmetrical and beguilingly similar twi-lights, dawn and dusk. This version of the figure is hardly com-patible with the other. The force of the figure may depend on the reader's not noticing this and thinking of it in both ways at once, in defiance of a logical impossibility not even noticed.

As a two-faced figure facing outward the Janus or Hermes is not the model of narcissistic knowledge only of oneself. It figures rather knowledge of what is outside the self. Only a two-faced vision can see the duplicity hidden from the vision of a single face, for ex-ample, the fact that dawn and dusk look the same. They are the same mixture of half light, half dark, but they are in different places in relation to the dark and light of which they are made. Only the Janus-Hermes can interpret the mixture of sameness and difference that is the basis of all metaphorical substitutions. Only such four-eyed vision can work as a reliable hermeneutical tool for gaining accurate knowledge of a duplicitous world, the world as it is according to Red Scharlach.

It is impossible, however, at least impossible logically, to have the figure of the mirroring Janus both ways at once. Nor do Borges's formulations allow a choice between them or the estab-lishment of a priority, hierarchy, or dialectical movement between them. This apparently final figure deconstructs all the other prior ones, the triangle, the rhomb, the centered and lawful labyrinth. But it also deconstructs itself. It doubles itself within itself. Each version of it disqualifies the other, while being disqualified itself by that other. The figure of the Janus-Hermes, far from giving the reader mastery of figure and mastery through figure of a narrative considered to be made of a system of figures, leaves the reader unable to move forward, rendered hermeneutically powerless by what may be Borges's final cunning trick on the reader—to provide an apparently reliable tool of interpretation that turns inside out and disintegrates in the reader's hands.

At this point, the reader may remember Lönnrot's final speech

presenting one further figure, an apparently superfluous image beyond the figure of Janus-Hermes. This is the figure of the labyrinth
"consisting of a single line which is invisible and unceasing
(que consta de una sola línea recta y que es invisible, incesante)"
(E2, 87; S, 163). What is the reader to make of this concluding
trope? After Lönnrot's proposal of this image the story ends with
Scharlach's firing his gun at Lönnrot: "He moved back a few steps.
Then, very carefully, he fired (Retrocedió unos pasos. Después,
muy cuidadosamente, hizo fuego)" (E2, 87; S, 163). Is this ending
no more than a clever conclusion, making "Death and the Compass" a detective story that ends with the murder of the detective
at the moment he has just solved the murder that has not quite yet
happened? Or does it have a further meaning in relation to the
reading of narrative or of the world by means of one figure or
another? Why is this enigma emphasized in the title? Why is the
story called "*Death* and the Compass," just as the anecdote on
which "A New Refutation of Time" is based, the story of the
experience of an exact duplication of two events, is, strangely,
called "Feeling in Death": "That pure representation of homogeneous objects—the night in serenity, a limpid little wall, the provincial scent of the honeysuckle, the elemental earth—is not merely
identical to the one present on that corner so many years ago; it
is, without resemblances or repetitions, the very same. Time, if we
can intuitively grasp such an identity, is a delusion: the difference
and inseparability of one moment belonging to its apparent past
from another belonging to its apparent present is sufficient to
disintegrate it" (E2, 226–27). What does this experience of identity
have to do with "feeling in death"? I have figured out the use in
"Death and the Compass" of various sorts of compasses, literal
and figurative, to plot the figures and measure their meaning, but
what is the relation between figures and death? What is the compass to measure that ratio?

The labyrinth made of an "invisible and unceasing" straight
line is appropriate as an endpoint for this book. It is the ultimate
reduction of narrative theory's tangled labyrinth to the simplicity
of a straight line. The one-line labyrinth is not the liminal line of
the Janus face Scharlach proposes and the ville of Triste-le-Roy
embodies. It is a line going from here to there along which one
can move only in that one dimension, back and forth. Such a
labyrinth is the obverse of the infinite labyrinth made of the bland
expanse of a trackless desert or sea. In both cases the labyrinth is

invisible and everlasting. It is invisible, in the case of the desert, because there are no lines at all on it. Lönnrot's labyrinth is "invisible," presumably, because the line exists only as generated by imaginary lines between various points. It is incessant in both cases, in a different way in each case, both because the desert and the line go on and on and because the labyrinthian movement generated by the play between points is unceasing. It is a dizzying movement in place or an infinite regression, as Borges shows.

What does it mean to say that a straight line can be a labyrinth? "In your labyrinth there are three lines too many," says Lönnrot to Scharlach just before the latter fires his gun. "I know of a Greek labyrinth which is a single straight line. Along this line so many philosophers have lost themselves that a mere detective might well do so too" (E, 141). No doubt the Greek one-line labyrinth Lönnrot has in mind is the figure used in the paradoxes of Zeno. These are discussed by Borges in "Avatars of the Tortoise." One paradox shows Achilles can never catch the tortoise. Another shows neither Achilles nor the tortoise can ever even get started, since any runner at some point will be half way there, before that half of that distance, before that half of that quarter, before that half of that again, and so on, ad infinitum, without ever being able to budge from the beginning. To be lost in this labyrinth is to use it as a figure of thought that boggles the mind and entraps it in an endless sterile meditation, like a computer caught in a looping repetitive feedback. "Scharlach," says Lönnrot, "when, in some other incarnation you hunt me, feign to commit (or do commit) a crime at A, then a second crime at B, eight kilometers from A, then a third crime at C, four kilometers from A and B, half way enroute between the two. Wait for me later at D, two kilometers from A and C, half way, once again, between both. Kill me at D, as you are now going to kill me at Triste-le-Roy" (141). Lönnrot's proposal gives a geometric model for an infinite regression of thought, broken in this case by the punctual execution of Lönnrot at point D. There is no reason why the division and subdivision should not go on incessantly, with a point E, a point F, and so on. "The next time I kill you, " Scharlach answers Lönnrot just before he fires, "I promise you the labyrinth made of the single straight line and which is invisible and everlasting" (141). Here is Lönnrot's figure:

AED C   B

Another celebrated Greek straight line exists, however, one offering a model for thought differing from the invisible line of

Zeno's paradoxes. I mean the twice-bifurcated line of Plato's *Republic*. A comparison of the two lines may help the reader understand why Borges's invocation of Zeno's paradox, or rather Borges's invocation through his narrator through Lönnrot, is an appropriate endpoint, or point before the end in the firing of the gun, for this story. "Death and the Compass" has proceeded from point A to point B to point C, and so on, by the successive presentation of geometric figures, each one disqualifying and abolishing the one before, only to be dismantled in its turn by the next, just as the story is made of consciousness within consciousness within consciousness.

Plato's twice-bifurcated line is a visual metaphor for all those metaphorical ratios drawing analogies between the physical and the metaphysical realms, the realm of things and the realm of ideas. These metaphors take the form of a proportional analogy. The latter is proposed in Aristotle's section on metaphor in the *Poetics* as the ideal and proper form of a metaphor: as A is to B, so C is to D. As the soul is to the body, so the One is to the world. Far from being invisible and unceasing, such a twice-bifurcated line and the thought to which it corresponds are controlled and logical. The line comes to an end at both ends with a satisfying click, like a riddle solved. It is logical because it is controlled by the logos. It has the form of logical thought as defined by Plato, model both for mimetic representation and for controlled, delimited, and definable figures of speech. Such a conception of figure is the source of our assumption that metaphor is not one trope among many but the model or type of trope. Metonymy and synecdoche are no more than defective metaphors. Plato's twice-bifurcated line is "invisible" in the sense that, for Plato, an *idea* is both an appearance and a thought. The line is visible, but part of what it stands for can never be seen, except metaphorically. The figure is disabled by what it names, the impossibility of naming the transcendent world except through metaphor. It is a condition of thought, for Plato, that the objects of thought be invisible. They are in the sunlight of reality outside the cave, where we would be blinded. As the physical eye is to visible objects, so the inner eye, insight, is to the invisible spiritual shining forth of the idea.

Zeno's line, or Lönnrot's, on the other hand, is a geometrical model for that most defective of metaphors, the one in which one of the four elements in the proportional analogy is missing. A fictive personification of this is the asymmetrical ratio among the four principle characters in Goethe's *Wahlverwandtschaften*. Another way to put this is to say that Lönnrot's line is the geometrical representation of the figure called catachresis. If the governing or head term, the logos, is missing, invisible, not available as an *idea* in either sense of the word (as concept or as eidos, visible form), the remaining three terms set up an incessant movement among themselves, a painful alogical oscillation of thought, as in the paradoxes of Zeno. Such oscillation is painful because it is undecidable and inescapable, like being caught in a revolving door, a door, moreover, that someone or something is pushing faster and faster, with infinite acceleration. One knows, or thinks one knows, that Achilles will catch the tortoise, but Zeno shows that can never happen. In "Death and the Compass" the labyrinth made of a single straight line, invisible and everlasting, is the geometrical model of a catachresis. This is so not because for Borges figurative language can be known to be a human artifice cast over a passive, indifferent, and chaotic world, but because it is impossible ever to be sure whether the two-faced Janus-Hermes faces inward or outward. If it faces inward it confronts the endlessly self-reflecting fabricating powers of consciousness as a specular structure. If outward it is oriented toward a possible revelation, by way of some magical correspondence, of a secret truth about the universe, something already there in things as they are, but hidden. To put this another way, it is always possible, for Borges, though never possible to know for sure, that the secret name of God has in fact been uttered, either by one or another of the figures Borges presents, or by the whole story taken as a single figure of thought. The whole interpretation of the story depends on deciding about this. The validity not of this or that figure but the validity of figure as such depends on it. Is the story a catachresis for some hidden knowledge that can be expressed in no other way, or is it a catachresis of nothing? Nothing is more important for the reader to know, and yet it is impossible to know. Only an ungrounded and arbitrary choice can decide, though the choice must be made. It must be made as a performative speech act for which the critic must take responsibility, since the choice has ethical and social consequences. Far from leading at last to a mastery of narrative theory, the exploration of figure as a mode of interpreting stories has led, in this case at least, to the experience of a rendering impotent of this last interpretative strategy. Like the Greeks and Lönnrot, we have become lost in a labyrinth whose particular horror is its extreme simplicity. This is the endpoint of the exploration of figure in "Death and the Compass."

———

Or rather it is the penultimate point. The story takes one more step. After promising Lönnrot the one-line labyrinth the next time he kills him, Scharlach fires his gun: "hizo fuego." After this the text ends, presumably in the blank of the protagonist's death. What is the reader to make of this ending? How can it be fitted into the interpretation of figure as the ultimate form of undecidability in narrative I have just proposed?

The story is called "Death and the Compass (La muerte y la brújula)" as if to call attention to this problem. The function of the compass we know. It is a means of measurement and orientation, a means of laying out maps and establishing lines between points to make designs. All I have called "figure" can be put under the aegis of the compass. But what of death?

A clue may be given by the exploration of another question. Who is the narrator of "Death and the Compass"? It can hardly be the man Jorge Luis Borges himself, since the narrator has extraordinary powers of penetration and ubiquity normally designated as omniscience. He (she?) knows what Lönnrot thought to himself as he explored the villa of Triste-le-Roy: "The house is not this large, he thought," among other things. He or she must have been present, as a kind of ghostly spectator, at the shooting of Lönnrot, though no person was present but Scharlach and his two toughs. Like other narrators of this type, this ungendered person is gifted with total memorial knowledge of all that made up this "periodic series of bloody acts (periódica serie de hechos de sangre)" (E, 129; S, 147). Whatever has happened, the narrator can make go on happening eternally within the covers of a book by telling it over again in the past tense, that is, in the verbal mode of having all already happened. This tense is essential to storytelling. The "historical present" is no more than a variation on this convention, the signal of a power of memorial resurrection that the past tense also implicitly has. In the historical present what has happened is overtly asserted as happening over again now, in the words.

To put this another way, the narrator of "Death and the Compass" is the survivor of the firing of Scharlach's gun at Lönnrot. All narration has this structure. All narrative is a species of epitaph, a memoir or memorial, an oblique act of mourning, just as all photographs of people, it has been observed, presuppose the actual or eventual death of those photographed. Photographs are at least proleptically pictures of the dead. All narrative, in fact all literature, is an assertion of what Maurice Blanchot calls "the right to death (le droit à la mort)." For Borges, as for Blanchot or for Derrida, all literature is inhabited by death, by the death of the other, as are reading and interpretation, in their turn, or as is the act of reading the work of criticism.[6] Each link in the chain going from author to protagonist to narrator to reader-critic to readers of the critical essay re-forms this epitaphic or memorial structure. Someone is dead and someone has survived that death to mourn and to narrate the dead person's story. This narration leads to further retellings. The series corresponds, as I shall show, to the endless repetitive series in Zeno's paradoxes that Lönnrot figures as the labyrinth made of a single straight line.

If all narration is memorial, or, to borrow a word from Borges, "memorious (memorioso)," it remembers a death that has always already happened and that is therefore only symbolized or figured by any death, real or imagined, such as the murder of Lönnrot. Such a death, death as the other of consciousness and language, the blank undermining both, can never be identified as having occurred at any present moment in the past as a punctual event. However far back one goes, it has always already occurred, or has always already not quite yet occurred. Any actual or imagined death in storytelling is only the memorial of this immemorial non-event. If narration is memorial in this sense, the memory of a past that was never present, narration too is deprived of presence. Narration takes place in a literary present, simulacrum of the real present we think we inhabit. Mallarmé calls this place of literature "a false appearance of the present (une apparence fausse de présent)."[7] Narrative memory is always of some figure, whether of person or of tropological design. Memory may be put with figure under the aegis of the compass. Death, on the other hand, names the otherness that inhabits any figuration and makes its validity and purport uncertain. They are uncertain because the figure's ground cannot be reached and ascertained. Death labels the missing fourth term in the proportional analogy, the unidentifiable X at the end of the series A, B, C, D, . . . X that turns the twice-bifurcated line, delimited and neat, into the invisible and unceasing one-line labyrinth, figure of an eternal repetition.

Death is never experienced as an event. What can be seen is the change of the other from live body to dead body, corpse, inanimate matter. We call that change death, but what we want to experience and be able to name is the transition from life to death. We want to follow someone from one realm to the other, but be able to come back and tell the story of this journey. We want to die and yet still be alive, as Wordsworth imagines himself as the survivor of his own death in an episode in *The Prelude,* "the Boy of Winander." As Paul de Man puts this, "Death is a displaced name for a linguistic predicament."[8] "Displaced name," that is, a substitutive trope for what has no proper name. The word *death* indicates a blind spot within knowledge. This blind spot de Man calls "a defacement of the mind" (ibid.). The word *defacement* names both a disfiguring of the mind, as vandals disfigure a statue, and a disabling of the trope of prosopopoeia that projects a human face and a human personality into the mind. Death is an area in the mind that cannot be humanized. This defaced area is a product of the inherence of language in consciousness and of consciousness's dependence on language. This place cannot ever be faced and named directly.

The fact that this blind spot cannot be faced means that any displaced name for it, "death," for example, covers over what it names as much as it reveals it. Death is a figure too, like the one-line labyrinth. The word *death* has the same misleading tendencies to be taken literally as giving epistemological certainty as any other figure. It is almost impossible to detach the name "death" from the pathos of mortality and from the beguiling implication that there must be some metaphysical realm of death, before, below, above, ahead, a place we could reach and know if we could only take one more step, that *pas au delà* of which Blanchot writes. But this is just what can never be known for sure one way or the other. "Death" names this uncertainty, but only if the name is read rightly. My final pages here cannot have escaped from a misleading humanizing pathos in the word *death,* any more than Borges can evade it in naming and ending as he does "Death and the Compass." After Scharlach fires, the story ends. Of death nothing can be said, though all the figures following one another and the story as a whole taken as a single figure are catachreses of death, a tropological way of saying "death." Just what this saying means cannot be further determined. Any attempt at determination could be nothing but another figure. It would be another throwing out of a configuration toward the unknown X at the end of the line.

It cannot even be said for certain whether anything is there or not, whether the X preexists the figures for it or is generated by them.

Thinking of a narrative as a whole as a catachresis shifts from the apparent spatiality of catachresis when it is a trope present in a single word (for example, "eye of a hurricane") to figuration as movement along a temporal line. The twice-bifurcated line of proportional metaphor is intimately related to a conception of narrative as having an origin, as oriented toward a goal, and as having a logos, a determinate transcendent base. The other figure, proportional metaphor with a missing fourth term (A is to B as C is to X), generates the model of another kind of temporality, narrative not logocentric but without center, without ascertainable origin or goal. In such a time death is not origin or end but is a perpetually displaced inherent absence. Of this absence it cannot even be said for certain whether anything is absent or not. The basic resource of narrative is prosopopoeia, that is, the invocation of the absent, dead, or inanimate by personifying them as characters who interact in a story figuring a linguistic predicament.[9] Such prosopopoeias are a temporal allegory, a saying it otherwise, of the catachresis in the word *death*. As Walter Benjamin puts this: "The reader of a novel actually does look for human beings from whom he derives the 'meaning of life.' Therefore he must, no matter what, know in advance that he will share their experience of death: if need be their figurative death—the end of the novel—but preferably their actual one. . . .What draws the reader to the novel is the hope of warming his shivering life with a death he reads about (Das was den Leser zum Roman zieht, ist die Hoffnung, sein fröstelndes Leben an einem Tod, von dem er liest, zu wärmen)."[10] I would modify this only by saying that the reader's desire to warm his or her life by experiencing the death of another through reading about it can never be satisfied. The hope remains unfulfilled, hence the perpetual need for more stories.

Any story is a catachresis for the unrememberable, that is, for what can never be remembered or narrated because it was never present, can never be present—for example, the death of Lönnrot in "Death and the Compass." Of more importance than the fact that there are always local tropes in a narrative is the way any narrative as a whole is tropological. If this is so, then the most literal narrative is therefore the most figural. Any story, novel, tale, narrative, account, or recounting, can be shown to be another example of this. All stories are apparently some form of memory as diegesis. They retrace a track already laid down by event following event in the past, but the event of most importance cannot be narrated. In narrative the distinction between literal and figurative disappears as the local figures are absorbed into the larger figuration. The figures of speech within a narrative are subsidiary figures of figure, or rather figures of what Blanchot might call the "figure sans figure" that the narrative line as a whole traces out in all its fictive verisimilitude.

How are these theoretical observations pertinent to the reading of "Death and the Compass"? The uncertainty inherent in any catachresis, especially in the large-scale catachresis of a narrative line taken as a single figure, is inscribed within the text of "Death and the Compass" as the concluding disfiguration of figure. The story ends with a final use of figure as the "defiguring" of the uncertainties apparently expressed in narrative figuration. So far I have tended to speak as if "Death and the Compass" ends unequivocally with the death of Lönnrot. Is that so certain?[11] The story ends not with the death of Lönnrot but with Scharlach's firing. "Hizo fuego": literally, "he made fire." The story concludes not with a literal statement, but a figure even beyond the image of the labyrinth made of a single straight line. "He fired" is a figure of speech in both English and Spanish, but it is even more obviously so in Spanish. The locution is a metonomy turned into a catachresis. It displaces the actual expulsion of the bullet from the barrel to a prior act, the striking of a spark. In antique pistols, that spark starts a fire that ignites the fuse that ignites the gun powder that expels the bullet. What is temporally contiguous to the movement of the bullet, prior to it and its proximate cause, then becomes the normal "literal" word for the pulling of the trigger in a more modern weapon. By another series of mechanical displacements pulling the trigger strikes the cartridge and "fires" the gun. To say "hizo fuego" is, strictly speaking, a catachresis, since it is not really "making fire," but saying that does not substitute for some other more literal word or term. "He made fire": that is the proper way to say it. The effect of this figure is to hint that a potentially endless series of delaying relays intervenes between the intentional act of pulling the trigger and the actual speeding of the bullet to its goal.

This perpetual intervention of yet another delay is like the first paradox of Zeno. If one applies to Scharlach's firing of his gun that paradox as rehearsed in Borges's "Avatars of the Tortoise," one can say that Red Scharlach's bullet will never reach Lönnrot. Even if the firing is not abortive, a flash in the pan, the bullet can never make it out of the barrel. It will never even get started out of the cartridge on its way down the barrel. "Almost no one recalls," writes Borges, "the one preceding it [the paradox of Achilles and the tortoise]—the one about the track—, though its mechanism is identical. Movement is impossible (argues Zeno) for the moving object must cover half the distance in order to reach its destination, and before reaching the half, half of the half, and before half of the half, half of the half of the half, and before . . . "[12]

The story just after "Death and the Compass" in *Ficciones*, "The Secret Miracle," may be read as another oblique commentary on Zeno's first paradox. The hero of that story prays for time to finish a verse drama he is writing before he is executed. God freezes time just at the moment the executioners are about to fire or perhaps have even pulled the triggers of their rifles. The miracle is "secret" because there is no way for anyone but God and perhaps Hladik to tell that time has been interrupted in this way. At the end of a "year," during which Hladik finishes his plan, down to the last half line, time starts again, the rifles fire, and Hladik is dead. "Death and the Compass" ends, one might say, at just that moment when a perpetual delay of time may be about to begin, or when it is impossible to be sure whether or not such a delay is about to begin. The last moment of "Death and the Compass" may be an intervention of eternity within time in the form of an infinite regress inhibiting movement from ever getting started.

The first presentation of the one-line labyrinth is made by Lönnrot in his final speech to Scharlach. The second is enacted by Scharlach when he speaks and then fires his gun. This doubling turns on a repetition of the Spanish word meaning "other" or "next," *otro*. Lönnrot says: "Scharlach, when in some *other* incarnation you hunt me . . . Kill me at D, as you are now going to kill me at Triste-le-Roy. (Scharlach, cuando en *otro* avatar usted me dé caza . . . Máteme en D, come abora va a matarme en Triste-le-roy)" (E2, 87; S, 162, 163, my italics). Scharlach answers: "The *next* time I kill you . . . I promise you that labyrinth, consisting of a single line which is invisible and unceasing. (Para la *otra* vez que lo mate . . . le prometo ese laberinto, que consta de una sola línea recta y que es invisible, incesante)" (E2, 87; S, 163, my italics).

Lönnrot's "otro" appears to mean "in another avatar or repetition." That would presuppose a theory of the eternal return not as the same but as variation. The same events occur and reoccur with every possible variation in their circumstances, as in the theory of narrative and time proposed in "The Garden of the Forking Paths." Scharlach's "otra," on the other hand, suggests the next time that is about to occur now, when he fires. This now is the eternally suspended moment of the bullet's trajectory that will never reach Lönnrot, if Zeno is right.[13] Scharlach's bullet will be lost on its own one-line labyrinth. Scharlach's response presupposes a different theory of the eternal return, the eternal return not as repetition with a difference, but as the same, the "now" as the locus of an unceasing repetition, like that line, invisible and unceasing, along which no movement can occur.

The title of Borges's "New Refutation of Time" is, says Borges, a *contradictio in adjecto*. If there is no time, there can never be anything new. The essay "refutes time" by combining Berkeley's idealism (nothing is except as it is perceived, *esse est percipi*) with the Leibnizian principle of indiscernibles (if no difference between two things or events can be discerned, then they are the same). If I experience an event as the exact repetition of something that happened to me before, then it is the same event. Since such experiences do occur, time therefore does not exist. In "Death and the Compass," this form of the eternal return, the present doubled in an unceasing repetition of itself, occurs not as a present experience, but as a nonpresent present which is never present as such, since it is always mediated by language or generated by language or "present" within language as a blank place within the syntax that can only be filled by a placeholding catachresis. An example is the word *death* as Borges or I use it, or rather abuse it. The etymological definition of catachresis is "abusive transfer," or "against usage." Such a linguistic present is always either future or past, either always about to be or the place in the past where narrative memory fails. Since it is a moment in the past that was never present as a *now* experienced as an event, it cannot be remembered and retold. In "Death and the Compass" that nonpresent present, a present that never is, was, or will be is represented by Lönnrot's death. As in Zarathustra's image of the present as a *Torweg*, a Janus-faced gateway facing outward toward the past and future but also inward toward that infinitely narrow dividing line between past and future, the present for Borges is always not quite yet or already no longer.[14]

Lönnrot's always imminent death fulfills Scharlach's vision of time as governed by Janus, god of doubling, facing inward toward an incessant repetition and outward toward a dawn and dusk that cannot be distinguished. For Lönnrot and Scharlach or for the reader who makes his or her way along the line of the story, the nonpresent present is a future now which is always not quite yet, the moment the bullet will reach Lönnrot. The story is a remembering of a future that can never be present or named except indirectly and uncertainly. The text taken as a whole, with its infinite regress of each new figure dismantling and replacing the figure just proposed, figures that time of infinite repetition, time as an eternal not-present present.

"Death and the Compass" as a whole is an allegory of this predicament. I use *allegory* here to name an extended narrative catachresis. The story as a whole is put in the place of something that has no name and cannot even be said for certain to exist. Each stage in the allegory provides an illusory mastery over the illusions of the previous figure it reads. Lönnrot "reads" Treviranus, Scharlach "reads" Treviranus and Lönnrot, the narrator "reads" Treviranus, Lönnrot, and Scharlach, and we then read the story. Each seeming clarity is open to yet another allegorical reading of its failure to apply to itself the act of reading it performs. "Death and the Compass" expresses this in the infinite regress of the perpetual refutation of the figure that has just been posited by the next figure that also is refuted in its turn. This narrative process is ultimately figured as the bullet that never reaches its target, never even starts towards its goal. The story, like that bullet, perpetually moves toward a future that would be the present achieved at last, the moment of Lönnrot's death now open at last to narrative memory. The past and future, origin and goal, would coincide at that impossible endpoint. There the consciousnesses of narrator, protagonist, and reader would come together. The story and its final trope figure the eternal return not outside the text as recurrence in a different avatar, but within the text as the play between *next* and *next, otro* and *otra*. Word following word make up the invisible, unceasing line of a perpetual repetition. The discomfort of this infinite regress is assuaged by the knowledge that certainty would be death, the loss of consciousness. Consciousness is not separable from the pain of being forced to play an endless game of odd and even.

―――――

Any reading of the story, such as this one, is a further displacement of the displacements within the story, another link in a potentially endless chain. I can conclude both this chapter and the book by showing how this is the case. Borges's "Death and the Compass" has served as a figure of thought allowing me to figure out certain implications of the word *figure* and to test the proposition that a mastery of rhetoric as analysis of figures of speech would be the true Ariadne's thread at last. Borges's story is a complex configuration generating thought about figure. Reading it allows me to try out a theoretical hypothesis about figures.

If all narrators are survivors and if all narration is therefore memoir, memorial epitaph, criticism in its turn is a repetition of that memorial act. The reader puts himself or herself in the place of the narrator. But both narration and reading reveal a peculiarity of such remembering. In remembering they forget. They cover over what they remember with some linguistic artifice. To put this another way, figure disfigures. Each figure is a mask that deforms what it covers. Behind each disfiguring mask only another mask can be uncovered. The reader is always left face to face with what Henry James, in a splendid phrase in *The Golden Bowl*, calls a "figured void," though whether or not the apparent void is really empty is not certain. Narration and criticism disfigure what the tracks or traces of the story reveal. They do this in putting forth words that seem devoted to tracking the quarry down, tracing out the meaning the figures reveal. But these words create new patterns of their own, covering the tracks they would elucidate, as a detective may make tracks of his or her own obliterating the tracks of the criminal.

"Death and the Compass" is a means of thinking something out, but that thinking puts the reader in a double double bind. If you do not interpret, you are out of it entirely, therefore safe, but dead. Not to interpret is death, like a computer with no files open, empty "random access memory" with nothing to remember. Life is the continuation of interpretation. Interpretation, on the other hand, is also death, in one of two ways, in a double bind within the double bind. If you interpret the text, if you make it make a figure, and if you are so foolish as to think you have mastered the work by means of that figure, you end up with a a fake configuration in your hands, like the *Kalevala* or like the gibberish uttered by a man who thinks he has found out the secret name of God. In the case of this chapter this moment might be represented by the implication that one has finally reached some triumphant endpoint in uttering the name *death,* forgetting that the dismantling of figure generally must apply to this figure too. If, on the other hand, you follow through the chain of figures as far as they will go, to the point where their inadequacy is recognized, you are led by that to something a displaced word for which is "death." "Death" here names the end of reading in one or another form of a failure to comprehend clearly. The reader comes to recognize through the reading the impossibility of deciding whether or not the figure made by "Death and the Compass" corresponds to something that can be named in no other way or whether it is a mere dead artifice.

I promised at the beginning of this chapter that I would show whether analysis of figures in narrative is a way out of the labyrinth. I have not kept the promise. Such a promise can never be kept. All we learn is that we do not know for sure whether figure will work or not. I have not reached an end in the sense of a goal, a satisfying endpoint. I have only made another reading that shows once more the asymmetry between theory and reading. But each such reading is generative. It keeps reading going and more than reading. Each reading enters back into social life and has such effects there as it may have, effects for which the reader must take responsibility. Each reading reveals something more about the role of language in human life. If I have not escaped from the labyrinth nor found Ariadne's thread at last, the secret clue of narrative theory, I have at least mapped part of the maze.

Notes

Preface

1 See Richard Lanham, "The Electronic Word: Literary Study and the Digital Revolution," *New Literary History* 20 (Winter 1989): 265–90; and Lanham, "The Extraordinary Convergence: Democracy, Technology, Theory, and the University Curriculum," *South Atlantic Quarterly* 89 (Winter 1990): 27–50. See also George P. Landow, *Hypertext: The Convergence of Contemporary Critical Theory and Technology* (Baltimore: Johns Hopkins University Press, 1991).

2 I have attempted to think through further the implications for humanistic study of the new computer technology in "The Work of Cultural Studies in the Age of Digital Reproduction," forthcoming in *Genre,* and, in longer form, as the first section of one of the four books to come from my Ariadne project, *Illustration* (Cambridge: Harvard University Press, 1992).

Chapter 1: Line

1 For the illustrations to which Ruskin refers in the first sentences of the citation, see figs. 1 and 2 here, from his *Works,* vol. 27, ed. E. T. Cook and Alexander Wedderburn (London: George Allen, 1907), pp. 407–08. Ruskin's commentary on the inscription beside the labyrinth in fig. 2, from the door of the cathedral at Lucca, is as follows: "The straggling letters at the side, read

259

straight, and with separating of the words, run thus:—'HIC QVEM CRETICVS
EDIT DEDALVS EST LABERINTHVS./DE QVO NVLLVS VADERE QVIVIT QVI FVIT
INTVS/NI THESEVS GRATIS ADRIANE STAMINE JVTVS,' which is in English:—
'This is the labyrinth which the Cretan Dedalus built,/Out of which nobody
could get who was inside,/Except Theseus; nor could he have done it, unless
he had been helped with a thread by Adriane, all for love'" (p. 401).

2 See Paul Ricoeur, *Temps et récit,* vol. 1 (Paris: Editions de Seuil, 1983), pp.
19–84; Ricoeur, *Time and Narrative,* vol. 1, trans. Kathleen McLaughlin and
David Pellauer (Chicago: University of Chicago Press, 1984), pp. 5–51.

3 See, for example, Susan Gubar, "'The Blank Page' and the Issues of Female
Creativity," *Critical Inquiry* 8 (Winter 1981): 243–63.

4 Gerard Manley Hopkins, "To R. B.," ll. 3–5, in *Poems,* 4th ed., ed. W. H.
Gardner and N. H. Mackenzie (London: Oxford University Press, 1987), p.
108.

5 Thomas Hardy, *Tess of the d'Urbervilles,* New Wessex edition (London: Macmillan, 1974), p. 107.

6 Sigmund Freud, *The Problem of Anxiety,* trans. Henry Alden Bunker (New
York: Psychoanalytic Quarterly Press and W. W. Norton, 1936), p. 15.

7 See Jacques Derrida, "Mes chances: Au rendez-vous de quelques stéréophonies
épicuriennes," trans. Irene Harvey and Avital Ronell as "My Chances/*Mes
Chances*: A Rendezvous with Some Epicurean Stereophonies," in Derrida,
Taking Chances: Derrida, Psychoanalysis, and Literature (Baltimore: Johns
Hopkins University Press, 1984), p. 16: "The paradox here is the following (I
must state it in its broadest generality): to be a mark and to mark its marking
effect, a mark must be capable of being *identified,* recognized as the same,
being precisely *re-markable* from one context to another. It must be capable
of being repeated, re-marked in its essential trait as the same. This accounts
for the apparent solidity of its structure, of its type, its *stereotypy.* It is this
that leads us here to speak of the atom, since one associates indestructibility
with indivisibility. But more precisely, it is not simple (Mais justement ce n'est
pas simple) since the identity of a mark is also its difference and its differential
relation, varying each time according to context, to the network of other marks.
The ideal iterability that forms the structure of all marks is that which un-
doubtedly allows them to be released from any context, to be freed from all
determined bonds to its origin, its meaning, or its referent, to emigrate in order
to play elsewhere, in whole or in part (en totalité ou en partie) another role. I
say 'in whole or in part' because by means of this essential insignificance
(insignifiance essentielle) the ideality or ideal identity of each mark (which is
only a differential function without an ontological basis) can continue to divide
itself and to give rise to the proliferation of other ideal identities. This iterability
is thus that which allows a mark to be used more than once. It is more than
one. It multiples and divides itself internally. This imprints the capacity for
diversion within its very movement. In the destination (*Bestimmung*) there is
thus a principle of indetermination, chance, luck, or of destinerring (destiner-

rance). There is no assured destination precisely because of the mark and the proper name; in other words, because of this insignificance."

8 Monteverdi's "Lament of Ariadne" is all that remains of his opera on Ariadne. Jiří Benda (1722–95) was a Czech musician and composer, more important than Rousseau in the development of the melodrama, or recitation with musical accompaniment, though Rousseau is also associated with the history of this form. Benda's *Ariadne auf Naxos* (1774) influenced Mozart, who planned to write a "duodrama" modeled on those of Benda. For a history of melodrama, duodrama, and monodrama in its connection with Tennyson's "Maud: A Monodrama," see A. Dwight Culler, "Monodrama and the Dramatic Monologue," *Publications of the Modern Language Association* 90 (May 1975): 366–85.

9 Geoffrey Chaucer, *The Legend of Good Women,* in *Works,* 2d ed., ed. F. N. Robinson (Boston: Houghton Mifflin, 1961), p. 513.

10 Walter Pater, "A Study of Dionysus," in *Greek Studies* (London: Macmillan, 1895), p. 16. For the paintings Pater mentions, see figs. 3 and 4.

11 For a valuable analysis of the motif of the crane dance, see Hubert Damisch, "La Danse de Thesée," *Tel Quel* 26 (1966): 60–68. Damisch refers to passages in Pausanias and in Plutarch's *Theseus.* See esp. p. 61: "L'élément dionysiaque qui transparaît ici pourra sembler timide, mesuré qu'il était par la cithare de l'aède (accompagné, il est vrai, de deux porteurs de tambourins): il importe à notre propos de souligner que pareille farandole, au moins si l'on en croit Plutarque, ne reproduisait pas tellement le cheminement du héros qu'elle ne redoublait le labyrinthe lui-même par le détour d'une danse qui mettait en mouvement tous les membres des corps entraînés par elle dans une course sans autre terme assignable que l'étourdissement ou l'ivresse légère qui ne pouvaient manquer de s'emparer des danseurs livrés à ses méandres, leur individualité étant appelée à se consommer dans des figures collectives dont l'entrelacement et la succession, entraînant la rupture répétée de la chaîne, étaient faits pour évoquer la structure de ce lieu obscur et sauvage, saturé d'un réseau de chemins sans mémoire bientôt refermés, pour ne le laisser plus échapper, sur celui qui en avait passé le seuil."

12 I. A. Richards, so far as I know, was the first to accept "Ariachne's" as the correct reading and to interpret its "bifold" meaning. See *"Troilus and Cressida* and Plato," in his *Speculative Instruments* (London: Routledge & Kegan Paul, 1955), p. 210. See also my "Ariachne's Broken Woof," *Georgia Review* 31 (Spring 1977): 44–60.

13 Friedrich Nietzsche, *Also Sprach Zarathustra,* pt. 3, in *Werke in Drei Bänden,* vol. 2, ed. Karl Schlechta (Munich: Carl Hanser, 1966), p. 474; translation from *The Portable Nietzsche,* trans. Walter Kaufmann (New York: Viking Press, 1954), p. 340.

14 Nietzsche, *Werke,* 2:1259, my translation. Unless otherwise noted, all subsequent translations are my own.

15 Ibid., p. 1257.

16 Henry James, *The Golden Bowl,* vol. 24 of the New York edition of *The Novels and Tales of Henry James* (New York: Charles Scribner's Sons, 1907–17), p. 187. Another explicit reference to Ariadne is made later. Maggie, betrayed by her husband, feels herself to be like "Ariadne roaming the lone sea-strand" (24:307).

17 I investigate this region of narrative criticism in a book entitled *Illustration* (Cambridge: Harvard University Press, 1992).

18 Wallace Stevens, "The Man with the Blue Guitar," in *The Collected Poems of Wallace Stevens* (New York: Alfred A. Knopf, 1954), p. 175.

19 Wallace Stevens, "An Ordinary Evening in New Haven," in Stevens, *Collected Poems,* p. 274.

20 *The Letters of Wallace Stevens,* ed. Holly Stevens (New York: Alfred A. Knopf, 1966), pp. 783, 360. I note, by the way, that my concern for X has been anticipated by Edgar Allan Poe. See his "X-ing a Paragrab," in *The Complete Works of Edgar Allan Poe,* vol. 6, ed. James A. Harrison (New York: Thomas Y. Crowell, 1902), pp. 229–37. The story has to do with a printer's devil who substitutes x's for o's in setting an article. The story is a cascade of x's. It ends with the following paragraph: "The opinion of Bob, the devil (who kept dark 'about his having X-ed the paragrab'), did not meet with so much attention as I think it deserved, although it was very openly and very fearlessly expressed. He said that, for his part, he had no doubt about the matter at all, that it was a clear case, that Mr. Bullet-head never *could* be 'persvaded fur to drink like other folks, but vas *con*tinually a-svigging o' that ere blessed XXX ale, and, as a naiteral consekvence, it just puffed him up savage, and made him X (cross) in the X-treme.'"

21 Elizabeth Gaskell, *Works,* Knutsford edition, vol. 2 (London: Smith, Elder, 1906), p. 77.

22 Both these geometrical figures have one focus at infinity.

23 Gaskell, *Works,* 2:77.

Chapter 2: Character

1 In a book of that name, forthcoming.

2 See, for example, F. R. Leavis, *D. H. Lawrence* (London: Chatto & Windus, 1955; New York: Alfred A. Knopf, 1956); W. J. Harvey, *Character and the Novel* (London: Chatto & Windus; Ithaca: Cornell University Press, 1965); Barbara Hardy, *The Novels of George Eliot* (New York: Oxford University Press, 1963); Hardy, *The Moral Art of Dickens* (New York: Oxford University Press, 1970); Martin Price, *Forms of Life: Character and Moral Imagination in the Novel* (New Haven: Yale University Press, 1983).

3 Virginia Woolf, *Collected Essays,* vol. 1 (London: Hogarth Press, 1966–67), pp. 319–37.

4 Sigmund Freud, "Constructions in Analysis," in *The Standard Edition of the Complete Psychological Works of Sigmund Freud,* trans. James Strachey, 24 vols. (London: Hogarth Press and the Institute of Psycho-Analysis, 1953–74),

17:269; Freud, "Konstructionen in der Analyse," in *Studienausgabe,* 11 vols. (Frankfurt: S. Fischer, 1970–75), 11:406.

5 Philippe Lacoue-Labarthe and Jean-Luc Nancy, "The Nazi Myth," trans. Brian Holmes *Critical Inquiry* 16 (1990): 291–312.

6 See Søren Kierkegaard, *Either/Or,* vol 2., trans. Walter Lowrie (Garden City, N.Y.: Anchor Books, 1959), p. 164: "Or can you think of anything more frightful than that it might end with your nature being resolved into a multiplicity, that you really might become many, become, like those unhappy demoniacs, a legion, and you thus would have lost the inmost and holiest thing of all in a man, the unifying power of personality?"

7 David Hume, *A Treatise on Human Nature* (Oxford: Clarendon Press, 1965), pp. 159–60.

8 "On Colleges and Philosophy: Jacques Derrida with Geoff Bennington," in *Postmodernism: ICA Documents,* ed. Lisa Appignanesi (London: Free Association Books, 1989), p. 224. For an earlier use of the word *paleonomy,* see Derrida, *Positions* (Paris: Editions de Minuit, 1972), p. 96; Derrida, *Positions,* trans. Alan Bass (Chicago: University of Chicago Press, 1981), p. 71.

9 I follow the traditional and problematic ordering of the "Nachlass" made by Nietzsche's sister after his death.

10 Friedrich Nietzsche, *The Will to Power,* trans. Walter Kaufmann and R. J. Hollingdale (New York: Vintage Books, 1968), pp. 263–64, henceforth "E." For the German original, I have followed Friedrich Nietzsche, *Werke in Drei Bände,* 3 vols., ed. Karl Schlechta (Munich: Carl Hanser, 1966), 3:673–74, henceforth "G." Subsequent references to these editions appear in the text. I have sometimes slightly altered Kaufmann's translation to make it conform more closely to Nietzsche's German—for example, by restoring his italics (or underlinings in the original manuscript). Like any great writer, Nietzsche is in a sense untranslatable, and I have woven some words and phrases from the original German into my citations in order to give some indication of Nietzsche's vocabulary, especially where the metaphorical force of conceptual words is different in German from the corresponding English, or where Nietzsche is playing on aspects of German words which do not carry over into English.

11 Friedrich Nietzsche, "On Truth and Lies in a Nonmoral Sense," in *Philosophy and Truth: Selections from Nietzsche's Notebooks of the Early 1870s,* trans. Daniel Breazeale (Atlantic Highlands, N.J.: Humanities Press, 1979), p. 80. For the German, see Nietzsche, *Werke,* 3:311.

12 Walter Pater, *The Renaissance: Studies in Art and Poetry* (London: Macmillan, 1910), pp. 235, 236.

13 Sigmund Freud, *New Introductory Lectures on Psychoanalysis,* in *Standard Edition of the Works of Freud,* 22:72–73. Susan Rogers called this passage to my attention.

14 See, for example, Jacques Lacan, "Ronds de ficelle," in *Encore, 1972–1973,* Le Séminaire, 10 (Paris: Editions du Seuil, 1975), pp. 107–23.

15 See Marc Shell, *The Economy of Literature* (Baltimore: Johns Hopkins University Press, 1978), p. 64.

16 Speaking of the opposition between grammar and reference, Paul de Man formulates succinctly in "Promises (*Social Contract*)" this contradiction between the material means of making meaning and the referential meaning any configuration of characters generates: "There can be no text without grammar: the logic of grammar generates texts only in the absence of referential meaning, but every text generates a referent that subverts the grammatical principle to which it owed its constitution"; de Man, *Allegories of Reading* (New Haven: Yale University Press, 1979), p. 269.

17 Walter Benjamin, *Reflections: Essays, Aphorisms, Autobiographical Writings,* trans. Edmund Jephcott (New York: Schocken Books, 1986), pp. 304–05; Benjamin, *Gesammelte Schriften,* vol. 2 (Frankfurt: Suhrkamp, 1977), p. 172.

18 Charles Baudelaire, *Edgar Allan Poe: Sa vie et ses ouvrages,* ed. W. T. Bandy (Toronto: University of Toronto Press, 1973), pp. 3–4; Baudelaire's italics. By chance, by a fortuitous conjunction of atoms, or by one of those crossings of one life line by another that John Keats describes in a passage cited at the beginning of chapter 3 here, Jacques Derrida, I have happened to discover, has cited this passage and commented on it in "Mes chances: Au rendez-vous de quelques stéréophonies épicuriennes," trans. Irene Harvey and Avital Ronell as "My Chances / *Mes Chances*: A Rendezvous with Some Epicurean Stereophonies," in Derrida, *Taking Chances: Derrida, Psychoanalysis, and Literature* (Baltimore: Johns Hopkins University Press, 1984), pp. 13–14.

19 Jacques Derrida, "'Il faut bien manger' ou le calcul du sujet: Entretien (avec J.-L. Nancy)," *Confrontation,* cahiers 20 (Winter 1989): 97.

20 Jacques Derrida, "Interview with Jean-Luc Nancy," trans. Peter T. Connor, *Topoi* 7 (1988): 117.

21 See Derrida, "My Chances," p. 16. This passage is discussed in the first chapter here.

22 See Jacques Derrida, *Parages* (Paris: Editions Galilée, 1986); Derrida, "Fors," in Nicolas Abraham and Maria Torok, *Cryptonymie: Le verbier de l'homme aux loups* (Paris: Aubier Flammarion, 1976), pp. 9–73. See also his "Living On: Borderlines," in *Deconstruction and Criticism* (New York: Seabury Press, 1979), pp. 75–176.

23 Anthony Trollope, *An Autobiography* (Oxford: Oxford University Press, 1980), p. 175. Subsequent references to this edition appear in the text.

24 George Eliot, *Daniel Deronda* (Oxford: Oxford University Press, 1984), p. 97, henceforth "DD." Subsequent references to this edition appear in the text.

25 Maurice Blanchot, *Death Sentence,* trans. Lydia Davis (Barrytown, N.Y.: Station Hill Press, 1978), pp. 10–11; Blanchot, *L'arrêt de mort* (Paris: Editions Gallimard, 1948), pp. 21–22.

26 See Geoffrey Hartman's introduction to a portion of the Lydia Davis translation, *Georgia Review* 30 (1976): 343–44.

27 Edgar Allan Poe, "A Chapter on Autography," in *The Complete Works of Edgar Allan Poe*, 17 vols., ed. James A. Harrison (New York: AMS Press, 1965), 15:141. Subsequent references to this edition appear in the text.

28 François Rabelais, *The Histories of Gargantua and Pantagruel*, trans. J. M. Cohen (Harmondsworth, Eng.: Penguin Books, 1955), pp. 356–59; Rabelais, *Oeuvres complètes*, vol. 1 (Paris: Editions Garnier Frères, 1962), pp. 505–11.

29 "What the Rose Said to the Cypress," *The Brown Fairy Book*, ed. Andrew Lang (New York: Dover, 1965), pp. 26–27.

30 Ludwig Wittgenstein, *Philosophical Investigations*, trans. G. E. M. Anscombe (Oxford: Basil Blackwell, 1968), p. 151e. Subsequent references appear in the text.

31 Ludwig Wittgenstein, *The Brown Book*, in *The Blue and Brown Books* (New York: Harper and Row, 1965), 2:16:162–63. For a German translation by Petra von Morstein, see *Schriften*, 5, *2nd* ed., ed. Rush Rhees (Frankfurt am Main: Suhrkamp, 1982), 250–52. Subsequent references appear in the text. A similar use of crudely drawn faces occurs in the "Lectures on Aesthetics," in *Lectures and Conversations on Aesthetics, Psychology and Religious Belief*, compiled from notes taken by Yorick Smythies, Rush Rhees, and James Taylor, ed. Cyril Barrett (Berkeley: University of California Press, 1967), p. 4: "If I were a good draughtsman, I could convey an innumerable number of expressions by four strokes— [three faces follow]. Such words as 'pompous' and 'stately' could be expressed by faces."

32 Paul de Man, foreword to Carol Jacobs, *The Dissimulating Harmony* (Baltimore: Johns Hopkins University Press, 1978), p. xi.

33 See, for example, *Philosophical Investigations*, paragraph 258, and the surrounding paragraphs. For essays on Wittgenstein's arguments against the possibility of a private language, see *Wittgenstein and the Problem of Other Minds*, ed. Harold Morick (New York: McGraw-Hill, 1967); also John Wisdom, *Other Minds* (Oxford: Basil Blackwell, 1956 and 1965).

34 E. H. Gombrich, *Meditations on a Hobby Horse and Other Essays on the Theory of Art* (London: Phaidon, 1963), pp. 1–11.

35 Charles Dickens, *Great Expectations* (London: Oxford University Press, 1953), p. 1.

36 George Eliot, *Middlemarch* (Oxford: Oxford University Press, 1986), p. 13.

37 Joseph Conrad, *Lord Jim* (Oxford: Oxford University Press, 1983), p. 3.

38 Walter Pater, "The Myth of Demeter and Persephone," in *Greek Studies* (London: Macmillan, 1910), p. 100.

39 George Meredith, *The Egoist*, vols. 13 and 14 of *The Works of George Meredith*, Memorial edition, 27 vols. (London: Constable, 1910), 13:2. Subsequent references to this edition appear in the text. This is a characteristically Meredithian way of saying "from one end of England to the other." The "Lizard" is at the extreme southern tip of England.

40 Here this chapter overlaps with the next, "Anastomosis," according to that law of narrative theory's labyrinth whereby each way of reading novels cannot be kept uncontaminated, detached from the others. Each is not a separate

corridor in the labyrinth but one way of retracing the whole maze. "Presentation of character" cannot be kept separate from "interpersonal relations."

41 See Ramon Fernandez, "Le Message de Meredith," in *Messages,* première série, 4th ed. (Paris: Librairie Gallimard, 1926), pp. 120–46. As an example of the extraordinary phenomenological verve and penetration of Fernandez's criticism, I cite the following paragraph from this essay: "Le principe d'activité concrète qui commande le jeu des images chez Meredith commande également—et dans une mesure qui le distingue de tous les autres romanciers—l'évolution physique et morale de ses personnages. Le tout-fait, le vécu, le monument sont radicalement bannis de son oeuvre. Point de déductions, de documents, de coordonnées abstraites. Ses personnages sont parce qu'ils sont et ne tirent leur raison d'être que d'eux-mêmes; mais—et ceci est de la première importance—ils ne sont que parce qu'ils agissent, *leur être dépend de leur activité.* Activité toute extérieure, toute physique, activité de relation; activité interne des sentiments que telles circonstances portent au point d'ébullition; réactions, adaptations, contractions et détentes; épreuve incessante de l'élasticité et de la trempe des ressorts vitaux; palpitations, émanations psychiques et physiques de fluide dramatique, chocs de paroles et de volontés; zig-zags de la pensée qui se cherche, vacillements de la conscience: le monde humain de Meredith est un monde de vibrations, ses créatures sont en perpétuel *déplacement,* elles miroitent comme les vagues au soleil. Mais le centre de leur activité—par conséquent la base de l'équilibre qui assure leur situation, leur existence, leur résistance—est en elles-mêmes, non pas dans la zone de leur action extérieure. Celle-ci, d'abord spontanée, est immédiatement réfléchie par leur sensibilité à la faveur d'un choc qui paralyse ou ralentit l'élan vital" (pp. 133–34).

42 Walter Pater, *Appreciations* (London: Macmillan, 1910), p. 207.

43 Eugene Vance informs me that St. Augustine glosses the fig leaves in Genesis as "rhetoric."

44 The modern locus classicus for this myth is a passage in Sigmund Freud's essay of 1933, "Femininity," in *New Introductory Lectures on Psychology,* trans. James Strachey (New York: W. W. Norton, 1961): "The effect of penis-envy has a share, further, in the physical vanity of women, since they are bound to value their charms more highly as a late compensation for their original sexual inferiority. Shame, which is considered to be a feminine characteristic *par excellence* but is far more a matter of convention than might be supposed, has as its purpose, we believe, concealment of genital deficiency. . . . It seems that women have made few contributions to the discoveries and inventions in the history of civilization; there is, however, one technique which they may have invented—that of plaiting and weaving. If that is so, we should be tempted to guess the unconscious motive for the achievement. Nature herself would seem to have given the model which this achievement imitates by causing the growth at maturity of the pubic hair that conceals the genitals. The step that remained to be taken lay in making the threads adhere to one another, while on the body they stick into the skin and are only matted together. If you reject this

idea as fantastic and regard my belief in the influence of lack of a penis on the configuration of femininity as an *idée fixe,* I am of course defenseless." This passage, and the essay of which it is a part, has received much sharp comment from recent feminist critics, as indeed it should. An example is Leslie Camhi's discussion in a brilliant dissertation on the history of hysteria (Yale University, 1991): "Women's single technological invention and contribution to the history of civilization would then be like hysterical fantasies; a woven tissue, derived from the body, to cover and repress their own 'genital deficiency'; like the knitted or embroidered symptomatic text of the pathologically feminine hysterical body, Freud's myth of origin, locating women's cultural achievements in their 'aberrant' bodies, was hysterically symptomatic of psychoanalysis itself. The mythic veil of shame which Freud would have had women draw across their bodies was a tissue of his own weaving, drawn to protect him from their difference. The lifting of this veil and exposure of these foreign bodies left him, as he himself wrote, 'defenseless'" (pp. 36–37). My reading of *The Egoist* might be described as a demonstration that Meredith in this novel dismantles before the fact Freud's assumptions of women's "original sexual inferiority" and "genital deficiency," along with all the social, interpersonal, and psychological power structures that accompany these assumptions. Particularly interesting for my purposes is Camhi's association of the weaving image in "Femininity" with thread images in *Studies on Hysteria* (1895) and with Freud's resistance to the recognition that the source of hysteria might be projected within the patient rather than found there. As Camhi puts this, Freud recoiled "from his realization that the 'foreign body' lodged in the hysteric might have been placed there by the physician himself" (p. 39). In *Studies on Hysteria* Freud and Breuer speak of following the thread of symptoms and memories back to the "pathogenic nucleus" that causes hysteria. They use my guiding image of Ariadne's thread, but as against Freud and Breuer I contend that the thread of analysis, for example analysis of novels, never leads back to a single univocal explanatory origin. For a discussion of such images in Freud's work see my "Constructions in Criticism," *Boundary 2* (Spring/Fall 1984): 157–72, reprinted in *Theory Now and Then* (New York: Harvester Wheatsheaf; Durham: Duke University Press, 1991).

45 George Meredith, *The Poems,* vol. 1, ed. Phyllis B. Bartlett (New Haven: Yale University Press, 1978), pp. 405, 408.

46 For an authoritative account of earlier stages of this dissolution, see Lawrence Stone, *The Family, Sex and Marriage in England, 1500–1800* (New York: Harper and Row, 1977).

47 For high points in the history of speech act theory and controversies about it, see J. L. Austin, *How to Do Things with Words,* 2d ed. (Oxford: Oxford University Press, 1980); John R. Searle, *Speech Acts: An Essay in the Philosophy of Language* (London: Cambridge University Press, 1970); Searle, "Reiterating the Differences: A Reply to Derrida," *Glyph* 1 (1977): 198–208; Jacques Derrida, *Limited Inc* (Evanston, Ill.: Northwestern University Press, 1988); Paul de Man, "Promises (*Social Contract*)" and "Excuses (*Confes-*

48 George Meredith, *The Ordeal of Richard Feverel* (New York: Modern Library, 1950), p. 331. Subsequent citations are from this text, the only widely available one that reprints the original version of 1859 rather than the new version of 1878. The latter severely truncates the crucial opening chapters and makes other changes obscuring Meredith's original conception. See Lionel Stevenson's introduction, pp. xxv–xxvi, for a discussion of the changes.

sions)," in *Allegories of Reading* (New Haven: Yale University Press, 1979), pp. 246–301.

49 See the discussion of two forms of repetition in my *Fiction and Repetition* (Cambridge: Harvard University Press, 1982), pp. 1–21.

50 Friedrich Nietzsche, *On the Genealogy of Morals,* trans. Walter Kaufmann and R. J. Hollingdale (New York: Random House, 1967), p. 57, henceforth "E"; Nietzsche, *Werke,* 2:799, henceforth "G." Subsequent references appear in the text.

51 Walter Benjamin, *Charles Baudelaire: Ein Lyriker im Zeitalter des Hochkapitalismus* (Frankfurt: Suhrkamp, 1969), pp. 111–64; for the English version, see Benjamin, *Illuminations,* trans. Harry Zohn (New York: Schocken Books, 1969), pp. 155–200.

52 Werner Hamacher, in an admirable essay in part concerning *On the Genealogy of Morals,* presents an analysis of this passage in terms of Nietzsche's insight into the power of language to posit fictitious entities that are then hypostatized. I am pleased to find that his reading of the *Genealogy* overlaps to a considerable degree with mine, though he does not focus on the question of gender difference. See Werner Hamacher, "The Promise of Interpretation: Reflections on the Hermeneutical Imperative in Kant and Nietzsche," trans. Jane O. Newman and John H. Smith, in *Looking After Nietzsche,* ed. Laurence A. Rickels (Albany: State University of New York Press, 1989), pp. 19–47, esp. 29–43.

53 The reasons for my awkward insistence on the gender alternatives will be made explicit later.

Chapter 3: Anastomosis

1 See Avital Ronell, *The Telephone Book: Technology—Schizophrenia—Electric Speech* (Lincoln: University of Nebraska Press, 1989).

2 Ambage: a roundabout way; the passages of a labyrinth; a circumlocution, ambiguity; puzzle.

3 John Keats, *The Letters of John Keats,* ed. Robert Gittings (London: Oxford University Press, 1975), p. 66.

4 See A. G. Ward, ed., *The Quest for Theseus* (Praeger Publishers, 1970), for further ancient representations of the story of Theseus and Ariadne, along with a series of learned essays on Theseus. Apollodorus and Plutarch are the chief ancient sources for the life of Theseus.

5 Søren Kierkegaard, *Either/Or,* vol. 1, trans. Walter Lowrie (Garden City, N.Y.: Anchor Books, 1959), p. 35: "My life is absolutely meaningless. When I consider the different periods into which it falls, it seems like the word *Schnur*

in the dictionary, which means in the first place a string, in the second, a daughter-in-law. The only thing lacking is that the word *Schnur* should mean in the third place a camel, in the fourth, a dust-brush."

6 See Marc Shell's brilliant and wide-ranging study, *The End of Kinship:* Measure for Measure, *Incest, and the Ideal of Universal Siblinghood* (Stanford: Stanford University Press, 1988).

7 Jacques Lacan, "The Function of Language in Psychoanalysis," trans. Anthony Wilden, in Lacan, *The Language of the Self* (Baltimore: Johns Hopkins University Press, 1968), p. 40.

8 François Rabelais, *The Histories of Gargantua and Pantagruel,* trans. J. M. Cohen (Harmondsworth, Eng.: Penguin Books, 1955), p. 468, henceforth "E"; Rabelais, *Oeuvres complètes,* 2 vols. (Paris: Editions Garnier Frères, 1962), 2:59, henceforth "F." Subsequent references appear in the text.

9 Martin Buber, *Between Man and Man,* trans. Ronald Gregor Smith (London: Kegan Paul, 1947); John Wisdom, *Other Minds* (Oxford: Basil Blackwell, 1956).

10 Jacques Lacan, *Encore 1972–73,* Le Séminaire, 10 (Paris: Editions du Seuil, 1975).

11 See Paul de Man, *Allegories of Reading* (New Haven: Yale University Press, 1979), pp. 160–220; Jacques Derrida, *La carte postale* (Paris: Flammarion, 1980), pp. 11–273; Derrida, *The Post Card,* trans. Alan Bass (Chicago: University of Chicago Press, 1987), pp. 7–256.

12 Erving Goffman, *The Presentation of Self in Everyday Life* (New York: Doubleday, 1959); Georg Simmel, Conflict *and* The Web of Group Affiliations (Glencoe, Ill.: Free Press, 1955), pp. 125–95.

13 See Louis Althusser, "Ideology and Ideological State Apparatuses: Notes towards an Investigation," in *Lenin and Philosophy and Other Essays,* trans. Ben Brewster (New York: Monthly Review Press, 1972), pp. 127–86.

14 Don Gifford with Robert J. Seidman, *Notes for Joyce: An Annotation of James Joyce's* Ulysses (New York: E. P. Dutton, 1974), p. 523.

15 Joyce, *Ulysses* (Harmondsworth, Eng.: Penguin Books, 1971), p. 139 henceforth "U." Subsequent references appear in the text.

16 James Joyce, *Finnegans Wake* (London: Faber & Faber, 1950), p. 584, henceforth "FW." Subsequent references appear in the text.

17 For the play on Greek and Latin here I am following the leads in Brendan O'Hehir and John M. Dillon, *A Classical Lexicon for* Finnegans Wake (Berkeley: University of California Press, 1977), pp. 507–08.

18 Jacques Derrida, *Glas* (Paris: Editions Galilée, 1974), p. 248, my translation. "Temps de famille: il n'y a de temps que de la famille. Le temps ne se passe qu'en famille. L'opposition du déjà, du pas encore, du déjà-plus, tout ce qui forme le temps de n'être pas présent (pas-là), tout ce qui constitue le temps comme Dasein d'un concept qui (n') est pas là, l'être-là du pas-là (un pas de plus—pas-pas-là—ou de moins), c'est une scène de famille."

19 Walter Benjamin, "Goethes *Wahlverwandtschaften,*" in Benjamin, *Illuminationen* (Frankfurt: Suhrkamp, 1969), p. 126, my translation.

20 For an excellent recent essay on the novel connecting it to Goethe's *Zur Farbenlehre*, as I have also done in *Illustration* (Cambridge: Harvard University Press, 1992), see Claudia Brodsky, "The Coloring of Relations: *Die Wahlverwandtschaften* as *Farbenlehre*," in Brodsky, *The Imposition of Form: Studies in Narrative Representation and Knowledge* (Princeton: Princeton University Press, 1987), pp. 88–138.

21 Johann Wolfgang von Goethe, *Elective Affinities*, trans. James Anthony Froude and R. Dillon Boylan (New York: Frederick Ungar, 1962), p. 139, henceforth "E"; Goethe, *Die Wahlverwandtschaften* (Munich: Deutscher Taschenbuch, 1975), p. 115, henceforth "G." Subsequent references appear in the text. Two other translations of *Die Wahlverwandtschaften* exist, one by R. J. Hollingdale and one by Judith Ryan. I shall discuss these later in this chapter.

22 This is discussed by Heinrich Nüsse in *Die Sprachtheorie Friedrich Schlegels* (Heidelberg: Carl Winter, Universitätsverlag, 1962); see esp. chaps. 6–8, pp. 68–97.

23 Goethe's statement is cited in Benjamin, *Illuminationen*, pp. 134–35, my translation.

24 "Topography," in a book in progress on the relations of narrative to what is presumed to be outside language and referred to by it.

25 Johann Wolfgang von Goethe, *Elective Affinities*, trans. R. J. Hollingdale (Harmondsworth, Eng.: Penguin Books, 1983); Goethe, *Elective Affinities* (with *The Sorrows of Young Werther* and *Novella*), trans. Judith Ryan (New York: Suhrkamp, 1988).

26 The corresponding text in English literature is the great lament for the fragility of signs at the opening of Book 5 of *The Prelude*:

Thou also, man! hast wrought,
For commerce of thy nature with herself,
Things that aspire to unconquerable life;
And we feel—we cannot choose but feel—
That they must perish. . . .

. . . .

Oh! why hath not the Mind
Some element to stamp her image on
In nature somewhat nearer to her own?
Why, gifted with such powers to send abroad
Her spirit, must it lodge in shrines so frail? (1850, 5:18–22, 45–49)

27 This is Goethe's reading. The picture does not represent father, mother, daughter at all but a bawd offering a prostitute to a client. The former was, however, the standard bowdlerizing interpretation in Goethe's day. Could Goethe have known what the real subject was, or suspected it? In both readings, though in different ways in each case, the woman as either daughter or prostitute is a medium of exchange, a living trope, a back with no front. For a discussion of Goethe's novel and this painting see Michael Fried, *Absorption and Theatricality: Painting and Beholder in the Age of Diderot* (Berkeley: University of

California Press, 1980), pp. 171–73. See esp. p. 241, n. 11: "By a historical irony that both Goethe and Diderot would have appreciated, the painting is today understood to represent a scene in a bordello."

28 Goethe's opposition here anticipates Walter Benjamin's distinction between cult value and exhibition value (Kultwert and Ausstellungswert) in "Das Kunst-werk im Zeitalter seiner technischen Reproduzierbarkeit (The Work of Art in the Age of Mechanical Reproduction)." Benjamin, *Illuminationen*, pp. 156–57; Benjamin, *Illuminations*, pp. 224–25. I have discussed Benjamin's essay in *Illustration*.

29 Benjamin, "Goethes *Wahlverwandtschaften*," pp. 114–17.

30 "Den mythischen Motiven des Romans entsprechen jene der Novelle als Motive der Erlösung. Also darf, wenn im Roman das Mythische als Thesis ange-sprochen wird, in der Novelle die Antithesis gesehen werden. Hierauf deutet ihr Titel. 'Wunderlich' nämlich müssen jene Nachbarskinder am meisten den Romangestalten scheinen, die sich denn auch mit tiefverletztem Gefühl von ihnen abwenden. Eine Verletzung, die Goethe, der geheimen und vielleicht in vielem sogar ihm verborgenen Bewandtnis der Novelle gemäß, auf äußerliche Weise motivierte, ohne ihr damit die innere Bedeutung zu nehmen" (Benjamin, "Goethes *Wahlverwandtschaften*," p. 117). There would be much to say about Benjamin's word "Verletzung," wound.

31 Cited by David Wellbery, in Goethe, *Elective Affinities,* trans. Ryan, p. 294. Wellbery goes on to observe that its name associates the novella with the "new" and with the unprecedented case that defies normal laws of narration or conceptual accounting.

32 Wallace Stevens, "The Red Fern," in *The Collected Poems of Wallace Stevens* (New York: Alfred A. Knopf, 1954), p. 365, l. 12.

33 Here is the passage in Aristotle: "By metaphor formed on the basis of analogy or proportion is meant the case when a second term, B, is to a first, A, as a fourth, D, is to a third, C; whereupon the fourth term, D, may be substituted for the second, B, or the second, B, for the fourth, D. . . . Hence one will speak of the evening (D) as the old age (B) of the day—as Empedocles does; and of old age (B) as the evening (D) of life—or as 'the sunset of life.' In certain cases, the language may contain no actual word corresponding to one of the terms in the proportion, but the figure nevertheless will be employed. For example, when a fruit casts forth its seed the action is called 'sowing,' but the action of the sun casting forth its flame has no special name. Yet this nameless action (B) is to the sun (A) as sowing (D) is to the fruit (C); and hence we have the expression of the poet, 'sowing a god-created flame.'" Aristotle, *On the Art of Poetry,* trans. Lane Cooper (Ithaca: Cornell University Press, 1947), p. 69.

Chapter 4: Figure

1 See Pliny, *Natural History,* 35, section 43: "Quae capta amore invenis, ab eunte illo peregre, umbra ex facie eius ad lucernam in pariete lineis circum-

scripsit." (He did this owing to his daughter, "who was in love with a young man; and she, when he was going abroad, drew in outline on the wall the shadow of his face, thrown by a lamp.") See also John Hollander's poem on this, "To a Sculptor (An Essay on the Origin and Nature of Relief)," in *Harp Lake* (New York: Alfred A. Knopf, 1988), pp. 30–33; and Jacques Derrida, *Mémoires d'aveugle: L'auto-portrait et autres ruines* (Paris: Editions de la Réunion des musées nationaux, 1990), pp. 54–56.

2 Jorge Luis Borges, *Ficciones* (Madrid: Alianza Editorial; Buenos Aires: Emecé Editores, 1982), pp. 147–63, henceforth "S"; Borges, *Ficciones,* trans. Anthony Kerrigan (New York: Grove Press, 1962), pp. 129–41, henceforth "E." Some English citations are made from the translation by D. A. Yates in Borges, *Labyrinths* (New York: New Directions, 1964), pp. 76–87, henceforth "E2." Subsequent references appear in the text.

3 This appears in a volume of 1941 called in English *The Garden of the Forking Paths.* See E, 3–18.

4 Cited from a note Borges wrote for the American edition by Emir Rodríguez Monegal, *Jorge Luis Borges: A Literary Biography* (New York: E. P. Dutton, 1978), p. 64.

5 See Paul de Man, *Allegories of Reading* (New Haven: Yale University Press, 1979), p. 204.

6 Maurice Blanchot, "La littérature et le droit à la mort," in *La part du feu* (Paris: Editions Gallimard, 1949), p. 293; Blanchot, "Literature and the Right to Death," in *The Gaze of Orpheus and Other Literary Essays,* trans. Lydia Davis (Barrytown, N.Y.: Station Hill Press), p. 21. See, among other works by Derrida, esp. *Mémoires pour Paul de Man* (Paris: Galilée, 1988) and *Memoires for Paul de Man,* trans. Cecile Lindsay, Jonathan Culler, and Eduardo Cadava (New York: Columbia University Press, 1986).

7 Stéphane Mallarmé, *Oeuvres complètes* (Paris: Editions de la Pléiade, 1965), p. 310.

8 Paul de Man, *The Rhetoric of Romanticism* (New York: Columbia University Press, 1984), p. 81.

9 I have investigated this in *Versions of Pygmalion* (Cambridge: Harvard University Press, 1990).

10 Walter Benjamin, *Illuminations,* trans. Harry Zohn (New York: Schocken Books, 1969), p. 101; Benjamin, *Illuminationen* (Frankfurt: Suhrkamp, 1969), p. 428.

11 I am grateful to Claudia Brodsky for observations that led me to raise this question.

12 Jorge Luis Borges, "Avatars of the Tortoise," trans. James E. Irby, in *Labyrinths,* p. 203.

13 More than one logician has "refuted" Zeno. Common sense indicates that he
    must have been wrong.
14 See Friedrich Nietzsche, "Vom Gesicht und Rätsel," in *Also Sprach Zarathus-tra*, in Nietzsche, *Werke in Drei Bänden*, vol. 2, ed. Karl Schlechta (Munich: Carl Hanser, 1966), pp. 406–10; and Nietzsche, "On the Vision and the Riddle," in *Thus Spoke Zarathustra*, trans. Walter Kaufmann (New York: Viking Press, 1954), pp. 267–72. I have read this text in *The Linguistic Moment* (Princeton: Princeton University Press, 1985), pp. 424–33.

Index

Adam Bede (Eliot), 99–100
Ahasuerus and Esther (Poussin), 200
Allegories of Reading (de Man), 152
Also Sprach Zarathustra (*Thus Spoke Zarathustra*) (Nietzsche), 15, 254–55
Althusser, Louis, 67, 153
Anthon, Charles, 78
"Apollo in Picardy" (Pater), ix–x, 2–4, 6, 50
Arachne, 14, 16
Archer, Isabel (*Portrait of a Lady*), 105
Ariadne, 10–17, 146–47, 150
Ariadne auf Naxos (Strauss), 10
Ariadne Florentina (Ruskin), 20
Aristotle, 6, 213
Arrêt de mort, L' (*Death Sentence*) (Blanchot), 74–75, 83
Ästhetik (Hegel), 173
Augustine, Saint, 6
Autobiography, An (Trollope), 67–72
"Autography" (Poe), 58, 75–79, 86–87, 101
Awkward Age, The (James), 103

Bacchae (Euripides), 13–14
Baudelaire, Charles, 63–64, 65, 66, 83
Belisarius (formerly ascribed to Van Dyck), 200
Benda, Jiří, 10
Benjamin, Walter, 61–63, 64–65, 66, 110, 132, 164, 169, 210–13, 251
Bennet, Elizabeth (*Pride and Prejudice*), 97
Berkeley, George, 254
Bible, 169–70
Birth of Tragedy, The (Nietzsche), 37
Blanchot, Maurice, 74–75, 83, 232, 249, 250, 252
Bleak House (Dickens), 5
Blue and Brown Books (Wittgenstein), 83–94, 101, 117
Booth, Wayne, 154, 225
Borges, Jorge Luis, x, xi, 228–57. Works and characters: *Artificios*, 234; "Avatars of the Tortoise," 245, 252–53; "Feeling in Death," 244; *Ficciones*, 242, 253; "The Garden of the Forking Paths," 254; Hladik ("The Secret Miracle"), 253; Lönnrot, Erik ("Death and the Compass"), 229–56; "La muerte y la brújula (Death and the Compass)," x, xi, xv, 228–57; "A New Refutation of Time," 244, 254; Scharlach, Red ("Death and the Compass"), 229, 231–32, 233, 236–45, 248, 250, 252–55; "The Secret Miracle," 253; "Tlön, Uqbar, Orbis Tertius," 229; Treviranus, Commissioner ("Death and the Compass"), 230, 232–33, 234, 237, 255

"Brook, The" (Tennyson), 226
Brooke, Dorothea (*Middlemarch*),
  30, 56, 64–65, 95–96, 97
Buber, Martin, 152

Carlyle, Thomas, 59
Carte postale, La (Derrida), 152
Cartesian Meditations (Husserl), 152
Casaubon, Edward (*Middlemarch*),
  30
Centuries of Meditation (Traherne),
  162
Cervantes, Miguel de, 34
Charles I of England, 208–09
Chartreuse de Parme, La (Stendhal),
  96
Civilization and Its Discontents
  (Freud), 132
Condillac, Etienne Bonnot de, 19,
  177
"Constructions in Analysis" (Freud),
  34
Cranford (Gaskell), ix–x, 2, 17, 25–
  27
Crime and Punishment
  (Dostoevsky), 96

Daedalus, 11–12, 14
Daedalus, Stephen (*Ulysses*), 162
Daniel Deronda (Eliot), 72–73, 99–
  100
Dante Alighieri, 206
De la grammatologie (Derrida), ix,
  xii
de Man, Paul, 89, 90, 250
Derrida, Jacques, ix, xii, 9, 10, 35–
  36, 64–67, 89, 116, 140, 152,
  155–56, 160, 249
Diana, 238–39
Dickens, Charles, 112–13
Diderot, Denis, 34
Dionysos-Dithyramben (Nietzsche),
  1, 15
Dionysus, 10–17, 146

Don Quixote (Cervantes), 95
Doyle, Arthur Conan, 231, 233–34
Dr. Jekyll and Mr. Hyde
  (Stevenson), 59
Dupin, Auguste, ("The Murders in
  the Rue Morgue" and "The
  Purloined Letter"), 230–31,
  233

Ecclesiastes, 16
Echo (*Metamorphoses*), 124, 183,
  205–06
Either/Or (Kierkegaard), 147
Eliot, George, 64–65, 72–73, 95,
  99–100, 187
Emerson, Ralph Waldo, 76
"Envois" (Derrida), 152
Eperons: Les styles de Nietzsche
  (Derrida), 140
Erigone, 13
Escher, M. C., 156, 238, 242
Euripides, 13–14

Father's Admonition (Terborch),
  200–202
Faulkner, William, 179
Fernandez, Ramon, 108–09
Feuerbach, Ludwig, 152
"Figure in the Carpet, The" (James),
  226–27
"Final Problem, The" (Doyle), 231
Finnegans Wake (Joyce), 156–61
Flint, Timothy, 77
"Fors" (Derrida), 67
Fors Clavigera (Ruskin), 1–2
Freud, Sigmund, 7, 25, 33–34, 52,
  132, 152

Gargantua and Pantagruel
  (Rabelais), 79–83
Gaskell, Elizabeth, ix–x, 2
Gide, André, 96
Girard, René, 154
Glas (Derrida), 10, 160

Goethe, Johann Wolfgang von, xi, 96, 146, 149, 164–222, 247. Works and characters in *Die Wahlverwandtschaften:* Architect, 175, 191–92, 198, 204; Assistant, 166, 193, 203–04; Baroness, 177, 193; Captain, 165, 167, 169, 171–74, 178–79, 186–87, 189, 205, 212, 216, 220–21; Charlotte, 165, 167–68, 171–74, 177, 178–92, 194, 196, 198, 202–05, 207, 212, 214, 216, 217–18, 220–21; Edward, 164–65, 166, 168, 170, 171–77, 178–91, 195, 203, 204–07, 209, 211, 212, 214–19, 220–21; Luciana, 193, 200–202, 206; Mittler, 176–77, 212, 214, 215; Ottilie, 164–65, 171–77, 178–83, 185, 189, 193–99, 200, 201, 202–09, 211, 212, 213–19, 220–21; Otto, 165, 177, 193, 205, 212, 216; "Die Wunderlichen Nachbarskinder (The Strange Neighbor Children)," 210–13

Goffman, Erving, 152

"Gold Bug, The" (Poe), 233

Golden Bowl, The (James), 16–17, 256

Golding, William, 33

Gombrich, Ernst, 95

Grandcourt, Henleigh (*Daniel Deronda*), 72–73

Great Expectations (Dickens), 95–96, 98

Grosz, George, 1

Harding, Septimus (*The Warden*), 71

Hardy, Barbara, 29

Hardy, Thomas, 7, 62, 179

Harleth, Gwendolen (*Daniel Deronda*), 72–73

Hartman, Geoffrey, 75

Harvey, W. J., 29

Hasidim, 235–36, 237

He Knew He Was Right (Trollope), 71

Hegel, G. W. F., 152, 173, 219

Heidegger, Martin, 6, 35

Hermes, 238–40, 243–44, 247

Hölderlin, Friedrich, 89

Holmes, Sherlock ("The Final Problem"), 231

Holquist, Michael, 232

Hopkins, Gerard Manley, 7

Hume, David, 34–35, 95, 116, 152

Husserl, Edmund, 35, 152

In the Penal Colony (Kafka), 138

Ingarden, Roman, 152

Innomable, L' (Beckett), 95

Iser, Wolfgang, 154

Jacques le fataliste (Diderot), 96

James, Henry, 103, 124, 226–27, 256

Janus, 239–40, 243–44, 247, 254, 255

Jim (*Lord Jim*), 95–96, 97

Jocasta, 147–48

Joyce, James, 144, 146, 149, 156–64, 209

Julie (Rousseau), 152

Kafka, Franz, 138

Kalevala, 233, 237, 257

Keats, John, 145–46

Kierkegaard, Søren, 34, 147, 152

Lacan, Jacques, 52–53, 148, 152

Lacoue-Labarthe, Philippe, 29, 34

Laius, 147–48

Leavis, F. R., 29

Legend of Good Women, The (Chaucer), 11

Leibniz, Gottfried Wilhelm, 254

Light in August (Faulkner), 179

Locke, John, 34, 152

Lönnrot, Elias, 233
Lord Jim (Conrad), 60, 95–96
Lord of the Flies (Golding), 33
Luther, Martin, 169–70
Lycidas (Milton), 226

Mallarmé, Stéphane, 249
"Man with the Blue Guitar, The"
(Stevens), 24–25
Marivaux, Pierre Carlet de
Chamblain de, 96
Marlowe, Christopher, 56
Mary, 202–07, 216
Mayor of Casterbridge, The
(Hardy), 62
"Meditations on a Hobby Horse"
(Gombrich), 95
Meredith, George, xiii, 9, 66, 80,
100–43, 188. Works and
characters: *Amazing Marriage,
The*, 104; Dale, Laetitia (*The
Egoist*), 129; De Craye, Colonel
(*The Egoist*), 103, 107, 129;
Desborough, Lucy (*The Ordeal of
Richard Feverel*), 127–28; *Diana
of the Crossways*, 104, 111; *The
Egoist*, xiii, xv, 9, 32, 66, 100–
43, 164; Feverel, Richard (*The
Ordeal of Richard Feverel*), 127–
28; "Hymn to Colour," 119;
Jenkinson, Mrs. Mountstuart (*The
Egoist*), 115, 130, 131; *Lord
Ormont and His Aminta*, 104;
Middleton, Clara (*The Egoist*), 9,
66, 97, 101, 102–03, 104–31,
133, 134, 136, 139–43, 164;
Middleton, Dr. (*The Egoist*), 101,
124, 129; *One of Our
Conquerors*, 104, 111; *The
Ordeal of Richard Feverel*, 127–
28, 132, 224; Patterne, Sir
Willoughby (*The Egoist*), 97, 101,
102, 103, 104–31, 141, 164;
"The South-Wester," 119, 129;

Whitford, Vernon (*The Egoist*),
101, 106–08, 109, 110, 116, 122,
124, 125, 128, 129, 130, 141,
142
Merleau-Ponty, Maurice, 109
Metamorphoses (Ovid), 122–23
Middlemarch (Eliot), 30, 64–65,
95–96, 98, 99–100, 187
Milton, John, 226
Montaigne, Michel Eyquem de, 233
Monteverdi, Claudio, 10
Moriarty, Professor ("The Final
Problem"), 231
"Mr Bennett and Mrs Brown"
(Woolf), 29
"Murders in the Rue Morgue, The"
(Poe), 230–31
"Musgrave Ritual, The" (Doyle),
233–44

Nancy, Jean-Luc, 29, 34
Narcissus, 122–23, 124, 141, 183,
185–89, 190, 193, 199, 205–06,
220
"Nazi Myth, The" (Lacoue-Labarthe
and Nancy), 29, 34
Nietzsche, Friedrich, xiv, 1, 34, 36–
54, 72, 92–93, 94–95, 99–100,
116, 131–40, 141
Novalis, 62

Odyssey (Homer), 95
Oedipus, 147–48
Oedipus the King (Sophocles), 231
On the Genealogy of Morals (*Zur
Genealogie der Moral*)
(Nietzsche), 131–40
"On Truth and Lies in a Nonmoral
Sense (Über Wahrheit und Lüge
im Außermoralischen Sinne)"
(Nietzsche), 43, 132–33, 137
"Ordinary Evening in New Haven,
An" (Stevens), 25
Ovid, 122, 124

Oxford English Dictionary, The, 55–60, 154–56, 225–28

Panurge (*Gargantua and Pantagruel*), 80–83
Paradise Lost (Milton), 122–23, 206
Parages (Derrida), 67
Pater, Walter, ix, x–xiv, 2–4, 6, 11, 49–50, 64, 96, 110–11, 131
Pentheus, 13
Pericles (Shakespeare), 226
Philosophenbuch, Das (Nietzsche), 37, 93
Philosophical Investigations (Wittgenstein), 83–85, 94, 101
"Philosophy of Furniture, The" (Poe), 79
Pip (*Great Expectations*), 95–96, 97
Plato, 26, 122, 180, 241, 246
Pliny the Elder, 227, 241
Poe, Edgar Allan, 58, 64, 75–79, 86–87, 101, 230–31, 233
Poetics (Aristotle), 213
Pope, Alexander, 121
Portrait of a Lady, The (James), 105
Portrait of the Artist as a Young Man, A (Joyce), 163
Poulet, Georges, 154
Poussin, Nicolas, 200
Prelude, The (Wordsworth), 250
Presentation of Self in Daily Life (Goffman), 152
Price, Martin, 29
Problem of Anxiety, The (Freud), 7
"Purloined Letter, The" (Poe), 233
Pygmalion (Rousseau), 152

Quart Livre, Le (Rabelais), 147–52

Rabelais, François, 79–83, 147–52
"Rape of the Lock, The" (Pope), 121
Renaissance, The (Pater), 49–50
Republic, The (Plato), 26, 246

Return of the Native, The (Hardy), 179
Ricoeur, Paul, 6, 152
Robinson Crusoe (Defoe), 98
Rossetti, Dante Gabriel, 110–11
Rousseau, Jean-Jacques, 19, 152, 177, 225
Rousset, Jean, 154
Ruskin, John, 1–2, 4, 10, 16, 20, 22

Saint-Jean, Prior ("Apollo in Picardy") x, xi–xiv, 2–4, 6
Sartre, Jean-Paul, 35, 152
"Schicksal und Charakter (Fate and Character)" (Benjamin), 61–63
Schlegel, Friedrich, 177–78
"Secret Writing" (Poe), 79
Sedgewick, C. M., 77
Sein und Zeit (Heidegger), 6
Shakespeare, William, 14, 51, 104, 134, 226
Shell, Marc, 55
Sigourney, L. H., 77
Simmel, Georg, 152
Sir Thomas Overbury His Wife, 28, 31, 55, 57, 60
Socrates, 101
Song of Solomon, 162–63
Sophocles, 231
Sterne, Laurence, 34
Stevens, Wallace, 24–25, 213
Stevenson, Robert Louis, 59
Strauss, Richard, 10
"Style" (Pater), 131
Symposium (Plato), 122

Tamburlaine (Marlowe), 56, 58
Temps et récit (Ricoeur), 6
Tennyson, Alfred, Lord, 226
Terborch, Gerard, 200–202
Tess of the d'Urbervilles (Hardy), 7
Thackeray, William Makepeace, 112–13
Theseus, 11–13, 146, 150

Tintoretto, 11, 15

Titian, 11

To the Lighthouse (Woolf), 98

Tolstoi, Leo, 242

Traherne, Thomas, 162

Treatise on Human Nature (Hume), 35

Troilus and Cressida (Shakespeare), 14, 51, 104, 134

Trollope, Anthony, 67–72, 73, 95, 112

"Über einige Motive bei Baudelaire" (Benjamin), 132

Ulysses (Joyce), 95, 144, 146, 156, 158, 161–64

Van Dyck, Anthony, 200

Warden, The (Trollope), 71, 95

Waves, The (Woolf), 95

"Web of Group Affiliations" (Simmel), 152

What Maisie Knew (James), 103, 124

"What the Rose Said to the Cypress," 83

Whitehead, Alfred North, 108

Will to Power, The (Nietzsche), 36–54, 136, 140

Wisdom, John, 152

Wittgenstein, Ludwig, 66, 80, 83–94, 95, 101, 116, 117, 152, 196

Woolf, Virginia, 29

Wordsworth, William, 250

Yeats, W. B., 45

Zarathustra (*Also Sprach Zarathustra*), 254–55

Zeno, 245–47, 249, 252–54